The Po Man's Guide to Breaking the Poverty Cycle

REALITY Cannot Be Opposed!

This book was dictated, so if you are looking for literary excellence look elsewhere, I'm working on it. But I ain't there yet.

The Po Man's Guide to Breaking the Poverty Cycle

Table of Contents

Introduction Pg.3

Chapter 1 Budget! Adjust! Budget! Adjust! This is the Long Game! Pg.6.

Chapter 2 Skills! Skills! Skills! You have to GROW!! Pg.35.

Chapter 3 The Credit Game Pg.70.

Chapter 4 Why You Need a Computer Pg.109.

Chapter 5 Dealing with Self-Destructive Behaviors Pg.123.

Chapter 6 Knowing How and When to Ditch that Dead-end Job! Pg.134.

Chapter 7 Research! Research! Research! Pg.163.

Chapter 8 Plan! Evaluation! Make Adjustments! Plan Again! Pg.167.

Chapter 9 Miscellaneous Topics - Things YOU NEED TO KNOW! Pg.178.

Alphabetical Index Pg.225-227. Helps with Quick Referencing Topics

The Po Man's Guide to Breaking the Poverty Cycle

Introduction

This book is a how-to manual. The aim is to change your mindset while attempting to expose you to proven methods that will assist you in achieving your goals. Nobody can stop or slow down your personal growth unless you allow it! Nobody has that kind of power! Learn to think differently! Learn to dream differently! Reality is not your enemy! When you fully embrace this concept, no one will impede your progress for long or stop you from growing into the person you wish to become!

People who didn't know me labeled me as a born loser based on my family and surroundings. Start somewhere. This book isn't for all those people who were born on the right side of the tracks. This book is for the ghetto hood rat, poor white trash people who had three strikes against them before they were born. People who have no reason to hope but dare to do so each day. Who are determined to wash away the designation engraved in their psyche by those who consider themselves to be your betters?

Through trial and error, I made many needed changes over time or as my shortcomings became painfully obvious to me. I employed many diverse spot corrections to negate my upbringing and break me out of the poor man's thought process. My methods have helped many young men and women to make the changes they could not do on their own. I'm no guru. I am simply a regular guy who sticks to what works.

Being the smartest guy in the room has never been the blessing of the poor man. Most of us are byproducts of our upbringing and we have to wake up each day struggling to learn what we need to do to get ahead. It sucks when your parents teach you everything but how to succeed in life.

My realistic outlook on life has always been simple but complicated: suffer more or make a change!

Having the right teachers/mentors changed my life! Those who have the ability to master the plan should help those who struggle! What sets a poor person and a rich person apart? The answer is not cash! The answer is options! Poor people have very few options available to them. A rich man has unlimited options! Long ago, I had an epiphany.

What are the options available to a poor man without money? The poor man gains options with skills! Your earning potential is directly proportional to the number of skills you possess. The more money you make, the more doors will open! Every rich man we celebrate started with a multitude of options. Poor men can become rich when they possess mad skills! It's a myth that problems will work themselves out. Unfortunately, wealth does not just appear from innovative ideas or heavy wishes. You have to put in the work! Quick fixes do not exist and should not be your go-to! There are no shortcuts. Unless you're not a real adult, or you are a minor, in which case your problems are someone else's responsibility.

You are in financial trouble because you did not budget properly. Short of extenuating circumstances, such as being born crippled, the blame falls squarely on your shoulders. Even if no one taught you how to manage cash or you had no cash to manage, there are

The Po Man's Guide to Breaking the Poverty Cycle

tools and a multitude of ways in this modern era to gain knowledge about anything and everything. If you did not take the time to get whatever experience or knowledge you are missing, you are choosing ignorance and you are choosing financial failure.

No angels will come down from heaven to give you money. Expect: Don't expect a millionaire stranger to give you money; instead, be wary of those who might try to scam you. No one wants to give you anything. They want you to take what is yours and they do not care if you do not have money for your bills. It will only be possible for you to change things around if you exercise self-discipline, make smart choices, and practice self-denial. You must have an overwhelming desire to change your present circumstances. The changes you need to make to change your circumstances are painful at first, but later, these changes will become your strength, your armor. Those things you are good at, naturally, will become beneficial habits.

You remember that nothing worth having comes easy. Make no mistake, I'm not promising you easy. I'm promising you results! The entire purpose of this book is to teach you how to plan and/or budget, stick to it and change your plan and/or budget religiously. This will ensure that it is always up-to-date. You need to figure out how to set reachable goals. You need to learn how to start with the insignificant things first! And while you are learning, your money will grow! Your knowledge and your ability will grow, and so will your ability to gain the things you desire most! Little by little, remember this mantra. You should repeat this mantra often "little by little" to stay grounded.

Now let's be realistic here. I'm not an expert at generating money, having money, saving money, or even keeping money! What I have become is proficient, disciplined, and aware. And before you go thinking I was born with a silver spoon in my mouth, remember the title of this book is "The Po Man's Guide to BREAKING The Poverty Cycle". Therefore, I must have grown up poor. I didn't learn from any gurus or money-making masters. I learned it the hard way, just like everyone else! You are lucky, my friend! I want to give you the benefit of my experience from all my mistakes I've made and everything I've ever done wrong. If you allow it, I will walk you through this process, including the mistakes I made along the way. I hope you can take this knowledge, learn from it, and make it your own. This will enable you to adapt to any situation or circumstance that may arise. Imagine, if you will, someone taking your hand and guiding you through the financial pitfalls this life might try to throw at you.

In the following chapters, I will try my best to explain many of the things I've learned. And even touch upon those instances where I merely got lucky. The advice others have given me. Only the stuff that actually works. I will be your chaperon and hopefully, when we are done, you can no longer call yourself a poor man.

So, if you're willing to put in the work, I will do everything within my power to help you reach your goals!

The Po Man's Guide to Breaking the Poverty Cycle

The Elephant in the Room
Before we get started, I would like to address the elephant in the room. Many of the things I'm going to lie out in the following pages are still possible for, say, someone in their late 40s to begin implementing. I have found the key age for most Americans to wake up and say, "Hey, I need to do something with my life!" is between the ages of 33 and 35 years old. It is not until then, most Americans wake up, look around and decide their lives are going nowhere fast. Once panic ensues, they look for help, but everyone else is stuck in the same position. I'm no expert, but I've noticed this mainly begins at age 35. If the epiphany occurs younger, that's great! This book primarily targets those aged 17 to 43, as it gets progressively harder to escape the cycle of poverty beyond that age. I'm not saying it can't be done. I'm just saying it is harder.
   A friend of mine and I have concluded that the small amount of information given at the right time has the greatest impact!

I've always believed that words hold power. Names have meanings. So, how can I use "your words" to express who and what I have become or will become? Things that work for Steve don't work for me. The things that work for Adam won't work for Sheila! Sheila can teach Brian how to be Brian, but George can't teach Philip how to be Philip! From beginning to end, it's you! You are the only person on this planet who knows how to be you. You are the only person on this planet who knows how things work for you! The twelve steps that work for Philip won't work for Brian. Ryan's rules for his life won't work for Paula. It's simple! We are all unique. "The struggle" is the only thing we have in common. How we approach our struggles must be unique. We must all find the things that work for us! If it doesn't work, throw it away and keep looking until you find those things that will! I haven't spent my life trying to find what works for others. I have spent my life trying to find what "works for me." Your job in life is to find what works for you, taking everything that works for everyone else and personalizing it so it always works for you!
I'm not trying to be rude or exclude anyone! I'm writing this book mainly for men because I have struggled my entire life with being a man. I don't know how to be a woman. I don't want to know because I'm not a woman. I saw a need. So, I drafted this book. And as the experts always teach you, write what you know,

BRAIN HACK: In this book, I will supply Brain Hacks and Mind Training Tips. Your Brain is a computer. You can program it to do whatever you want; it's physical and touchable. You can program it to do whatever you want; it's physical and touchable. Your MIND is an inner extension of self. Order your brain to subconsciously work on a problem. It may take a while, but eventually, you will have "a ha moment" or an epiphany! Once your brain has finished its job, your mind will tell you how to properly apply the solution to the problem your brain has solved. It takes PRACTICE but once mastered, this skill will be invaluable! Your brain does its thing without your input. Are you telling yourself to breathe? Do you have to think about walking? Your MIND must be engaged! It takes an act of will! The two are NOT synonymous. And they are NOT the SAME!

The Po Man's Guide to Breaking the Poverty Cycle

Another thing, I intend to shove so much needed information down your throat that you will be defecating GREATNESS! You will be like that YouTube guy who wears the shirt that says, "I PISS EXCELLENCE!" It will seem as though I'm bouncing all over the place. Just grind it out! There is a method to my madness! If you were born with a silver spoon in your mouth, then I could understand your trepidation! Yes, REALITY is where we are going and I intend for you to take up residence in a suitable domicile. This isn't a low-content eBook. Buckle up, it's about to get bumpy! If you are anything like me, you hate liars! So be certain if I'm asking you to do something, it's because it works!

The Po Man's Guide to Breaking the Poverty Cycle

Chapter 1: Budget! Adjust! Budget! Adjust! This is the Long Game!

Do I know Where My Money Is Going?

Before we get started. The lesson of this book briefly: break your cycle of bad decisions. A cycle is a circle! A circle is a choice. Break the circle! Break the cycle! Learning to make good, well thought out decisions will end your cycle! So, I will point out circles and hopefully, when we are done, you will pinpoint your circles and break your poverty cycle.

The first thing we need to learn about breaking out of the poverty cycle is if you have to budget! Budget! Budget! There is no way anyone can make it in today's world without "knowing" where their money is going. I've spoken with many people and it is astonishing how many of them will say that they never budget or will openly admit they have no budget at all. I've even had people tell me flat out that until payday, they wouldn't know where their money was going. Flying by the seat of their pants, just making it up as they go along. This is okay if you have rich parents, a sort of trust fund, or a money tree in the backyard. For those of us who are not living in the land of make believe or have a guardian angel standing on our shoulders, we can't afford to make those types of mistakes. There is no one I know who has so much money. They can afford to throw thousands of dollars away!

You must get into the mindset or habit of "knowing" where your money is going, down to the nearest dollar. Even the Bible tells us we must count the cost, and the only way to do that is to budget. Like most people, you are probably thinking you don't have any money to budget. I say you can't afford to not budget. Even a slight savings of $10 a week is enough to change your entire life. Think of it this way: there are 52 weeks in a year. Do the math, $10×52 weeks equals savings of $520 a year. Are you starting to get the picture now? Don't wait until your income tax check comes at the end of the year. Start saving your money all year long.

*Luke 14:28 **For which of you, intend to build a tower, sitteth not down first and counteth the cost, whether he have sufficient to finish it?***

No, this is not going to be a spiritual book! And no there will be no bible thumping.

Budgeting is counting the cost and the best way to manage your money. As you may have noticed, the average person just waits until payday and only then will they recognize their error and only then will they contemplate whether they will fall short on their bills and be able to afford the new thing they have been wanting to buy. Yes, I am repeating myself! I tend to "when" I need to drive a point home! And repetition is the fastest way to get the latest information to stick! Everyone has at least 30 minutes during the day they can set aside to get their money in order.

The Po Man's Guide to Breaking the Poverty Cycle

But most people never take the time. I do not like surprises, but they happen. With a budget, you can make minor adjustments here and there and presto, like magic, you have enough money to cover your expenses. You can resolve most problems by simply moving money around, although it takes work and sometimes imagination. But timing is always crucial. (I will get to that later).

The whole idea behind budgeting is to know and fully understand where your money goes and what you spent it on. You should always be able to tell "where" your money went. Simple stroll through your home and you should be able to see with your eyes and touch with your hands the items you have spent your money on. You should also never feel guilty; because each item you bought was a justified purchase! A "need" and not a want! Again. Budgeting takes time, energy and effort! And in the end, you will be glad you did it!

A well-laid budget gives you the illusion of control. You will stay on top of your bills, everyday expenses, your grocery spending, medical bills, and so on. Budgeting puts you in the position of never having to guess! You can find the exact amounts you can pay on your bills! The amounts you intend to pay, with a mind to reducing any remaining balances and/or any fees that may be due by anticipating bills that can fluctuate (go up and down on you)! Such as your light bill, your water bill and, in other cases, your phone bill. Most bills follow patterns. Correctly learning these patterns and making the needed adjustments is a must. Every time you access your online accounts, you must be able to accurately estimate the amount of these bills. You must get into the habit of looking into the amounts you have already paid each month the year before the current year.

However, looking at your past spending should give you insight and the ability to gauge how much you will need to spend in the future, allowing you to create a reliable plan of action. An action plan that will help you decide how and when you are going to pay for them. You will also be able to forecast "what" if anything you may have to sacrifice, to enable you to meet your budgetary goals for that pay period. You must always balance everything out or be able to account for your incoming monies versus the total funds you have going out. Overspending should not occur if you are paying attention or if by mishap, you somehow missed it the first time when you were balancing out your funds. You must develop the ability to catch any mistakes. This is why **I adjust my budget after every expenditure to prevent me from overspending or counting on money I have already spent.**

To create a well-rounded budget, one must distinguish between wants and needs. A need would be something like gas, food, light bills, car notes, rental insurance, medical bills, vehicle maintenance, etcetera..... A want would be something like a bag of chips, a candy bar, fast food, a new pair of jeans, or anything else you don't need, but you simply want these things. While we are on the subject, let's discuss impulse buying: impulse buying is a byproduct of excitement. You see something someone else has and you get excited. When a man gets excited, he wants to do something about his excitement. This usually involves making an on-the-spot decision.

The Po Man's Guide to Breaking the Poverty Cycle

Later, after the impulse is satiated, he has regret. The cure for any impulse is to analyze "what" you are excited about until **you are** no longer excited. Then, once you are no longer excited, you must be able to logically convince yourself that this action is the correct action. If you cannot logically convince yourself, this action is reasonable and needed, take no action.

Scenario #1: You have $30 remaining after you somehow managed to pay all your bills. While window shopping, you notice a nice pair of jeans on sale for $25. With your bills paid and a desire for the jeans, you can easily afford this impulse purchase.

Scenario #2: Barely, you've managed to balance your incoming and outgoing funds. You have no money left to spare and on impulse; you buy the same pair of $30 jeans, now you are in the hole for thirty bucks and you have no incoming funds! Now you are in jeopardy of a bill (let us say a light bill) not being paid. Now, you are going to have to borrow the same $30 from your next check. You are thinking, *hey, I should be able to cover thirty dollars.* Enter Murphy's Law (Anything that can go wrong will go wrong)! A couple of days later, one tire blows on your vehicle. Now, you must replace the tire and it is $50. Now you are $80 in the hole! Your light bill is higher than expected and it is due. The power company will turn off your lights if you don't pay $80. While this may be an unpleasant thought, it is just one example of what one little impulse buy can do to you. If it is not a need or a literal must-have because your job requires it, you must always refrain from impulse spending!

Overtime

WEALTH NOTE: How long and how hard you work has nothing to do with gaining wealth. You are simply working harder and longer for a lower wage. A higher-paid wage means that the more money you make, the less you should have to physically work! Let that sink in!

And since we are on the topic of budgeting let's address one of my pet peeves: under no circumstances should you ever and I mean never ever make any purchases, as in a car, a house, or anything involving a payment plan, based on projected overtime! All businesses have their highs and lows and eventually that overtime is going to evaporate! Overnight, you are going to find yourself overextended and in a very precarious position. Not only will you not be able to afford a new car, new house, or whatever it is you were counting on your overtime to cover, you will have no new money coming in. What will you do then...? Let us continue on with this train of thought. Your job has been slow and now they are sending everyone home early, so you are not even making your regular pay. Now, you have put yourself in a position where you could lose your vehicle. Now you are going to lose a house or whatever it is you are making payments on, which you can no longer afford. Depending on overtime is counting your chickens! If you are working overtime, great! Knock several dream

The Po Man's Guide to Breaking the Poverty Cycle

items off your list; but under no circumstances make it a part of your budget as in the money you depend on!

Your Next Raise
Another one of my pet peeves: You expect that every year you will get a raise. It is like clockwork. You know exactly what you are going to get, how much in taxes they are going to take out and exactly how much you will have left to spend. The smart person would wait until they have a raise or bonus in hand. But the impulse buyer will spend away, counting their chickens before they hatch. They will assume money will be there as they make an impulse purchase. Let us say, they spent $500. Then, when the time comes: no raise, no bonus. Now, you are $500 in the hole. Are you starting to see a pattern here? Count no money until it is in your hands! Nothing is certain! Not bonuses! Not raises! Not safety bonuses! Nothing! Never spend money you do not have on hand. Wait until payday!!

Let us say, I lent this guy 50 bucks and I'm counting on that money. If you cannot afford to lose it, don't lend it! Let us say this is a close friend to whom you have lent money in the past and they always pay it back on time and you have never had any problems. Your friend is in a bind so you lend them $50 from your light bill and when the time comes for your friend to repay the debt, he loses his job and cannot afford to pay you $50 back. Now your lights are in jeopardy. Whatever can go wrong will go wrong!

If you are like most of us, meaning you cannot go running to mommy or daddy for money or anyone else for that matter, then you are all you have. You cannot afford to make reckless mistakes. Don't: You must avoid impulse buys! It's unwise to count your chickens before they hatch! You cannot afford to count on overtime, which may go away as fast as it materializes! You cannot afford to spend money you do not have on hand! In short, you cannot afford to make stupid mistakes! You need to think hard before doing anything that might jeopardize your budget!

Budgeting enables you to communicate with your significant others about money. Instead of trying to explain your situation to your spouse, you can simply go over the line items in your budget. You will not have to depend on them to read your thoughts accurately as you draw pictures in the air which no one other than you can see. With the help of your spouse, who can point out savings you may have missed, you will GLEAN ANY ADDITIONAL SAVINGS! Your spouse should be able to point out expenses you have overlooked or bring up shortfalls in your budget you may have to cover. Budgeting allows you to know in advance what you can and cannot afford to buy. And allow you to make adjustments if the need arises.

I will not go into tiny details here about how to make your budget. If you have a computer and Microsoft Excel, this will be easier for us. If you do not have a computer, I hope you like writing. You'll require a notepad. This notepad is only to be used for budgeting. You will also need a second notepad for your goals. Start small with the

The Po Man's Guide to Breaking the Poverty Cycle

things you want to accomplish and as time goes by only, you will know when those goals can gradually get bigger and bigger!

No two people can agree on everything, but we can agree on those things which affect us all. Remember, your budget, your goals, your bills and your debt are specific to you and you alone. Please do not waste your time comparing yourself to other people! No two people can take the same path, nor will they be in the same shape financially. One person will be in better shape and the other person not be so much. Everything you do **must** cater to you specifically! Your goals! Your needs! Your wants! If you try to keep up with the Joneses, you may find yourself worse off than the Smiths.

The Real Reasons Most Budgets Fail

Big Money Sunny Syndrome

Now, we're going to discuss some of the bad habits that often get us into some form of trouble. One of these forms of trouble, I would like to call Big Money Sunny Syndrome. Big Money Sunny Syndrome is at work when you have a guy who behaves normally until he gets paid. Once paid, he spends a lot of money trying to impress people. Guys suffering from this illness will often overdress and spend a lot of money on drinks. He hands out money to women, hoping to get a date or something more. These guys are always broke after the weekend.

On Monday they will return to work suddenly cured, returned to normal. No money. No woman. And nothing to show for the money he spent. Big money sunny syndrome sufferers always borrow money at the beginning of the week, usually on Wednesday. These syndrome sufferers brag a lot about what they did on the weekend. They lack impulse control and this often stems from a feeling of self-hatred. They can see that they are failing in life, so they have to do something to make themselves feel better on Friday night. Once payday comes, they can be the life of the party again! And when the party is over and the high is gone, they are broke. I will address the cure for this illness when I give The Rules of Clubbing.

You Spend All of Your Money at the Club

Clubbing and bar hopping: I will attempt to give you rules for this because there's no point in trying to stop you. Let's face it: everyone goes through the clubbing and partying phase! All I'm saying is if you are going to do it anyway, do it smart! Make sure you can actually go out there, enjoy yourself, and come back without feeling the dread of losing your paycheck! You don't need to overspend on the club! There is nothing wrong with wanting to have some fun, just don't do it at the expense of your goals! Let's be real about this: now and then you are going to want to celebrate. Maybe you got promoted. Maybe you reached a milestone and overcame something big. You're getting married. Your old boss died, whatever!

The Po Man's Guide to Breaking the Poverty Cycle

The Rules for Clubbing (I hope I didn't make you wait too long!)

If you must go clubbing then you are going to have to follow some self-imposed rules:

1. Always have a designated driver if possible or get a ride.
2. If you drink, have a set limit you will spend leave the rest of your money at home!
3. See paragraph on Big Money Sunny Syndrome
4. If you and your friends are going to buy each other rounds, have it sorted out before you get to the club. Do the math. It works out in the end.

Once you are mature enough to realize you are going to meet the same ole people with different names, faces and bodies you won't want to go anymore.

Fixing Up Your Ride
Now, everybody knows that guy, the one who has a nice ride with the sweetest sound system. He spends all of his money fixing up his vehicle. Men overcompensate when they lack in a highly visible area. Nice ride says, "Yeah, I know I'm poor, but look at this ride! You will look good riding in it next to me!" Let's be honest, women fall for it all the time! Invest your money, time and energy in something that will pay you back! But if you're still making payments on all that stuff, you're riding around now that's a problem. Ideally, you want to save up your money and buy your vehicle outright and fix it up, as they say once you own it! Buying super expensive rims and then having to pay for those rims for the next two years is not smart. Don't even get me started on the sound system. I remember being at my mother's funeral reception and my cousin, whom I hadn't seen in years, asked me, "Whatcha driving?" I pointed at my used, beat-up 1996 Nissan pickup that I owned. He smiled and said, "It's ok. You'll do betta!" He was implying he was better than me. He lived in the hood and had a low-paying job, lived in a broken-down apartment and drove a nice vehicle. I simply smiled and said, "Yeah. One day". Later that night, I parked my used, beat-up 1996 Nissan pickup in the driveway of my brand spanking new two-story, four-bedroom house in the suburbs. Yeah. I was the loser.

The Po Man's Guide to Breaking the Poverty Cycle

Don't Fall for Get Rich Quick Schemes!

Finally, we get to the MEAT of this thing! I have fallen prey to these fake dream pushing charlatans for years! If I have any part to play in the GREAT AWAKENING of the American people, this is where I intend to WARN any and EVERYONE I possibly can! The truth about getting rich quick infomercials! I don't know if anyone remembers I'm older than you, but back in the 90s was the heyday of the 900 number! Fraud and schemes were everywhere! And since it was all so new, almost everyone fell for them! There was an onslaught of phony get rich quick schemes! These frauds would acquire slots on TV and peddle their wares, write any nonsense book, and they sold off the shelves! If it was on TV, it had to be true! It wasn't like the days of the good old-fashioned pyramid schemes where you would use Amway!

These guys were different! New and exciting, they were! They weren't trying to sell you a product they were selling "the dream!" They upped the ante! Now-a-day all advertising is selling the dream! But, back then, in the 90s, it was all new! People didn't care about the products; they were buying into "the dream!" They had products sure, but people were buying the advertising! Their products never worked! But people bought into it, anyway! Because it was on TV! They'd offer you a sham product and make an upsell! We will send you this product that won't work, but wait! If you act now, I'll throw in more garbage! Don't allow this incredible opportunity to pass you by!

They offered government reports that no one had ever heard of! They offered phony forms that no one could use! Yes! I have issues with these characters. I hate liars! I was going to write this epic chapter telling you not to buy into the lies! A friend of mine suggested a better idea! He said, "Instead of telling people what you think, use reviews!" The lightbulb went off and here we are! I will not tell you anything! I found the reviews: They're the ones you need to read. I haven't changed a word! I only changed the names or removed them so others can tell you how they got duped! You don't need to listen to me. But read the reviews or the articles that follow! I didn't change a thing! So, if they seem broken up, it wasn't me. I wanted to write about each of these guys. Instead, I simply took the words of other victims from multiple sites! Read what they had to say and make up your own mind.

Carlton Sheets
Unknown Author

Remember that guy? He was on TV all the time. He talked about buying houses and making a fortune. He never talked about tenants, repairs, evictions, problems and so forth. I wonder what happened to him. I know that Tom Vu went to prison and now plays poker. Dave DelDotto went out like Vin Diesel. McCorcoran clown went to prison. Those guru sideshows used to crack me up. How about Armando Montelongo?

The Po Man's Guide to Breaking the Poverty Cycle

Haven't heard his name in years. I get emails all the time from Than Merril peddling his products.

Good times.... ... Ann Bellamy Lender from Tyngsboro, MA
replied about 7 years ago, well, I'll give credit to Carlton Sheets for one thing: he inspired people to get involved in real estate investing, even if his stuff was bs. I was among them. I bought his course, started it and said "That's crap, it will never work" but went out and educated myself on buy and hold because I was bitten by the bug.

Armando Montelongo must be alive and well and selling lots of mentorship programs because I have two current customers doing deals as a result of his programs. They are thin deals, but ok for a first deal. One of them found me here on BP and his project is coming along nicely, looking good.

As for Than Merrill and Paul Esajian, I have a great deal of respect for them, actually and know them both from multiple points of contact. Yes, they sell courses, boot camps, mentorship programs, etc., but I consider them to be among the best of the gurus and I work with several investors who are in their program. I don't like the hard sell, but their stuff is good. Of course, real life is never like the seminar, but I think they do their best in preparing the students for reality. Out of the guru that is.

Updated over 1 year ago

Looks like this thread still gets traction. I want to update my opinion: I have nothing good to say about Montelongo. As for Fortune Builders, it seems they have gotten far from their roots. I'm sure they are making money. I'm not sure their new students are. I think their early students who made good decisions are doing very well.

By Unknown Author
Back when the flipping TV shows were big, I ran across a webpage with hundreds of comments on Armando Montelongo.
http://www.flipthislawsuit.com/2007/04/anyonepurchasedarmandomontelongosrealestatepackage/

The "Flip This Lawsuit" website was created by fans of the show and Richard from SC's Trademark Properties to track the developments in his lawsuit with A&E, but the Armando Montelongo page has been buzzing for over 5 years now. It's on the first page of Google when you search Armando's name, but I guess a lot of folks don't do much research before whipping out the credit card, or they simply want to believe so badly they disregard all the negative critiques.

A couple of local San Antonio guys ("Mike Voss" and "Steve in Texas") made a habit of DVD Ring the shows and figuring out exactly which house was featured in each episode. Then they'd search courthouse records, drive by, check the MLS and see how much BS the Montelongo's and A&E were shoveling that week.

The Po Man's Guide to Breaking the Poverty Cycle

Some houses were rehabbed on the show that the Montelongo's never owned, houses supposedly sold on the show but not in real life, improvements and landscaping were taken out after the show and a woman, if I recall correctly, was the mother-in-law one week and the open house buyer another week.

All part of "reality shows", I suppose, but Armando made it part of his credibility kit, claiming vast numbers of successful rehab flips despite a lack of evidence in the real world. He's turned it into a multimillion-dollar guru business, with all the worst guru tricks, getting people to shell out $25K or more to be gurus by a low-level flunky with unknown credentials. He's my poster child for evil gurus.

Russ Dalbey

The kicker, according to the complaint? "Defendant Dalbey has not earned millions of dollars from brokering promissory notes. Most of Defendant Dalbey's note related income for the past two decades has come from the marketing and selling of products and services purporting to teach consumers how to find and broker promissory notes."

Lori Bennett says, August 17, 2016, at 10:04 am
FYI to all people who got swindled by this jerk. I called the Colorado Attorney General's office (June 2016) and spoke to a lady who worked there. I told her that my husband and I lost close to $40,000. (sickening). Went to the seminars and boot camps, etc. Anyway, I asked her what was going on if he was in jail or whatever and she said he and his family fled to Belize. They said the wife and kids came back and she got arrested and spent time in jail. She is out now and her and her kids 'passports have been taken. So, he is hiding in Belize with the millions of dollars he defrauded from all of us and they cannot do a thing unless he comes back and gets caught. He's not worried about coming back to his family. He's celebrating with our money!! I'm sure we will never see our money again.??

Kevin Trudeau

Kevin Trudeau Sentenced to 10 Years in Prison
March 17, 2014, by Paul Lucas
I guess it will be another decade before we will see a new Kevin Trudeau infomercial on the air:

Chicago Tribune: TV ad person Kevin Trudeau sentenced to 10 years in prison. Congratulations to the Illuminati and Bilderbergers (with special help from Yale's Skull & Bones) for a job well done!

Update: Kevin Trudeau has made a post about the sentence on his Facebook page. Trudeau both consoles himself and polishes his ego with the words, "Mandela got 28 years, I was blessed to get only 10". He also tells us, "A 10year sentence means I will be

The Po Man's Guide to Breaking the Poverty Cycle

out between 68 years depending on certain things" and "There are people I must meet and who must meet me. There are experiences and emotions I must confront".

So as early as 2020 we might see an infomercial for Kevin's book revealing the "secrets" to not getting shanked by a burly 300pound sociopath!

Don Lapre

(CBS) Authorities say TV ad person Don Lapre was found dead after a clear suicide in an Arizona jail cell on Sunday morning. Officials say they are continuing to investigate the circumstances surrounding his death. It was only days before his $52 million fraud trial was set to begin.

The 47yearold had been charged with 41 counts of conspiracy, mail fraud, wire fraud and promotional money laundering with his company, "The Greatest Vitamin in the World."

Lapre called himself "The King of Infomercials" on his website; he gained notoriety from his numerous late-night advertisements, including "Making Money From A Tiny One Bedroom Apartment," where he claimed he made $50,000 a week from his small apartment. The infomercials were parodied on "Saturday Night Live," and made fun of on the "Late Show with David Letterman."}

The formal accusation claims the Arizona based TV pitchman received millions from his scam between 2004 to 2007. He was accused of tricking at least 220,000 people with worthless Internet based businesses mostly revolving around a pyramid scheme to sell vitamins did not supply the health benefits he claimed. His company was shut down in 2007 due to multiple complaints.

If convicted, he would have faced between $250,000 to $500,000 per count and five to 25 years in federal prison.

Matthew Lesko

Free Money? Don't Think So
Government grants out there for the taking? Think again
By Unknown Author

Multimillion dollar advertising and a new book by author Matthew Lesko are peppered with exaggerations and half-truths about government grants, according to a report released by the New York State Consumer Protection Board ("CPB").

The Po Man's Guide to Breaking the Poverty Cycle

In its report, "Secrets Revealed! "How Misleading Advertising Is Feeding a Nationwide Boom in Government Grant Scams," CPB says Lesko and others are feeding a growing number of government grant scams now hurting consumers across the country.

"Lesko is now promoting a new book, 'Free Money to Pay Your Bills,' by claiming the federal government has more than $350 billion in "hidden money" ordinary people can use to pay their credit card bills and 'get out of debt.' claim is simply not true," said CPB Chairman and Executive Director Teresa A. Santiago.

Santiago said, "Privately, this company admits there is no 'free money to pay your bills' despite advertising contrary information on radio, late-night TV and Internet advertising. This myth has helped to create a growing industry of books, tapes and websites and, unfortunately, some swindlers say they can help consumers find "hidden money" from the government."

The CPB is now helping New York consumers victimized by ongoing government grant frauds. These include at least four telemarketing networks that falsely "guarantee" government grants to consumers in exchange for an upfront fee of roughly $250. Many of these fraud victims said they were aware of Lesko's advertising claims.

The Federal Trade Commission and other agencies recently reached a half-million-dollar settlement with a telemarketer accused of deceptive practices in its telemarketing.

Lesko's book offers useful information about scholarships and other programs and his company offers refunds to dissatisfied customers, Santiago noted. "Many other government grant offers are outright scams, offering no benefit whatsoever to consumers," she said.

These frauds and other grant offers have benefited in some cases, directly from the business practices of Mr. Lesko's Maryland based company, Information USA Inc. For example, Information USA compiles and sells direct marketing lists with the names, addresses and other information of Lesko's customers. These lists have been used by other companies to sell services such as debt repair and, in at least two cases, Lesko customer lists were sold to outright scams involving government grant offers.

Two companies, Grant PAC and Grant Search Inc. were charged with deceptive practices in a $2.6 million complaint by the Federal Trade Commission. The firms both bought customer lists from Lesko and other government grant publishers.

Another buyer of Lesko customer lists is a Rochester, N.Y. company called National Grants Conferences. The seminars and high-priced products sold by National Grants Conferences have been the source of consumer complaints for several years.

The Po Man's Guide to Breaking the Poverty Cycle

The report also cites a New York City publisher, FPH Communications, for misinformation in at least one of its grant guides. The consumers who bought this paperback guide are now being targeted by grant scheme telemarketers. FPH says it sells its customer lists to other direct marketers.

In releasing a report on the activities of Lesko and other government grant companies, Santiago said the CPB hopes to dispel the myths the government is handing out or "hiding" billions of dollars that can be used to pay personal expenses. Lesko even advertises that these grants can help someone "stay out of debt forever."

Specialty Merchandise Corporation (SMC)

SMC specialty merchandise Corporation changed its name to smart living Corporation. My impression of SMC. I have read complaints posted on this site. I agree with them (if not all of them). I have lost around $18,000.00 during my "SMC experience" (In a year, I have not made one penny on this enterprise, nor have I made one sale). SMC would most likely explain I have failed at this because I am a loser. My advice to you would be, don't add your name to this VERY LONG list of losers. I feel I have received a Ph.D. in finding a fraud when I see one. I look at the positives of this experience. I tend to be a creature of observation. I have tried to list my observations of SMC below:

SMC will not allow the use of PayPal Pro. PayPal Pro is a gateway (with very reasonable charges). SMC "supplies" their "own" gateway company and of course, receives payment from this company for referrals. A typical gateway will cost around $40.00 to $50.00 per month (If you sell absolutely nothing). The price quickly goes up if actual products are sold. If you decide to sell SMC items at swap meets or markets, you will find 3 or 4 (or more) selling the same merchandise from SMS (at a greatly reduced price). Most, if not all of the products are made in China, I especially love the Harley Davidson coffee mug with "Made in China" stamped on the bottom (would get you killed at any Harley Davidson Rally.... lol). You will find all of the "tremendous success" stories SMC portrays are individuals are groomed and given unlimited support (SMC has to have marketing heroes to present to the general public to entice new victims, right?) Given the fact SMC is conducting fraudulent business practices across state lines, I am amazed the Federal Government has not become involved (Of course, SMC may have written this into their "terms and conditions" as well. Time will tell).

THE ULTIMATE HYPOCRITE: ROBERT KIYOSAKI AND HIS COMPANY'S BANKRUPTCY
Last Updated on November 8, 2018,

Financial Hypocrisy A story came across the news this weekend about Robert Kiyosaki, the author of Rich Dad, Poor Dad and how his company went bankrupt last month. The company didn't pay the proper royalties for its seminars and when they lost in court, they didn't have enough money to pay at all. It wasn't a personal bankruptcy, but rather, a corporate bankruptcy. However, a corporation with money should be able to

The Po Man's Guide to Breaking the Poverty Cycle

pay up for a minor royalty dispute (only $23 million compared to $400+ million in revenues). And when your name is attached to a company and your business is built around creating wealth, the word bankruptcy associated with it usually isn't a good thing.

However, minor you may consider it, I find it appalling as a personal finance writer. This guy made a living on selling "his story" and encouraging others to fork out tons of money to hear it. In the end, the story crumbles and it just makes him a hypocrite.

Practice What You Preach
What upsets me the most is Kiyosaki is portrayed by many as a financial guru. His Rich Dad, Poor Dad book made him famous because of the practical advice he pretended to gain throughout his life. He talks about life lessons learned and how that allowed him to do remarkable things in real estate and other ventures.

The problem?

Before his 1997 publication of Rich Dad, Poor Dad, Robert Kiyosaki never had any documentation of the wealth he supposedly amassed (Forbes)There wasn't a rich dad, even though his book specifically claims there was one (Smart Money Magazine, February 2003) In the end, this "nonfiction" story is just fiction and so it calls into doubt the advice he gives to readers and followers.

Even though his advice may sound good: be an owner, invest in cash flow investments, etc., the fact he (or his business) didn't support solid financial health is sad.

Don't Prey on Your Followers

Another big red flag for me is preying on your followers. This is hypocrisy at its worst. If you're selling yourself as a model for something (values, wealth creation, business, or even how you coach your kid's soccer team), don't use your followers and believers to empower them.

Robert Kiyosaki wrote and sold his book, which I consider to be honorable. He then tacked on a class, which was free, which is also honorable. But then he started preying on his followers

Class #1 Free Advice
Class #2 Paid Advice, $495 (However, extraordinarily little education and more marketing for class #3)
Class #3 Paid Advice $45,000 (Yes...'s not a typo)
If you're a financial planner, I think it is fair to charge for advice. However, it is important to be reasonable for your services. If you're trying to help someone, get rich and supply value, $495 could be reasonable. But how could $45,000 be reasonable for

any personal finance class? Furthermore, would you ever pay given the credibility issues raised by the teacher?

Kiyosaki Isn't the Only One

The sad fact is Robert Kiyosaki isn't the only one. There are hundreds of financial hypocrites out there. There are even more people out there who have hypocritical moments (I'm sure I have as well).

It doesn't take shelling out thousands of dollars for courses from potentially hypocritical speakers. Just earn, save, get out of debt and invest. Done.

The Po Man's Guide to Breaking the Poverty Cycle

Budgeting Examples

Now that we have that madness out of the way. Let us get into the budgeting examples. I will only cover Excel. On a notepad, it will be self-explanatory. If you do not have a computer or Microsoft Excel, you can skip over the example shows how to hit Auto Sum to get the total amount. Now, if you have a computer and believe that you cannot afford Microsoft Office, I may be of some help.
https://softwaresupply.net/product-category/cheap-microsoft-office/

For those of you who already have Microsoft Excel, you are going to create a new worksheet. Name the file after your current year i.e., 2020. Your file name should read Budget 2025-2026. What you are going to do is make up a monthly budget depending on how you get paid. You will either make a weekly, biweekly, or monthly budget.

Weekly Budget

Here you see the entire month represented in four weeks. The object is to have all your bills paid by the end of the month. There is more wiggle room when you have four weeks to move your money around. So, there is no confusion. Each week has its goal. Overtime in the past two weeks resulted in a negative balance. We can still plainly see that this person is going to need a better job or higher pay to drop his dependence on overtime. Another advantage of weekly pay, you will recover faster than say, someone who gets paid twice a week.

WEEK 1		WEEK 2	
Car Note	$ 190.00	Car Note	$ 190.00
CAR INSURANCE	$ 110.00	Food	$ 30.00
Food	$ 42.00	RENT	$ 220.00
Laundry	$ 10.00	Gas	$ 10.00
Gas	$ 10.00		
Cell Phone	$ 30.00		
Netflix	$ 11.00		
	$ 403.00		$ 450.00

WEEK 3		WEEK 4	
Food	$ 30.00	Food	$ 18.00
RENT	$ 300.00	RENT	$ 380.00
LIGHTS	$ 80.00	Gas	$ 10.00
Laundry	$ 10.00		
Gas	$ 10.00		
	$ 430.00		$ 408.00

The Po Man's Guide to Breaking the Poverty Cycle

Biweekly Budget

Here you see the entire month represented in bi-weekly increments. They are the same bills as above, same result. I'm just showing you how to set up a bi-weekly budget in Excel. We can still plainly see that this person is going to need a better job or higher pay to drop his dependence on overtime.

PAYDAY 1	
RENT	$ 220.00
Car Note	$ 380.00
CAR INSURANCE	$ 110.00
Food	$ 72.00
Laundry	$ 10.00
Gas	$ 20.00
Cell Phone	$ 30.00
Netflix	$ 11.00
	$ 853.00

PAYDAY 2	
RENT	$ 680.00
Food	$ 48.00
LIGHTS	$ 80.00
Laundry	$ 10.00
Gas	$ 20.00
	$ 838.00

Monthly Budget

Here you will see the entire month represented in Microsoft Excel. It is the same budget as above, and the object is to have all of your bills paid by the end of the month. This person relies on overtime, so the total is in the red. We can still plainly see this person is going to need a better job or higher pay to drop his dependence on overtime.

Month 1	
RENT	$ 900.00
Car Note	$ 380.00
CAR INSURANCE	$ 110.00
Food	$ 200.00
Laundry	$ 20.00
Gas	$ 40.00
Cell Phone	$ 30.00
Netflix	$ 11.00
	$ 1,691.00

The Po Man's Guide to Breaking the Poverty Cycle

Whip up A Quick Budget

Below is an example of how I began making my budget in Microsoft Excel. Enter all your items in a column and enter the amounts in the cells next to them, all in the same row. Next, you want to highlight all your weekly totals and click on the Auto Sum button at the top right side of the page. You can see the sums at the bottom of the highlighted column. This is just one week. Now highlight the entire thing, right click and select copy. Paste the first week three more times and then you have four weeks or one month. I hope this goes without me having to say if you get paid biweekly, you will only have to copy and paste once. Use dates instead of weeks 14. The date of payday, i.e., 11/26/2025. You are going to want to estimate your budget for the entire year. This will give you the ability to forecast bills and set financial goals, whether it is for the rest of the month or the rest of the year. Once you have your entire year planned out, you should be able to take a step back and see everything. The purpose of doing it this way is so you will move money around; if you need to, so you cover all your needs.

WEEK 3	
Food	$ 30.00
RENT	$ 300.00
LIGHTS	$ 80.00
Laundry	$ 10.00
Gas	$ 10.00
	$ 430.00

I did a video on YouTube

https://www.youtube.com/watch?v=ZB4FgOD_1Mg

Life happens. Expect the unexpected! Money and emotions don't mix! Here are a few examples of life choices and the financial consequences.

The Po Man's Guide to Breaking the Poverty Cycle

Example #1: Bob makes $15 an hour, and he gets a minimum of 10 hours of overtime each week. Bob is a smart guy; he understands sometimes his overtime is going to decrease and sometimes it will increase. He knows better than to count on overtime; but while he has it, he's going to use this as an opportunity to save money. His normal take-home pay with no overtime is $408 a week. This leaves him about $30 to $40 in the hole. With his overtime, he can easily compensate because he gets an additional $175 take-home. Bob saves the $100 a week and uses the remaining $70 to meet any unexpected needs or occasionally he buys something he wants. He has his 401(k) contributions set at 3% which is the maximum his company will match. He pays $50 a week for his medical insurance, which leaves him with approximately $408 take-home.

His rent is $850 a month, car insurance $88 a month, AAA costs him $10 a month and his light bill averages around $80 a month. Bob also knows the economy is not doing as great, so he spends an average of $60 a month on silver. This leaves him with a whopping $220 to enjoy a month. This year he began paying for a gym membership of $40 a month. So now, his splurge money goes down to $180 a month.

Bob likes to hang out with his friends. Occasionally, they will go out and hit the local bar scene. Bob's best friend is George, who never drinks (designated driver). This allows him to buy and consume a six-pack before they leave the apartment. He does this to get a buzz to save money on drinks. He will only spend $30 a night at the club on drinks. They usually go out on Fridays and Saturdays to blow off steam. Bob rarely eats takeout, but when he does, he saves all his change (coins). At the end of the month or when his change jar gets full, he simply takes it to the bank, pours all of its contents into the coin machine and adds the total to his savings account. Bob opted to wait on buying an iPhone, noting the cost would put him in a bind. (No one is saying you can't have an iPhone, just do it responsibly. If need be, wait until you are financially stable. This will put you into a position where this purchase is a win and not a loss). It's a want, not a need! Bob won't go out with his friends if he has no throwaway cash! And he does his best to never borrow money to spend on things he merely wants. He usually saves about $30 by the end of the month. Bob takes this throwaway money (throwaway money is money you won't miss even if things go wrong) and uses it for odds and ends.

The overtime has been flowing for two years. Bob has managed to buy 72 ounces of silver and save a whopping $9600. Year three is business as usual. Bob has managed to gain 108 ounces of silver and increased his savings to $14,400. Not bad for a single guy making $15 an hour. Bob usually buys an ounce of gold with his income tax check at the end of the year. Now, Bob has 4 ounces of gold totaling about $5000. He can liquidate in times of trouble.

The Po Man's Guide to Breaking the Poverty Cycle

One day, Bob meets Susan, who is very pretty and challenges Bob intellectually. He decided he could not live without her. Susan, unlike Bob, has four credit cards. And she is $30,000 in debt because of these credit cards. Her frivolous spending and failure to budget stem from an impulse-buying addiction. Bob is willing to overlook all these RED FLAGS because he is in love with Susan. Susan is a receptionist, and she earns $11 an hour. She lives with her parents because she cannot afford to make it on her own. (RED FLAG)

Bob is no longer saving as much as he used to save; because he has been taking Susan out regularly, trying to make her happy. The $400 a month he was saving is gone. They decide to get married. Susan's parents are also broke because they supported her for so long. Which results in Bob having to pay for the wedding. His gold and silver are liquidated. He also withdraws the $14,000 he had previously saved. He spent $25,000 on the wedding to make Susan happy. Now Bob has no savings! No cushion. Susan sees Bob as a great provider, so she decides they need a bigger place. Now, remember, Bob was not struggling before Susan's arrival. The overtime from work was helping him keep his head above water.

The couple decided most of the money Susan earns will be used to pay off her credit cards and to cover most of her impulse buying, severely impeding her ability to help Bob with their finances. Bob loved Susan in the beginning, but he began to resent her because he cannot see what, if anything, she had brought to the table but her outstanding bills. But he believes in keeping his vows and forces himself to look at everything positively. I will just need to work harder and put in more hours! Men are meant to suffer. Get err done and all...

One day, Susan comes home from her doctor's visit and tells Bob she's pregnant. Bob is ecstatic! But then reality sets in. Just in time, Bob got a $2 raise at work so he is thinking I might see some daylight. But we are going to need all this new stuff for the baby! Milk, baby food, diapers and childcare are some of these things that are cheap and if Susan does not change her spending habits, it is going to put us a little bit deeper into the hole.

Time goes on and Susan decides she no longer wants to work. Instead, she wants to be a stay-at-home mom. Her spending has not decreased, nor has her impulse buying. Now Bob is $40,000 in the hole because of her unpaid credit card debt. Bob is reeling. He has a child, a mortgage, two car payments, a high light bill and no help in sight. He takes out a 401(k) loan and pays off the credit card debt. Susan is ecstatic! Now they can plan! So, Bob gets a part-time job! She wants all new furniture and lots of toys for the baby and, of course, she tells Bob; she is feeling neglected. I hope you can see where this is going! It does not matter what Bob does the marriage will not work. He will have paid off all of Susan's bills, incurring massive debt which he alone must pay. Susan will file for divorce because she is not happy and feels neglected, stating Bob is always at work. She will get the house and one car in the divorce settlement. Bob will

The Po Man's Guide to Breaking the Poverty Cycle

be required to add the child to his medical insurance and pay the child's medical expenses. Bob will still be required to pay off the vehicle and pay child support and alimony. Bob will be financially devastated and left with nothing but bills that he is forced by law to pay. So much for love.

Example #2: Jill just got out of college and she majored in Women's Studies. With $30,000 in student loan debt and no realistic job prospects in her field, she faces a difficult situation. She has no one to help her pay off her loans. She moved in with her parents and took a job at the local Walmart at $8 an hour. Do I need to tell you where this is going? She is looking for a guy like Bob. If you have not been red pilled, get red pilled! I will not get into the whole MGTOW movement. Look it up and watch the videos. Now do not go buying into the narrative, just the facts. Make your own choices! I want to ensure you are well-informed!

Example #3: Paula comes from a wealthy family, but they disowned her because she married Dave. Her family taught her how to invest her money wisely and build wealth. Dave was a normal guy from a struggling family, but thanks to Paula, they never struggle. Paula and Dave are planning and budgeting superstars. In everything they do, they work together as a team. They live modestly, well below their means, and make it a rule to never borrow money unless it is necessary. They both have decent jobs. Paula makes $30,000 a year. Dave makes a little more at 45,000 a year. Their budget is extensive, covering everything they need, including food, water and all the necessities of life. They invest their money. They religiously track their 401(k) accounts. Paula likes to make necklaces, which she sells on eBay for extra money. Dave likes to work with his hands. He makes patio furniture out of wood in his spare time. These guys are the epitome of frugal and they know how to separate their wants from their needs. According to the plan, Paula and Dave also pool their money and invest it in real estate. They just started flipping houses.

Wealth Note: Wealthy people teach their children to use people as assets, doctors and so on. These assets get paid to help you. Wealthy people do not pay for anything they do not ask for. When you go to a doctor and they try to tell you what to do, it is because you are poor. They simply assume you do not know any better, so they will tack on extra tests, unnecessary prescriptions and give you misleading advice designed to keep you coming back more than you should. I have a wealthy friend **who scrutinizes all of her medical bills and disputes any and all charges she believes to be fraudulent.**

Example #4: Jeff and Monica Gleason, these two plan nothing. Monica is frugal and Jeff likes to pretend he is better off financially than he is, resulting in overspending. Jeff often borrows money from his friends and must pay them back on payday. It is an endless cycle that prevents them from saving money. Monica must nag Jeff to get him to do anything responsible. She is the only reason they still have a home. They both have decent jobs. Monica makes $45,000 a year. Jeff makes $18 an hour. He could

The Po Man's Guide to Breaking the Poverty Cycle

make more, but that would mean greater responsibility. Jeff will eventually lose Monica because of his carefree attitude about life and how he spends his money. They cannot afford to invest any of their money and only Monica has opted to contribute to a 401(k) account. Monica does not feel secure and is tiring of having to tell Jeff to be responsible. Jeff does not see the handwriting on the wall, he thinks: Monica just likes to nag; it is just her thing.

NOTE: Budgeting has one big drawback. For it to work properly, you must consciously choose to update and utilize it. Budgeting does not save you from bad spending habits, but it will point them out. Budgeting gives you a platform on which to plan out your financial goals and provides you with a handy reference model to help you stay on course.

There is nothing too small or important that you need or want, that should not be included in your budget.

The idea is to estimate the total of anything you desire and find a way over time to pay it off. But, before you go throwing money out there, you must remember to break down the total amount into payments if you cannot afford to buy it outright. Considerate it your form of layaway. When you buy something, you cannot afford to pay off in one lump sum, make sure the payments will not affect you financially. It must be as they say: throw away money.

Let us pretend you want a stereo that is on sale for $300. Got lucky at work and you are now guaranteed an additional 10 hours a week in overtime for the next three weeks! You will have paid all your real bills. After doing the math, you know you'll have $175 each week for spending money after taxes. You only need two weeks to pay off the stereo. After this is done, you will have an additional $50 to deal with. Instead of splurging or spend money, you decide to buy 2 ounces of silver. You decide to save the next $175 and put it into your Emergency Fund. After much deliberation, you decide that you cannot trust yourself to leave the saved money alone; therefore, to prevent spending it, you will buy more silver.

Silver cannot be spent at a store. No fast-food place will take it and your only recourse would be to cash it in if you wanted the money. But you bought silver to prevent you from being able to spend it. Once you have the silver in hand, you store it away and it is soon forgotten. You started the Emergency Fund knowing that it is money you have which you cannot spend! Its sole purpose is to be there, money you have put away for a rainy day. So, instead of blowing the money like you normally would, you elected to buy something you could always cash in, but you cannot spend. And like you expected before you knew it, you had a few thousand dollars of silver on hand to bail you out of most jams. You used your brain; you knew you would be tempted by cash on hand just sitting there already and available so you bought silver as a safeguard.

The Po Man's Guide to Breaking the Poverty Cycle

You must be smarter than the people around you! You must think ahead. I have purchased 200 or so ounces of silver! And there have been many occasions I have had to use silver to bail me out of minor financial jams! Stacking gold and silver is addictive! Gold and silver are the physical representation of your money, something you can always look at! You can also touch it! But you cannot spend it! And you must go out of your way to cash it in! You must learn to come up with new and more creative ways to Stash your money in such a way you cannot spend it, but it will always be available to you if you find yourself in a jam!

The idea is this: if you have money, you are never broke! Even if you cannot spend it, it is still money! I do not know why, but if you have money, it attracts more money. The "goal" is to never be without money! So, if you are anything like me, I say, if! You will need to be creative. Find many ways to have money you cannot spend. So be honest about this. Silver and gold are **real money!** You must be willing to do things that are a little outside of your comfort zone. You must find a way to put yourself in a position where you are able to give YOU something to hold onto! Because no one else will! I harp on about this because no one out there wants to help you! No one out there is going to do anything for you unless there is something in it for them! If you do not set yourself up ahead of time no one else will! What are you going to do, in your time of need, when you have to dig yourself out of a hole?

I have spent my entire life having no one to turn to! No one would or could give me useful advice! My goal in authoring this book is to ensure YOU cannot say the same! I have watched so many young men of this new generation destroy themselves before they ever got started. I believe someone needs to help them! Someone is going to have to tell them how things work! If this does not happen, then in their greatest time of need they will be lost. All you must do is go to California, walk along the sidewalks and see how many homeless people there are camped out on the streets. No one is going to rescue them from themselves and the lies they have been taught.

If you are of the mind, people are by nature good and generous. Go there! It will only take a day to destroy your delusion, for you to see the same destitute people being completely ignored. People passing by, pretending they do not exist! Nobody is going to help you! Nobody wants to care! No one will come and rescue you! Except YOU! Your past must feed your future, built and based upon your present actions. If you do not start now, tomorrow will be too late! Young men hate being told the truth. So talking to them is sometimes pointless, but I began to understand: If you can get a young man to read, you can also get him to listen to reason!

The Po Man's Guide to Breaking the Poverty Cycle

Grocery Lists

Your grocery list should be extensive. It should cover everything you normally buy! Up-to-date pricing for these items, the quantities you intend to purchase and which store you will visit to acquire these items. Plan your routes so you only make one trip. Start your errands at the store farthest away and make stops on the way home at the other stores on your list for the day. You will save gas and time! Have an estimated total so you know exactly what you are going to spend on food! Always know your total grocery bill before reaching the checkout line.

	7/12/2019	
Roast & Bag		HEB
Potatoes (1)		HEB
Welches Grape Juice(2)		HEB
Real Fruit Juice		Family Dollar
Fruit Punch/Lemonade(5)	$ 8.00	HEB
Chicken Thighs		HEB
Hot Wings (2)		HEB
Chicken Wings	$ 10.00	HEB
Drumsticks		HEB
Breakfast Sausage	$ 4.00	HEB
Chicken Tenders		HEB
OX Tails (2)		HEB
Swai Fillets	$9.00	HEB
Talapia Fillets		HEB
Egg Rolls	$ -	HEB
Steak Sirloin (2)		HEB
Hamburger Meat	$ 8.00	HEB
LAMB Chop		HEB
Lasagna		HEB
Bacon	$ 4.00	HEB
Hot Dogs		HEB
Lunch Meat (Turkey Ham)		HEB
Beef Sausage Links		HEB
Eggs	$ 3.00	HEB
Ice Cream - Vanilla	$ 3.00	HEB
Butter		HEB
TUNA (2)		HEB
Mayo		HEB
Sandwhich Spread		HEB
OJ	$ 3.00	HEB
Gravy		Walmart
Lemon Pound Cake	$ -	HEB

You should always be below your original budget projection. Avoid impulse buying unless you have saved enough money for additional purchases! You are good to go if those new items will not affect your estimated overall total. Be smarter, plan out all your meals, cutting back whenever possible! And never go shopping when you are hungry! Your goal when grocery shopping is to get in and get out, having purchased everything on your list. Remember, food prices tend to fluctuate, keep your listing updated. My grocery list is 122 lines long.

The Po Man's Guide to Breaking the Poverty Cycle

I have even gone as far as to make a budget for my dry cleaning. Factoring in the taxes and the number of garments, I could come up with a formula that would tell me how much everything will cost.

Dry cleaning is expensive! When you want to know how much everything is going to cost you beforehand. What will you do? Yeah, I know you are thinking, dry cleaning? Who has money for that!? You must keep in mind that the day may come when you are going to need a suit for an interview. Who knows, they may have a dress code. What are you going to do when you land an awesome job and they say you must dress better? You will need to know how much it is going to cost you. So, I tried my best to take a little bit of the guesswork out of it for you.

Dry Cleaning

Cleaning	Starch				Subtotal			
Dress Shirts	No	0	$	5.49	$ -			
Polo Shirts	No	0	$	5.49	$ -			
Silk Shirts	No	0	$	5.49	$ -			
Slacks	No	0	$	6.90	$ -			
Pants	No	0	$	5.90	$ -			
Dockers	Yes/Light	0	$	5.90	$ -			
Jeans	Yes/Med	2	$	6.29	$ 12.58			
Vest	No	0	$	1.50	$ -			
Blazer	No	0	$	7.41	$ -			
Leather Jacket	No	0	$	20.00	$ -			
Alterations	What Type							
Jacket Crest	Sew On	0	$	7.16	$ -			
Jacket Buttons	Sew On	0	$	7.16	$ -			
Jeans/Hem	Original	0	$	14.95	$ -			
Leather Jacket	No	0	$	20.00	$ -	TAX		TOTAL
		0			$ 12.58	$ 1.04		$ 13.62

Just in case you want to do the same, the two formulas you will need are below.

TAX=PRODUCT (E70, 8.25%)
TOTAL =SUM (E70:F70)

The Po Man's Guide to Breaking the Poverty Cycle

Moving Money Around

I suppose it is safe to say that you can never make the best use of your budget if you do not know how to move money around. There will always be situations and/or circumstances where you will not make your budget or balance out your checkbook. At these times, you are going to have to do what I call moving money around. You are going to have to become creative when finding new ways to spread things out or juxtapose money, so your credit card or loan payments are on time and your bills are being paid. Moving money around allows you to give yourself an unofficial extension. By moving money from this week, to let us say, the second week of another month. You can only do this if you've already budgeted for the entire year. A budget made out for the entire year gives you the budgeter insight. You can see where this bill can be substituted for another bill! A well-thought-out movement of funds will enable you to pay both bills on time and lose nothing. As you continue to forecast your budget for each year, you will get better and better at moving money around. Now, imagine if you will, attempting to have the same foresight with only a month budgeted. You cannot see clearly into the same future if you have nothing written down!

Placeholder: A want (pair of shoes, jeans, amino acids, or any item that is not a need). Placed into a budget simply causes the weekly sum to equal the expected amount of take-home money generated for the week. Call it "extra money" for lack of a better term.

1. Silver and gold make excellent placeholders:
   - You cannot just spend them you must trade them in.
   - They can go up in value.

Example: I have a $140 light bill due right now! But I cannot pay for it right now. Luckily for me, I have already added what I like to call placeholders to my budget. I begin to strike out these placeholders and a balance of money begins to form. Let us say, I had an item I wanted (not needed), which would have cost me $100 and another two items totaling $40. So I take the money from those placeholders and managed to come up with the money I needed to pay my bill! Losing the wants will not affect me. If I am able, I can put the placeholders somewhere else, so that I can still get what I want later, but only after taking care of my needs. Do not get caught up in big numbers, sometimes placeholders can be small, i.e., $8 here, $15 there, $20, etc. Doesn't matter, it is a placeholder. You total up your budget and you find: you have $30 extra (I still hate this saying, there is no such thing as "extra money"! You get what you work for so there is no such thing as extra money). Money left over, I will accept!

You have $30 left over and try as you might, you can't think of anything you might need. So, you decide to put the money into your emergency fund. Get it into your skull, there are going to be emergencies! There are going to be times when $20 or $30 will bail you out of the bind! Hold on to what you have whenever you are able! Don't just go out and buy stuff you don't need! You can do it later when you're prosperous.

The Po Man's Guide to Breaking the Poverty Cycle

Once again, I cannot stress enough the importance of the placeholder. I've found frequently, even during the writing of the book, I've had to continuously use the money I've gleaned from placeholders to counteract the chaos of unforeseen bills.

Let's see if I can explain placeholders a little better, to give you a clearer picture of what I'm trying to say here... Imagine yourself entering your yearly budget, week by week, month by month. And after you entered in all your big bills and estimated your overtime if you are getting overtime. Will you have money left over each week? I often put in a want, something I desire, but can completely do without. You can enter a BBQ pit for $200 if it is something you have been wanting on for a while. Remember, the object is to allocate the money. Whether you buy the BBQ Pit remains to be seen. You are entering the BBQ Pit into your budget as a placeholder: money you can glean if something goes wrong. If something goes wrong and it usually does, you can immediately adapt and change out the placeholder and put the new bill in its place. I have a habit of including quasi emergency money throughout my budget each week if possible. I add emergency money somewhere each month. Some months more than others. It must be done! You will thank me later.

Cast thy bread upon the waters: for thou shalt find it after many days.

Giving Money
I know that, in a lot of people's minds, giving away their hard-earned money is the last thing they want to do or believe they should do. I'm not going to start Bible thumping, so relax! Let's just say it works! Giving out of your need is ridiculous! Don't do it! But if you have a little extra and it will help someone who you know is trying their best and has no one else to help them, then by all means give! Don't give to a church. Don't give to an organization. Help people you know who will use the money to better themselves or meet their own or their family's needs with the money you have given them.

There are few among us who can say they don't know some child without a dad at home. It's an epidemic in America. Now I'm not trying to tell you to go out and make some grand Good Samaritan gesture! I am saying, however, I've noticed, over the years: when you do good for others, that same good returns to you! I'm sure every one of us knows some young children who have no dad. Sometimes it could be something as simple as giving your time, a word of inspiration, or a word of motivation! Our goal is to break the poverty cycle; therefore, we must hit it where it lives! This means each of us as we learn and grow will have the ability to teach others to do the same things you are learning from me! Mastering these lessons will enable you to positively impact many lives. Think about it. You see all these TV commercials promising to help children, and deep down you know that any money you donate will never reach them. These people rake in millions! If they solved the problems they so eloquently bring to YOUR attention, what happens to those millions? Think about it! Those clothing drives for little children. Those food drives for needy families! All you need to do is ask these people if they ever see any money! If you pay attention, you will see ninety percent of the time.

The Po Man's Guide to Breaking the Poverty Cycle

When you give to an organization, those little children may never even see money! They may never even come close to receiving anything you contributed! Stop! Take the time to research these organizations. Some of them have been around for decades and the commercials keep right on coming. The suffering is still present. Shouldn't you see people being helped all around you? Is it happening? Remove the blinders these liars have positioned over your eyes and stop pretending you don't see anything being done to truly help these people!

Then people will stop pretending that they don't see your struggles, they will take notice, they will want to help you! You get what you put out there! I've dedicated many years to assisting young children, giving help when and where I could. I started this thing long ago when I was working so many hours; I didn't get the chance to cash most of my checks, because I was always at work! I would get paid and make sure I had at least twenty $1 bills. Once: Once the neighborhood children gathered around the back of my truck, I began asking them questions. I asked questions about Science, English and anything else I could think of. If they got the question right, they got a dollar. I was trying to teach them: knowledge means money! And it seems as though I somehow managed to get my point across! I didn't find out until years later that some of them went on to become electronics guys, engineers and technicians of one sort or the other! They learned! They even tracked me down to thank me! The whole idea behind breaking the poverty cycle is that you must stomp it out wherever you find it! And before you know it, we all make it! True power is only given unto the weak, not to the STRONG! The STRONG wrest it from the weak, who allow it. The weak fear those they perceive to be STRONG. And Fear murders the hopes and dreams of all men!

There was this time...when the wife had just bought all four children new bedroom furniture and when I asked her what she was going to do with the used furniture, she simply said, "Throw it away." And I said, "I don't think so!" I asked her to call the children into the living room. Once there, I asked them, is there anyone you guys know who needed and would want the furniture we were going to throw away? Surprisingly, the children came up with the same name. So, my wife and I went over there, knocked on the door and asked the woman of the house if she could use four beds that were slightly used. It was like a light turned on inside of her and she smiled and then cry. I carried the heavy stuff. The wife and children carried the rails and everything else. Four little children received a bed to sleep in from us that night. We didn't spend any money, and it took us very little time to move the stuff! We were able to help those children by giving them furniture we were going to throw away callously. You don't always have to give people your best! Sometimes, the old saying is true: one man's trash is another man's treasure! Now that's just crazy!

Remember the Boy Scouts or even the Cub Scouts back in the day? They used to have this thing about helping little old ladies cross the street. I'm only bringing them up to

The Po Man's Guide to Breaking the Poverty Cycle

make a point. They were children; they did what little they could and sometimes a little goes a long way. And maybe one of your neighbors is one of those little old ladies. Five bucks here, a little extra food there. Check on them occasionally. Ask them how their day is going. Giving doesn't always mean money, but money is the easiest thing to give. If you have little, then give a little. If you have more then give more! We must learn to meet the need.

The cost of medicine has always been the biggest financial burden on most senior citizens. Talk to a few of the guys in the neighborhood and come up with a little fund you can use to help the needy in your area. Save leftover change you don't care about and when the need arises, you can cash in your change and buy a widow her medicine for the month. This might cost you a little of your time, but the effect would be huge! Money not spent on medicine could buy a widow a little more food! Or buy an extra blanket because she is so cold at night. You can't break a cycle you helped to perpetuate by doing nothing! Wherever you see needless suffering in someone else's life, stamp it out by any means necessary if it's legal! You have the power to change your environment. Be creative! Be good! Don't just look around and shake your head! Get it done!

Everyone has passed someone on the streets that you know is homeless. Don't ignore them! If you have a dollar or two, give it and when you need it, someone will give you a dollar or two! I know I can't convince you these things work, but I can tell you, this philosophy has worked for me! Help came to me during a time of need. When I needed food, someone fed me! When I needed clothing, someone gave me their spare clothes! I know we can't stomp out all the evils in the world! But I also know everybody has difficulties. No one is immune, we all suffer lack! Just not at the same time! Make it your business to do what little you can! And if we all rise and start helping one another, we will break the poverty cycle! I once met a homeless veteran on the street. I had five dollars in my pocket. We talked about the military and he was telling me how no one would even try to help him. I could also tell he was a little mentally unstable, but he was harmless. I couldn't do much, but I gave him three five dollars, and he seemed so grateful. When he asked why I had given him the money, I said, "Because I'm a veteran and I know if I was in the same situation." I would hope someone would show me the same kindness.

Using your 401(k) as an Emergency Savings Account

Over the years, I've learned one of the greatest weapons in your arsenal is your 401(k) account. Most people won't bother to sign up for the 401(k) account offered by their company, because they see no future for them at the company. While this may be true, you should still use what you have available, if given the opportunity to use it. Although you may never use your 401(k) as an actual retirement account, you can always use it as

The Po Man's Guide to Breaking the Poverty Cycle

an emergency savings account. Consider it as insurance to be used in case of termination or you quit.

I find myself telling everyone these days that they cannot afford to not have a 401(k) account! Based on math, how much you stand to lose by not having an account seems clear to me. When people say they can't afford to have a 401(k) account, it tells me they have done no research. They are unaware that the government only taxes 401(k) money after it is deducted. They don't realize that they are paying less in taxes, even if they could only afford a very minimal contribution, let's say 1%. For example, if you make $1000 a month, one percent of a thousand is $10. That's $10 you didn't have before and 3% is $30 you didn't have before. So, 30×12= $360 you saved in a year. So, if you get fired, you have an excess of $360 and after taxes it is $252. I averaged it out and can safely say, they charge you a 10% tax penalty when you do an early withdrawal. Now, who could use an extra $252? If enrolled in a 401(k) account and you stay at the company less than five years, you only get the money you invested, minus a 10% tax penalty. And the money your employer matched usually disappears. But let's say, you got lucky and got fired after six years, then you would get to keep all the money minus the 30% in taxes! When you stay with your company for more than five years, you get to keep the money your employer matched! So if your employer matches up to 3% it would be $502 a year!

They often say, "Any little bit helps!" This is especially true when you find yourself in need of emergency money and you have no job! If you were terminated and are ineligible for unemployment benefits due to your actions. I'm not judging, just pointing out some companies can be toxic to your health. I have gotten myself fired on purpose before and was so relieved once I walked out of the building. It happens to us all. But each time I had my 401(k) to fall back on.

Someone convinced a person who worked for their company for nine years or more that they couldn't afford a 401(k) during that time. So, when they left their company, they left with nothing. Consider their average paycheck would have been missing about $20 a week. It adds up! If you get fired, the money is still yours! Even if you count the taxes lost and pay the 10% early withdrawal penalty, it's a solution where everyone benefits. Person could have left with money in their pocket!

Yeah, I know I'm bouncing around a bit but bear with me, there is a method to my madness. The idea is to give your brain many different things to absorb all at once.

Later, your mind will begin to paint a picture and you will know what to do next after you have read the book. You will be able to apply what you have learned!

The Po Man's Guide to Breaking the Poverty Cycle

Chapter 2: Skills! Skills! Skills! You have to GROW!!

If you're not like most people I know and you work at a job that requires basic skills, such as a specialized laborer, someone who uses hand tools, you are going to have a leg up on the competition. You are on your way towards the desired outcome. If you are a general laborer and have no skills to speak of then you will need to decide or at least discover what you want to do with the rest of your life. What are your interests? What excites you? What motivates you? If you have no clue, pick something, anything and begin to acquire those skills. If you have or had the opportunity at work to learn a new skill set and declined to do so because you feel you're doing it for free! You are seriously listening to the wrong people! Free training is FREE TRAINING! You can add it to your resume!

Everyone else will drill it into your head that you need a job. Any job. I'm not trying to force the bible on anyone, but I noticed the book of Job is spelled the same, but pronounced differently. So, I looked up the meaning of his name and it means AFFLICTED. Suddenly, it occurred to me: a job is sort of an affliction. Low wages, demanding work and more hours than most of us want. Affliction! You are killing yourself and are barely able to make ends meet. So, I thought, this will not work for me. I need something that will pay me a decent wage and it needs to be something I will enjoy doing.

What skills do you possess? Can you take these skills with you to a new job? A new industry in a different location? Do you have the skills you need to move up? Can you become a supervisor with your present skill set? You are going to have to ask yourself, what do I want to do? What kind of career can I imagine undertaking for the next 25 years? What is it going to take to get me there? Am I going to need a special license? Do I need to attend some sort of trade school? The younger you start, the better off you will be.

For some reason, I had this thing where I would sort through Job Descriptions in the classifieds to see if I could find my dream job. A job I could grow into if given the chance and enough time. I would list all the skills required for the job and use my imagination to figure out what it would take for me to obtain those skills! At first it felt as though I was deluding myself until I got the first new skill under my belt. After that it was open season on my ignorance!

Based on all the job descriptions I'd read and the skills required, I decided I wanted to be an Industrial Maintenance Technician. Now, don't get me wrong, your goals must be realistic and obtainable with lots of planning, hard work and diligence. In my case, I had recently gotten out of the army, where I had been a 67U, which is a Medium Helicopter Repairman. Without a miracle, there was no realistic path for me to enter the field of industrial maintenance. My first break came when I walked into the Based on all the job descriptions I'd read and the skills required. I decided I wanted to be an Industrial

The Po Man's Guide to Breaking the Poverty Cycle

Maintenance Technician. Now, don't get me wrong, your goals must be realistic and obtainable with lots of planning, hard work and diligence. In my case, I had recently gotten out of the army, where I had been a 67U, which is a Medium Helicopter Repairman. Without a miracle, I had no realistic path to a career in industrial maintenance. My first break came when I walked into the Texas Workforce Commission office and entered the Workforce Innovation & Opportunity Act (WIOA) program! I don't know how or why, but someone established this program as an OJT (On-the-job training) program. WIOA focused on the acquisition of skills within the work environment, under normal working conditions (OJT). Through on-the-job training, workers acquire both general skills they can transfer from one job to another and specific skills are unique to a particular job). So, I took some tests, and they matched my aptitude scores and gave me a selection of fields from which to choose. And there it was, an Instrumentation Technician. I interviewed and got the job thanks to my years of helicopter maintenance and the electrical and electronics and hydraulic experience I had obtained in the military. There, I learned to build electrical and pneumatic control panels. I also got PLC experience, which was on my list.

I soon realized the field wasn't for me and became a full-time Control Panel Wireman for seven years; until it dawned on me: being a wireman was getting me nowhere. I went back to the classifieds and struck gold! I found a job listing that was too good to be true! This company wanted someone with PLC experience and proven mechanical ability and a willingness to learn. I was going to be a Maintenance Mechanic in a company that manufactured corrugated boxes! That job opened the door for me to get into Industrial Maintenance. I got sick breathing in welding fumes and missed over two days in 90 days (about 3 months), so they let me go. Anger wasn't what I felt. I hated my job! But I had acquired the title I had been after Maintenance Mechanic. Another interview and a new job title. I found myself at a glass manufacturing plant. The company needed someone with PLC experience, electrical ability and hydraulic/pneumatic experience with a lot of room to grow. I learned quickly and soon became the Senior Millwright. Over the years, I learned to order parts, add new vendors, build a Preventative Maintenance Program, and schedule maintenance on all machines in the factory. I loved everything about the place except my pay, but I was, after the experience, 3 to 5 years to be exact.

Before we get too deep into developing your skills, I have one question. Do you own a computer? You wouldn't believe the number of people who would say no and then make silly excuses like I can't afford one. And this self-same individual who is making minimum wage will go out and buy an iPhone! They are oblivious to the irony. If not an iPhone, some other high-dollar item, never realizing they could've bought a nice computer! It will never occur to them that if they had skipped the iPhone, bought a reasonably priced phone and saved the rest of their money, they would have a computer! Have you ever seen one guy who spends all of his money fixing up his vehicle? Somehow, he can afford high dollar tires, spinning rims and a stereo system that rattles his windows when he drives by you on the street! Yet this same guy will

The Po Man's Guide to Breaking the Poverty Cycle

always ask someone else for gas money because he can't afford to keep gas in his dream car.

I'm saying this to get one point across, there is no situation or circumstance where not having a computer is going to help you. I have just purchased a $215 computer and monitor with Microsoft Office 2016 on eBay for my sister, so I know what I'm talking about!

Let's say there is this job and the position will require him to know how to use Microsoft Office. What are the odds of him getting this job if he doesn't have a computer at home? How can he practice using MS Office? Let's say his competition is some person who has a computer at home. Let's assume this person knows almost nothing about Microsoft Office. But he can go online, take a few classes for free and get caught up to speed. Who do you think is going to get the job? To have what you desire, you are going to have to take the calculated necessary steps to ensure that when your time comes, you WILL BE READY!

In short, go for it! Live, learn and make mistakes; but NEVER give up! Seize any opportunity to learn a new skill! You don't stop learning; until you die. If your neighbor is a welder and wants to teach you LEARN! Enroll in free courses online and if you can afford it, pay for them. Allison and Udemy are excellent sites. The classes are affordable, if not free and very informative. Attend a Vocational College, find a Trade School, a Technical Institute and do whatever it takes (as long as it's legal)! There are no shortcuts, there are no easy roads and slow and steady wins the race! If you can see that you are still making progress, you are heading in the right direction.
If you want to be a plumber or an electrician, these are the steps in my state:

- Complete your high school education.
- Get Vocational Training.
- Complete an Apprenticeship Program.
- Get Licensed.
- Look for employment or open a business

Example #1: Jaime has a felony on her record. Instead of throwing her hands into the air and simply giving up any hope of having a decent future, she did some research and found out she could become a Dental Assistant. She went to a technical college, got her certificate and quickly found a job. Now she has a career! Hers isn't the most preferred method. But it worked out in the end because she wasn't willing to give up! And she wanted to make something of herself. She succeeded. I know this woman!

Example #2: I met an old guy while I was working at the glass factory and we became friends. Paul had worked there for 12 years and they were treating him like crap. One day during lunch, he was near tears when I asked him one simple question: "What do you want to do for a living?" "I want to drive trucks," he answered. "Then let's make it

The Po Man's Guide to Breaking the Poverty Cycle

happen," I replied. We closed the door to my office, got on the internet and searched for suitable truck driving schools until we found the right one for him. He needed a small loan to get started and then $125 for some new glasses. We got it done. Now he makes 70K a year driving his truck.

Example #3: I met a young guy. He was a friend of one of the young men I was mentoring in the neighborhood. He lived at home with his parents and needed a job. I spoke with my boss and we decided to give him a try as a Maintenance Helper. He only lasted six months, but he acquired many new skills.

Example #4: Remember, I spoke of the times I would give out money to the children in the neighborhood if they could answer my questions correctly? Well, one of these youngsters listened to me when I advised the older boys and told them to look into ITT Tech. He went to ITT Tech when he got older. He graduated, landed an excellent job at a company quickly, and they subsequently promoted him to a management position. Now he has multiple gigs on the side. He even has his own pool cleaning business. He never passes up on any opportunity to better himself! To be different, you must THINK differently!

The Copycat Wins in the End

Reality Hack: I'm always pushing my limits, constantly challenging myself. Lifelong learning and skill acquisition are important to me. I know there's no limit to what I can achieve.

In every group of ten people, you will find at least five of them are good at something different. One guy is the best salesman. One guy is the best at paperwork, and another is the best at getting things done. Your job is to figure out what those talents are and get them to teach you how they do things, whatever the "skill" may be.

Let's use me as an example. Years ago, when I was in training to become an Instrumentation Technician, there was this guy named Long who was the best at wiring control panels. Kahn was the best at pneumatic panels. Terrence was the best at reading prints and finding mistakes. I knew how to remove the doors without grinding or damaging the metal by removing the piano wire used to secure the hinges. I also had more experience working with hydraulic systems than most of the guys in the shop. Ted was the best at pneumatic tubing, layouts and tube fitting. When we were in doubt, we would make our rounds. We'd go to the guy we believe was the best at whatever discipline we were struggling with and ask them to teach us the ropes.

The objective is to gain a new skill. A skill you can use to get you closer to achieving your goal. Anywhere you go or on any job you take, you should be attempting to beef up your resume.

The Po Man's Guide to Breaking the Poverty Cycle

Warning: Not everyone is going to be keen on teaching you, so you are going to have to be creative in how you approach them and sincere when you attempt to convince them you are worth teaching. Remember, they must want to teach you the skills they know. When they start teaching, shut up and listen! Take notes. It tells people you are serious about learning. Never tell someone, "I was trying to see if you knew," because it's an insult. Joke with your friends later when you get home. You MUST take learning seriously. NO ONE will waste their time on some clown who thinks he's in elementary and he's treating them like a new substitute teacher. People consider their time to be valuable. It is something they can never get back! Behave yourself! Be mindful of their time! Be respectful! Learn.

Reality Hack: There is such a thing as a STUPID QUESTION! Don't ask them! Ask your question in your mind. If you can come up with a good and plausible answer and can find it easily online, don't ask it! Ask questions of others when you get stuck and can't figure it out on your own.

I'm having a hard time here and it may seem as though I'm rambling, but I'm trying to come up with every scenario I can think of that might help you.

Know Your STUFF!

Brain Hack: If you hate to read then read until you don't! At first, you will fall asleep or zone out after a few paragraphs. Later you will fall asleep after a few chapters until finally, you will read as much as you want without any unwanted side effects. I know you don't believe me, but it's NORMAL! It's a mental game you must win! It's your job to train your brain, to make it bow down to your will.

Mind Training Tip: I know you have heard of the term, "Think outside the box!" Well, we are not going to practice that...

You are going to have to retrain your brain. You will only be allowed to use the thoughts that are inside the box. The difference is that you are going to be the one building the box. Everyone you meet will attempt to tell you HOW to think or HOW you should think! Nothing is written in stone! True intelligence can't be measured because it grows as you grow. The more you question EVERYTHING the MORE answers you receive!

Mind Training Tip: This might sound unbelievable, but you actively choose what to remember. Tell your brain to commit it to memory. It might not seem natural at first, but with time, it will become habitual.

The Po Man's Guide to Breaking the Poverty Cycle

Self-discipline: the ability to control one's feelings and overcome one's weaknesses; the ability to pursue what one thinks is right despite temptations or the manipulations of others to get you to abandon which you believe is right for you and your circumstances.

Mind Training Tip: Controlling your emotions takes practice. You must think of yourself as two different people. The "at work you" should show no real emotions. The "at home you" can vent, rant and rave later so you can get it off your chest. Venting works. It allows you to hear yourself saying something stupid and/or emotional. I have rarely seen anyone (with a brain) remain angry after they have vented to the right person.

Discipline: 1: to punish or penalize for the sake of enforcing obedience and perfecting moral character. 2: to train or develop by instruction and exercise, especially in self-control.

Diligence: noun careful and persistent work or effort.

Effective communication: this is defined as verbal speech or other methods of relaying information that gets a point across... An example of effective communication is when the person to whom you are speaking listens actively, absorbs your point and understands it.

Mind Training Tip: Training yourself to think and speak at the same time is a choice. You tell your brain to think and have the words come out of your mouth at the same time. It's weird at first, but once you get the hang of it, it will become natural. There is a side effect. You will think aloud or as they say, talk to yourself.

Knowing your stuff will rely on you being able to perceive when and how to employ the Brain Hacks listed above. Mind Training Tips, self-discipline, diligence, and the ability to be able to effectively communicate. This will require considerable effort on your part. Change is sometimes slow. You must also abandon your use of slang at work. It will get you nowhere in the real world.

You need to spend your time becoming known for doing the right thing and making the right choices. Never go looking for attention. Knowing your stuff will bring you all the attention you need. Mind your own business and stay out of ALL drama!

Owe no man nothing. Never use someone else despitefully. Whatever resources you obtain, whether it be money or things you need, always pay what you owe! And as far as knowledge and skills go, whoever agrees to teach you what they know, your job is to drain them dry and pass them! The student must become better than their teacher!

The Po Man's Guide to Breaking the Poverty Cycle

When you don't know what you are doing admit it quickly and then ask as many questions as you need, until you understand the task at hand. Nobody likes a Know-it-all, who knows nothing!

The Rock, the Sponge and the Diamond in the Rough

Some people are just born talented and rarely make mistakes. They get all the best stuff, but you are not one of them, so we're not going to talk about them anymore.

If you're reading this book, it's because you are a rock. Your job is to become a sponge and after months, sometimes years, of just soaking things up, you will find you have become a diamond in the rough.

A rock is a hard-headed individual you can't teach. You can attempt to instruct them, but they won't listen. They are usually stubborn, opinionated, and for some unknown reason, arrogant. Most of these hard-headed individuals think they know everything, when in fact they know nothing.

A sponge: is a wounded rock, which has acquired so many pits and chips and holes over the years, they have become softer because of being drenched in their own sweat and tears. Experience has taught the sponge. And Experience is a **HARSH** teacher. They know how and when to shut up, listen and allow themselves to be taught. They have learned to follow instructions to the letter. They always listen intently and ask intelligent questions so they don't make stupid mistakes when assigned tasks. A sponge rarely gives their opinion because they understand what happens when they open their mouths without thinking things through. **A sponge knows it is better to be silent and be thought of as a fool rather than open their mouth and remove all doubt.**

A diamond: is an older sponge that's become hardened through adversity. Diamonds don't make stupid mistakes. They usually have a good idea of how things work. A diamond knows what is required, shows initiative and gets things done without ever having to be told!

The Po Man's Guide to Breaking the Poverty Cycle

Research! When You Don't Know!!

I can't explain why I've developed this pattern of tackling things I don't understand. I created it in a time of need; it's a mental construct, an inner drive, call it what you will. The teasing I experienced in my youth is what motivates me now. In situations where I lacked knowledge, words, or a course of action. Yet, I've developed an insatiable need for knowledge. Always be ready with an answer, the right answer.

In the Army, you'd have to do pushups if the Drill Sergeant asked you a question and you failed to give the correct answer. You were supposed to know your general orders. You were supposed to know your equipment. There was no room for anything except excellence. My curiosity has always driven me to learn about everything. My incessant questions drove my parents crazy. Physically and mentally, I was weak. So, I watched a lot of Kung Fu flicks. The hero would start out as puny and train until he was the strongest guy around. I've always attacked my weaknesses. Maybe it's because I'm the only person I've ever been able to depend on. But when I find something that I completely suck at, I feel this need to conquer it or develop what I call in my mind, acceptable mastery.

As I get older, I have realized that I do not give up on anything easily. I think I learned it somewhere along the way, and now I attack and attack anything that has a challenge in front of it. It doesn't matter if it is an issue, a task, a problem, or something else, it gets attacked until I'm ready to give up, or until finally, I get it. This doesn't always work for everyone, though. It takes a lot of effort and time to attack something until finally something clicks in your brain, and sometimes I will attack a thing as much as I possibly can, but no matter how much effort I put into it, I just won't get it.

I can't explain this, but it has happened to me too many times to be a coincidence. I think there is something to it. When I'm stuck on a question or puzzle, I start by trying to solve it myself. When I reach my limit, I give it up for a while, maybe a few months. Something will happen that will lead me to ask the right questions to figure out the puzzle. It's like a key that will unlock the information that I've been seeking. I don't have these "a-ha" moments where I suddenly understand everything all at once. Instead, the answers come in waves and I slowly put it all together until I finally get it.

Sometimes I bite off more than I can chew. A perfect example is when I decided that, no matter what happened, I was going to learn how to program PLCs. I researched the internet and found classes I could take. I also searched out websites that offered training programs. Still, I couldn't get it. I never had that revelation that makes something click. It didn't stop me from trying, though. I still believe that I will eventually master PLC programming. I've come to terms with the fact that it won't happen today. I have bigger fish to fry now. But it's still in the back of my mind. It's one more thing I

The Po Man's Guide to Breaking the Poverty Cycle

have yet to conquer! I don't know what your trigger is going to be, but I suggest you find it!

With this in mind, I will toss out some decent paying careers:

How do you become a Certified Safety Coordinator?
https://study.com/be_a_safety_coordinator.html

How to Become a Certified Project Management Professional
https://www.wikihow.com/BecomeaCertifiedProjectManagementProfessional

How to get into Human Resources
https://upstarthr.com/howtogetintohumanresources/

How to become a Registered Nurse
https://www.wikihow.com/BecomeaRegisteredNurse

How to Become an Accountant
https://www.wikihow.com/BecomeAccountantinTexas look up your state

How to Become a Radiology Technician
https://www.wikihow.com/BecomeaRadiologyTechnician

How to Become a Truck Driver Don't laugh, these guys make good money. I have a friend who makes 77,000 a year.
https://www.wikihow.com/BecomeaTruckDriver

Become a US Postal Worker
https://www.postalexam473e.com/jobs/index/?msclkid=b4f859d8e4a017dd338e07992c532a34

I can't list every career path you might be interested in but I can give you some advice. Ignore all the background noise. Look for entry-level positions. Not mediocre jobs, but really good ones, the kind that are hard to get. I know entry-level doesn't mean big bucks but when you're young and willing to learn there are a lot of opportunities out there. Entry-level jobs are becoming more common because today's colleges aren't churning out the kind of worker that businesses want. They don't need degrees anymore. They're looking for people with self-discipline and the ability to self-motivate. If you can show them that you're willing to learn, plus you have initiative, you're in. It's all about problem-solving ability, not parroting everything your professor said.

Note: Don't get discouraged, there's always a "back door" into almost any profession that requires a brain and pays less than one hundred thousand a year!

The Po Man's Guide to Breaking the Poverty Cycle

Karma (/ˈkɑːrmə/; Sanskrit: कर्म, Romanized: karma, IPA: [ˈkɐɾmɐ] (listen); Pali: kamma) means action, work, or deed; it also refers to the spiritual principle of cause and effect where intent and actions of an individual (cause) influence the future of individual (effect).

Whatever you put out there comes back to you! You cannot escape the consequences of your actions. You cannot reach any of your goals by stepping on someone else! Treat people the way you would have them treat you.

When it is time for you to train someone, do it with a good attitude. Later, when it is someone else's turn to train you, they will do it with a good attitude. Do not lord what you know over others. Be easy but firm. Let the people you train know you had to struggle to learn the things you are teaching them. I have found that people won't want to learn from you if you tick them off! They will learn nothing just to spite you and at the perfect opportunity use everything you did to them against you. Never burn bridges you might need to cross later. Just because you leave a place doesn't mean you might not need to go back later. Things change. Situations change. Always leave under good circumstances, even if you get fired. Leave with dignity. Don't resort to tattling on others or trying to get someone else fired. Be a man!

You have to progress until you "know better"
You are going to have to become a mad scientist of sorts. You must learn to observe people and predict their next move. Experiment with the many options available to you in order to find your way of doing things! Developing emotional detachment while interacting with others is a learned skill. Learning to anticipate their next move by adapting quickly. Anticipate their actions before they even understand their own responses. Formulate a question in a manner that you can foresee their response and the follow-up question they will pose.

You must become the king of mental multitasking, using all ideas as needed! You must master "when" to use what you know to ensure that you have a ready answer or have anticipated the outcome of any given scenario.

The smallest amount of information given at the right time has the greatest amount of impact! Sometimes you can read the smallest cues or gestures and immediately know what to do or how to react. It takes a lot of practice, but in time, you will get very good at reading people.

Trouble is so easy to get into and so hard to get out of! To succeed in life, you must have a sense of responsibility. It is your key to everything. There are many situations you will encounter in life, good and bad. The good situations are usually easy to handle, but you will find that bad situations can be very challenging. It is always best to anticipate bad situations from afar and try to ensure you are not involved. But, even if that happens, there's always the possibility of being involved, and you must be prepared to

The Po Man's Guide to Breaking the Poverty Cycle

address these situations. Never try to lie your way out of a bad situation because it will only make things worse. You must learn to take everything seriously, even when it's a joke. And never take any actions that might negatively impact or damage someone's livelihood. Take responsibility for your actions, and try to admit any fault that you may have. Never play the blame game. If the situation requires it, be the peacemaker, but most importantly, whatever the obstacle, get it done.

People show you who they are based on the jokes they tell.   Watch and observe!!

Your emotions are your enemy and should not be trusted under any circumstances, much less, be acted upon. Emotions are fickle at best and will always get you into trouble. Learn to get your emotions under control quickly by using logical thought.   When you get offended, agitated or just angry as hell, you must be able to think clearly!
Once you are calm enough to think, you can think your way out of a situation. And continue to think your way out until your emotions subside. When your emotions start to rise you must remember your emotions will catch up with your thoughts, and vice versa. Your emotions can be controlled and caused to subside by using logical thinking. When your emotions erupt, think of the consequences of whatever action your emotions are directing you to take! If the consequences outweigh the offense, your emotions will always subside! So, whatever you are feeling when your emotions attempt to take control, ignore them, think your way out of it! Your emotions will catch up! Emotions grow greater in strength the more you pay attention to them! And feeding into them only makes matters worse! Ignore them! They will go away! Take a walk! Remove yourself from the situation! Do whatever it takes, but never react!

 Conscience is the greatest gift you will ever receive, so trust it and learn to heed it! Not doing so can cause something bad to happen. When you have the sense that something is going to go wrong heed the warning! Before you do or say anything that gets you into trouble, pause and take a moment to run your thoughts through your mind, and then respond the best you can to resolve the situation. It's often too late when people say, "I shouldn't have done this or I shouldn't have done that!" So learn to avoid negative results by listening to your inner voice! If you begin to listen to your conscience, you will no longer get in trouble, and your life will thank you for it, trust me.

You MUST BE WORTHY OF THE JOB YOU HAVE BEEN HIRED TO DO! In most cases, everyone will tell you they didn't do anything wrong, but this is always a lie. You must learn to speak the truth in your inner mind and never lie to yourself. Don't try to lay blame on someone else when you know you are at fault. Admit you're wrong and move on. You must have integrity. Other people need to be able to trust what you say because you have become known for your honesty.
Your boss wants the truth from you, but don't be naive enough to think that they will be completely honest with you. They will play word games and give no straight answer to

The Po Man's Guide to Breaking the Poverty Cycle

your questions about money or promotions, and this is to be expected, so don't be surprised when it happens. You are the only one who has the power to control your actions.

No one makes you do anything.
You can choose what you do with your life.
It's important to live in reality and not just dream, because you can't live on dreams. If something looks like trouble, it probably is trouble. If something sounds too good to be true, it probably is too good to be true. If something seems too easy, it is because it is too easy, and it probably won't work. Positive fake thinking is just lying to yourself. Regardless of how you slice it, fake positivity will get you in as much trouble as a straight-up lie.

Murphy's Law should become your new mantra. Whatever can go wrong, will go wrong. You must learn to apply Murphy's Law to whatever you're attempting to do. To put it another way, you need to be able to think of anything that can go wrong, plan for it, and leave some sort of time cushion in all of your plans. This way, you have some room to adjust for whatever may go wrong. If you know that the attack is coming, and it is going to take you three hours to overcome it, tell them! The harder the task, the greater the time cushion you will need.

You must become tenacious, diligent, unable to quit and unwilling to lose! You must declare war on your ignorance and do whatever it takes to defeat your enemy! Meaning study, research use flashcards, post-it notes, whatever it takes for you to learn what you don't already know! After your emotions catch up, knowing will become a habit! You'll get angry if you're not learning something new! You will be addicted to LEARNING and it will also cause you to become more ambitious! You will seek to achieve greater goals conquer bigger challenges all while being confident in your ability to finish whatever you start!

Prudence

[ˈpro͞odns]

NOUN
1. the quality of being prudent; cautiousness.
"We need to exercise prudence in such important matters"
synonyms:
wisdom · judgment · good judgment · judiciousness · sagacity · shrewdness · advisability · common sense · sense · caution · cautiousness · care · carefulness · canniness · chariness · wariness · circumspection · far-sightedness · foresight · forethought · discretion · thrift · thriftiness · providence · good management · careful budgeting · economy · frugality · abstemiousness · forehandedness · sparingness

Experience is a harsh teacher!

The Po Man's Guide to Breaking the Poverty Cycle

Ever heard an older guy say, "I'm older than you so that makes me wiser?"
My elders have always launched their assault against me with, you don't get old by being a fool! And I always reply, it is also said, there ain't no fool like an old fool!

Knowledge, Wisdom and Experience are 3 different things.

Knowledge [hälǝj]

NOUN
   2.   facts, information and skills acquired by a person through experience or education; the theoretical or practical understanding of a subject.
"a thirst for knowledge" ·
[more]
synonyms:
understanding · comprehension · grasp · grip · command · mastery ·
[more]
   •   what is known in a particular field or in total; facts and information.
"the transmission of knowledge"
synonyms:
learning · erudition · scholarship · philosophy · lore
   •   philosophy
true, justified belief; certain understanding, as opposed to opinion.
   3.   awareness or familiarity gained by experience of a fact or situation.
"the program had been developed without his knowledge" ·
[more]
synonyms:
awareness · consciousness · realization · recognition · cognition · apprehension · perception · appreciation · cognizance

Wisdom ['wizdǝm]
NOUN
   4.   the quality of having experience, knowledge and good judgment; the quality of being wise.
"listen to his words of wisdom"
synonyms:
sagacity · sageness · intelligence · understanding · insight · perception · perceptiveness · percipience · penetration · perspicuity · acuity · discernment · sense ·
[more]
   •   the soundness of an action or decision with regard to the application of experience, knowledge and good judgment.
"some questioned the wisdom of building the dam so close to an active volcano"

The Po Man's Guide to Breaking the Poverty Cycle

synonyms:
sagacity · sageness · intelligence · understanding · insight · perception · perceptiveness · percipience · penetration · perspicuity · acuity · discernment ·
[more]
- the body of knowledge and principles that develops within a specified society or period.

"the traditional farming wisdom of India"
synonyms:
knowledge · learning · erudition · scholarship · philosophy · lore

Experience [ˌikˈspirēəns]
NOUN
5. practical contact with and observation of facts or events.
"he had already learned his lesson by painful experience" ·
[more]
synonyms:
involvement in · participation in · contact with · acquaintance with ·
[more]

VERB
6. encounter or undergo (an event or occurrence).
"the company is experiencing difficulties"
synonyms:
undergo · encounter · meet · have experience of · come into contact with · run into · come across · come up against · face · be faced with · confront · be forced to contend with · feel · know · become familiar with · live/go through · sustain · suffer · endure · tolerate · participate in · taste · try

Knowledge is everything that you have learned. Experience is gained by doing, knowing what will work and what won't. Wisdom is the ability to apply your knowledge and plan based on your experience, your next course of action.

Why am telling you all these things? Knowing how to apply knowledge is a <u>SKILL!</u>

The Po Man's Guide to Breaking the Poverty Cycle

Obtaining Computer Skills, YOU NEED and Lack

I am writing to you to explain the importance of knowing how to use the Microsoft Office suite. Almost every job you will ever have will require you to know how to use them, including Word, Excel, and Outlook. There's no getting around it: if you want the job, you will need to be adequately familiar with all three. I have never read a job description that didn't require at least the first three, and some even require PowerPoint. It can make or break you, it's that simple.
Here's the deal: if you don't already know how to use these programs, you will be on your own. Yes, you might be able to get your coworkers to give you tips here and there, but they're not going to hold your hand and walk you through the basics. It's your job to learn how to use Microsoft Office. No one is going to teach you. **But there is a YouTube video for everything.**

You will be hard-pressed to develop any of your computer skills if you don't have a computer at home to practice on. I learned Microsoft Excel at home, by practicing and using online activities to increase my proficiency. Once using Excel was required at work, I copied the formats already given and learned to make tweaks as necessary. On your job, you will only get a small amount of time to learn new stuff, not to learn the program itself. Your employer will expect you to already know how to use the program. This is problematic if you don't have a computer at home or if you never practice what you've learned, especially if you've never seen the format they use at work before. You may be required to create new forms as needed, and you will need to be well versed in using Microsoft Word to write memos or make forms and documents. Mastery of Microsoft Word will be needed when you must write letters and drive them up the email chain. Not every email you send will be informal! I hope you get the point. Don't get complacent; your new job may require you to know how to use Skype, so you can be added to conference calls. You are going to have to know these things! Years ago, I went online and learned how to build websites using HTML and JavaScript. The sky's the limit, but you must first know the basics.

Where to GO?

Udemy states on their homepage they have 45,000 courses and 15 million students. Given Udemy courses are always on sale, you don't have a valid excuse! Udemy is a very low-cost place to learn and grow your skill set. The problem with Udemy, is they're not considered to be an accredited institution, which means courses will not count toward college credit or even continuing education units (CEUs). So, what!? Udemy certificates are also not recognized by employers. So, what!? Now, don't get me wrong, not being recognized doesn't mean learning new things on Udemy can't massively help you advance your career. Their courses can give you real-world knowledge! Lots of companies have learned this the hard way and no longer require a degree. But you must have equivalent experience! There's rarely any

The Po Man's Guide to Breaking the Poverty Cycle

need to spend more than $50 on a course, so your knowledge will be more beneficial than producing a paper from a school that has yet to figure this out! And has only become a detriment to most of its students!

Here is an excellent article on Soft Skills. Check it out, most people overlook the importance of Soft Skills.
https://www.thebalancecareers.com/listofsoftskills2063770

The following sections are only inserted to get those brain gears to start turning! Don't copy me! Make a plan of your own! These classes are my way of attacking my weaknesses. Find the methods that work for you! But if you can learn from classes, you are going to love these sites!

The Po Man's Guide to Breaking the Poverty Cycle

My Courses on Udemy.   as in the courses I have purchased!

`https://www.udemy.com`

(I paid for these courses! Don't buy at full price, wait until they go on sale and you can pick up most classes for $12).

Mastering Microsoft PowerPoint Made Easy Training Tutorial

Description

Learn Microsoft PowerPoint 2010 with this comprehensive course from TeachUcomp, Inc. *Mastering PowerPoint Made Easy* features sixty-nine video lessons with over 6 hours of introductory through advanced instruction. Watch, listen and learn as your expert instructor guides you through each lesson step-by-step. During this media rich learning experience, you will see each function performed just as if your instructor were there with you. Reinforce your learning with the text of our two printable classroom instruction manuals (Introductory and Advanced), more images and practice exercises. You will learn introductory through advanced concepts from creating simple yet elegant presentations to adding animation, video and customization.

Whether you are completely new to PowerPoint or upgrading from an older version, this course will empower you with the knowledge and skills necessary to be a proficient user. We have incorporated years of classroom training experience and teaching techniques to develop an easy-to-use course you can customize to meet your personal learning needs. Simply launch a video lesson or open one of the manuals and you are on your way to mastering PowerPoint.

MS Outlook Training for Complete Beginners 2 Minute Videos

WHAT YOU'LL LEARN IN THIS COURSE

If you are thinking of starting a business, working for a business, working in a team, or working with others around the world digitally then you need to know how to use Microsoft Outlook! Microsoft Outlook makes communicating so easy. It allows you to send and receive emails, create appointments, organize meetings, receive and distribute files and so much more! Let me take you through how to start this amazing program. I will explain to you the basic interface, I'll show you how to write emails, reply, delete, forward, attach files and more! I will show you how to create a contacts list, set reminders, arrange meetings and appointments as well as create your very own digital signature! So come on in and let us have some fun!

The Po Man's Guide to Breaking the Poverty Cycle

Microsoft Excel 2013 Be the Excel master!!

Description

A complete guide to learning the essentials as well as the advanced features in Microsoft Excel 2013. This course starts right from the basics of entering data into a cell to the advanced features of excel. Learn how to enter Formulas and functions, insert and edit several types of shapes and learn the different Data Validation options. With the new and improved look of Excel 2013, working has just become easier. With new and advanced features like Flash Fill, recommended charts and the new quick analysis tool, life just got easier. Learning is easier with the exercise files provided along with each of the tutorials. Take this course and see yourself working more efficiently than ever!

Master Microsoft Excel Table Design in Under 30 Minutes

What you will learn

- Data Inputting
- Random Number Function
- Basic Arithmetic
- Cell Deletion
- Fill Handle
- Copying and Pasting
- Font Type and Size Selection
- Border Design
- Cell Alignment and Justification
- Bold, Italic and Underline Formatting
- Cell Coloring
- Text Coloring
- Cell Merging
- Text Wrapping
- Row and Column Control

The Po Man's Guide to Breaking the Poverty Cycle

Ultimate Guide to Microsoft PowerPoint for All Levels

WHAT YOU'LL LEARN IN THIS COURSE

I built this course so you can use PowerPoint once you finish the first section. It has all the basic elements you need to build and present your presentation. Following section, each section will get progressively harder until you become an expert. I will show you:

1. All basic elements of PowerPoint slide design
2. Image Control and Manipulation, Artistic Effects, Shapes and SmartArt
3. How to help yourself when you meet a specific problem
4. Standard Printing, PDF Printing Options, Email and Sharing
5. Quick Access Toolbar Setup, Productivity Techniques and Keyboard Shortcuts
6. Slides Transitions, Object Animations and Complete Effect Customization
7. Post Review Functions including Spell Checking, Thesaurus, Researching, Window Duplication and Password Protection Protocols
8. Video Uploading from your Computer and YouTube, Video Trimming, Audio Recordings and Screen Casting
9. Presentations Do's and Don'ts which teaches you Slide Design and Structure, Sequencing, Logistics and Communication Tips
10. Table Design, Object Linking and Excel Connections
11. Complete Chart Design including Elements, Styling and Control
12. Header and Footer Design for Document Tracking
13. Master Views for Template Control
14. And much more……

The Po Man's Guide to Breaking the Poverty Cycle

Complete Introduction to Business Data Analysis

What you will learn

- Learn eight different techniques for data analysis can be easily implemented in Excel 2010, 2013 and 2016
- Lifetime access to course materials and practice activities from an experienced Udemy instructor
- Transform Data into Insight and Intelligence using powerful methods of analysis, techniques and tools
- Learn to ask the right questions about your data using comparison, trend, ranking, variance, Pareto chart and other techniques
- Learn data analysis using easy to master drag and drop techniques no confusing formulas, macros, or VBA
- Learn best practices for data analysis and data presentation
- Learn best practices for the design and setup of interactive dashboards

Excel Pivot Tables Data Analysis Master Class

What you will learn

- Learn to create a pivot table and pivot chart reports in Excel
- Use Excel pivot tables tools for data manipulation and data analysis in Excel
- Hone your analytical skills using Excel Pivot Tables and Pivot Charts
- Multiply productivity when working on Excel pivot tables
- Save time in Excel by using built-in Excel pivot table functionality
- Master data presentation by using Excel Pivot Tables

The Po Man's Guide to Breaking the Poverty Cycle

Introduction to Finance, Accounting, Modeling and Valuation

What you will learn

- #1 Best Selling Accounting Course on Udemy (Learn Finance and Accounting the Easy Way)!
- Analyze and understand an income statement (even if you have no experience with income statements).
- Analyze and understand a balance sheet (even if you have no experience with balance sheets).
- Analyze and understand a cash flow statement (even if you have no experience with cash flow statements).
- Understand and use modeling best practices so you can create financial models.
- Know where to get data to build a financial model (In-depth understanding of identifying and using/navigating the best free websites and sources to build your financial model)!
- Create a financial model (projecting the future) for an income statement.
- Create a financial model (projecting the future) for a balance sheet.
- Create a financial model (projecting the future) for a cash flow statement.
- Understand valuation best practices so you can create target prices based on your financial models.
- How to use Discounted Cash Flow (DCF) and how to create the Weighted Average Cost of Capital and Terminal values to pick target prices.
- How to use P/E to pick target prices.
- How to use P/R to pick target prices.
- Other valuation methodologies, including EV/Sales, EV/EBITDA, P/B, EV/FCF, etc.
- Come up with a target price based on an average of several different valuation methodologies.
- Analyze the total addressable market for a company you are researching on.
- Analyze financial statements using profitability ratios: Gross Margin (Cost of Goods Sold / Revenue), Operating Margin (EBITDA/ Revenue), Net Profit Margin (Net Income / Revenue), Return on Assets (Net Income / Assets) and Return on Equity (Net Income / Equity).

The Po Man's Guide to Breaking the Poverty Cycle

- Analyze financial statements using debt and inventory formulas: Debt to Assets (Total Liabilities/ Total Assets), Debt to Equity (Total Liabilities/ Total Equity), Interest Coverage Ratio (EBITDA / Interest) and Inventory Days on Hand (Inventory / Cost of Goods Sold) * 365.
- Analyze and compare companies using the following formulas: Price / Earnings, PEG (P/E / Growth), Price / Revenue, EV/EBITDA, EV/Sales, Price/Free Cash Flow and Price / Book.
- We will do an extremely in-depth professional accounting, finance, modeling and valuation analysis of LinkedIn using the accounting and finance methodologies used in this course (you will also have many exercises to complete will help you understand accounting, finance, valuation and modeling).

Business Process Modeling AZ™: Learn BPMN 2.0 From Scratch

What you'll learn

- Model any real-world business process
- Have a comprehensive knowledge of BPMN 2.0 Elements
- Understand how to use "XOR" gateways
- Understand how to use "AND" gateways
- Understand how to use "OR" gateways
- Understand how to use event driven gateways
- Understand how to use Message events
- Understand how to use Compensation events

Learn AutoCAD from Scratch: Make Your Plans by Yourself

What you'll learn

- Learn how to make professional looking drawings with AutoCAD.
- No previous experience is required with AutoCAD, we begin at the very beginning.

AutoCAD 2D and AutoCAD Electrical 2017 for beginners

What you'll learn

- Work easily with any AutoCAD workspace
- Master the house plan designs using AutoCAD
- Draw advanced 2D shapes
- Learn about drawing tools provided by AutoCAD
- Draw maps for all types of facilities
- Designing electrical schematics for facilities
- Design master electrical panel

Certified Lean Management Professional

What you'll learn

- By the end of the course, you will be able to strategically implement the tools and techniques of Lean management.
- This course provides in-depth learning of all the concepts, tools and techniques of Lean management such as Value Stream Mapping, 7 wastes, 3Ms, Kaizen, Kanban, Poka Yoke, SMED and One-piece flow, Line stoppage and on, Autonomation, JIT, JIDOKA, etc.

Lean Manufacturing Simplified the Root of Lean Enterprise

What you'll learn

- Identify Wasteful Work Practices on a Production Floor
- Identify Production Value from the Perspective of the Customer
- Interpret a Value Stream Map
- Begin a 5S, Visual Management Initiative

The Po Man's Guide to Breaking the Poverty Cycle

Effectively Managing Employee Performance

What you'll learn

- This course will help you better manage and prevent performance problems through several strategies, from hiring the right candidate to delivering performance feedback. You will be able to identify performance problems and zoom in on their causes.

- You will have a thorough understanding of how to evaluate employee performance and identify any performance issues. You will have acquired the skills, knowledge and strategies that are used to discipline an employee experiencing performance issues.

- This course qualifies for 4.00 PDU credit hours toward the PMP® certification from PMI.

The Ultimate Microsoft Project 2013 Training Bundle 19 Hours

What you'll learn

- Calendars and timelines
- Learn critical paths
- Setting up tasks and tracing their paths
- Project costs
- Resource allocation
- Interim plans and baselines
- Safeguards and restrictions
- Consolidating multiple projects
- Learn to effectively split projects into subprojects
- Effective use of budgets
- Manage cost rate changes
- Import and exporting of project data

The Po Man's Guide to Breaking the Poverty Cycle

Project Management with MS Project Scheduling Master Class

What you'll learn

- Earn 8 PDUs towards your PMI certification.
- Learn how to use Microsoft Project.
- Learn Microsoft Project best practices.
- Gain Project Management knowledge.
- Improve Project Management skills.
- Develop skills in project scheduling.
- Learn the art and science of managing projects with Microsoft Project

SAP for Beginners Comprehensive Guide 2016

What you'll learn

- Identify SAP Applications and Components
- Explain the basic functionality of SAP Solutions
- Attend more detailed SAP courses and have the required baseline knowledge
- Learn effective techniques for navigating.
- Receive an overview of the development process in an SAP system landscape
- Support implementation, upgrade, customizing and development projects using the SAP software logistics concepts and tools
- Explain basic functionalities of Modern User Interfaces (Fiori and Screen Personas)

How to become an SAP Associate Project Manager (C_PM_71)

What you'll learn

- Understand the SAP Certified Associate Project Manager (C_PM_71) exam in detail
- Understand what is required to successfully become a Project Manager (C_PM_71)
- Get valuable tools and templates to help you sign up, prepare and pass the exam

The Po Man's Guide to Breaking the Poverty Cycle

The Complete Networking Fundamentals Course. Your CCNA start

What you'll learn

- This course is for anyone who wants to attain the Cisco CCENT or CCNA certification
- This course will prepare you for the CCNA 200125 certification exam; CCENT / ICND1 100105 certification exam; and ICND2 200105 certification exam.
- Describe network fundamentals and build simple LANs
- Explain IP addressing and subnetting
- Describe hubs, switches and routers
- Explain the OSI model
- Explain how addresses are allocated using DHCP
- Explain name resolution using DNS
- Explain Access Control Lists (ACLs)
- Introduce OpenFlow and Software Defined Networking topics

Investing 101: The Complete Online Investing Course 2019

What you'll learn

- Discover All The Secrets of The Stock Market & Start Generating Consistent Passive Income Online!
- Dedicated Support from the Course Instructors and the Learning Community. 100% Questions Answered Within 24 Hours!
- How to Turn 10% of Your Monthly Income into A New Source of Passive Income
- How to Make a Risk-free 10% Annual Return from the Stock Market By Just Using a Simple Strategy
- How to Build a $1,000,000 Net Worth (Proven Strategy)
- How to Invest in Exchanged Traded Funds and Use Them as a Way to Protect & Grow Your Money
- How to Invest in Stock Market Sector ETFs to Maximize Your Returns
- How to Build a Low-Risk Wealth Building Investment Portfolio

The Po Man's Guide to Breaking the Poverty Cycle

- How to Set Your Financial Goal and How to Develop an Effective Investment Plan
- How to Take Advantage of the Stock Market to Grow Your Money Effectively
- How to Invest Your Money The Right Way Stop Being a Loser!
- How to Take Advantage of Our Profitable Investing Experience to Make Consistent Profits From The Stock Market
- How to Discover The Best Opportunity to Make a Big Fortune from the Stock Market (Don't Get Left Behind!)
- How to Live Away from Debts and Financial Problems (Being Financially Free!)
- And a lot more... .

PLC Programming From Scratch (PLC I)

What you'll learn

- By the end of this course, you will be able to create a PLC program from scratch.
- The primary and overall objective of this course is to give a novice an understanding of PLC programming, ladder logic and the inner workings of a standard HMI (Human Machine Interface).
- Students will learn the difference between digital and analog signals and how to bring them into a PLC, process them and send them back out.
- Students will be familiarized enough with a sufficient variety of ladder logic instructions to create a complete PLC program from scratch.
- Students will explore basic, standard control techniques for things like HOA control, level control, pump control and (on at least an introductory level) PID control loops.
- Students will develop an understanding of alarm and notification programming and the relevant considerations to safety and operator usability.
- Students will be introduced to HMI development and given a general understanding of how an HMI program works.

The Po Man's Guide to Breaking the Poverty Cycle

Practical PLC Programming (PLC II)

What you'll learn

- By the end of this course, you will be both able and practiced at originating complex ladder logic applications.

- The primary and overall objective of this course is to give an INTERMEDIATE PLC programming student rigorous, practical experience in creating unguided, original ladder logic.

- Students will build on the knowledge and understanding of PLC programming they got from "PLC Programming from Scratch" by using those instructions and environments and techniques to create real-world solutions to problems defined throughout this course.

- Upon completion of this course, students will have the requisite skill set to translate a description of a process into a functioning logical solution.

Process Visualization with HMI / SCADA (PLC III)

What you'll learn

- By the end of this course, you will be able to create HMI / SCADA interfaces using various technologies allowing operators to interact with a live, running system.

- Using the provided PLC program as the basis for our interfaces, you'll be creating fully functional graphical interfaces to monitor the process, visualize alarms, provide control and even log periodic and on demand data storing it into a SQL database.

Advanced Programming Paradigms (PLC IV)

What you'll learn

- By the end of this course, students will be able to program nearly ANY modern PLC regardless of mfg.

- Students will be knowledgeable AND experienced with all five IEC programming paradigms.

- Students will know how to lay out a complex PLC program

Advanced AC Drive VFD, Servo & Stepper Power flex & Delta

What you'll learn

- To program the VFD and Servo with customized parameters suitable for the application
- To design turnkey circuits for VFDs and Servo Drives
- To interface VFDs and Servo with PLC for intelligent operation

Learn SCADA from Scratch Design, Program and Interface

What you'll learn

- Install SCADA on their computer
- Link it to the PLC and create tags
- Monitor and Control PLC operations

Excel Crash Course: Master Excel for Financial Analysis

What you will learn

- Perform professional level financial analysis in Excel
- In the end, the course students will be able to use industry best practices when building financial models in Excel

The Ultimate Microsoft Project 2013 & 2016 Mastery Course

What you'll learn

- How to effectively use MS Project 2013 & 2016 to manage a complex project.
- Consolidating multiple projects.
- Learn to effectively split projects into subprojects.
- How to track costs.
- Effective use of budgets.
- Manage cost rate changes.
- Import and exporting of project data.

The Po Man's Guide to Breaking the Poverty Cycle

- Includes exercise files.
- Learn valuable new skills for complex projects at work
- Discover how to work with costs and deadlines and overcome scheduling issues
- Learn critical paths
- Setting up tasks and tracing their paths
- Discover how to use subtasks, dependencies, deadlines and resources
- How to format a Gantt chart
- Resource allocation
- Interim plans and baselines
- Safeguards and restrictions
- Learn how to use Project 2016 on a touch device
- How to measure a project against a baseline project
- How to save your project as a template for future projects
- Utilize calendars and timelines in MS Project 2016
- Assign resources to a task
- Discover how to manage cost rate changes
- Use of outline codes and WBS codes
- How to use macros the speed up use and work more efficiently

The Po Man's Guide to Breaking the Poverty Cycle

Khan Academy Courses, these are free Courses! Not enough people know this site exists!

https://www.khanacademy.org/forgotpw

Science & engineering
Physics
AP® Physics 1
AP® Physics 2
Cosmology & astronomy
Chemistry
AP® Chemistry
Organic chemistry
Biology
High school biology
AP® Biology
Health & medicine
Electrical engineering

Computing
Computer programming
Computer science
AP® Computer Science Principles
Hour of Code
Computer animation

Arts & humanities
US history
AP® US History
World history
AP® World History
US government and civics
AP® US Government & Politics
Art history
AP® Art History
Grammar

Test prep
SAT
LSAT
Praxis Core
MCAT

Math
Early math
Arithmetic
Prealgebra
Algebra 1
Geometry
Algebra 2
Trigonometry
Precalculus
Statistics & probability
AP® Calculus AB
AP® Calculus BC
AP® Statistics
Multivariable calculus
Differential equations
Linear algebra

Math by grade
Preschool
Kindergarten
1st grade
2nd grade
3rd grade
4th grade
5th grade
6th grade
7th grade
8th grade
Illustrative Mathematics
Eureka Math/EngageNY
High school

Economics & finance
AP® Macroeconomics
Macroeconomics
Microeconomics
AP® Microeconomics

The Po Man's Guide to Breaking the Poverty Cycle

GMAT
IIT JEE
NCLEXRN

College, careers, & more
College admissions
Careers

Finance & capital markets
Personal finance

College, careers, & more
Entrepreneurship
Growth mindset

The Po Man's Guide to Breaking the Poverty Cycle

Alison Courses, these are free Courses! Not enough people know this site exists!

https://alison.com/courses/categories

IT
Network and Security
Hardware
Software Development
Game Development
Software Tools
IT Management
Mobile Apps
Software Engineering
Data Science
Databases
Core IT Skills

Language
English
Spanish
German
Irish
French
Chinese
Arabic
Swedish
Japanese

Health
Mental Health
Health Care
Nutrition
Fitness
Yoga

Humanities
Education
History
Politics
Sociology
Personal Development

Geography

Business
Human Resources
Operations
ECommerce
Leadership and Management
Entrepreneurship
Project Management
Sales
Finance
Tourism and Hospitality
Communications

Marketing
Social Media Marketing
Marketing Management
Digital Marketing
Public Relations

Software Development
Front End Languages
Back End Languages
Software Testing

Software Engineering
Operating Systems

Health Care
Nursing
Caregiving
Disease and Disorders
Pharmacology

Operations
Supply Chain Management
Business Process Management
Risk Management
Service Management
Management and Administration

The Po Man's Guide to Breaking the Poverty Cycle

Law
Psychology
Media and Journalism
Economics

Life Science
Biology
Environmental Studies

Science
Life Science
Physics
General Science
Chemistry
Engineering

Math
Core Maths Skills
Calculus
Probability and Statistics
Algebra
Geometry
Series and Sequences
Exam Prep

Finance
Finances and Banking
Accounting

Customer Service
Manufacturing
Health and Safety
Quality Control
Workplace Supervision
Critical Operations

Skilled Trades
Plumbing
Electrical
Carpentry
Masonry
Motor

Lifestyle
Food and Beverage
Art and Crafts
Music
Literature
Skilled Trades
Photography

The Po Man's Guide to Breaking the Poverty Cycle

Codecademy

Codecademy is a website dedicated specifically to teaching coding. Where other coding sites follow an example/practice session workflow, Codecademy includes a live practice window. This means you can practice coding while still viewing the lesson material.

The courses at Codecademy are well written and easy to follow and the website is organized very nicely. Codecademy features a centralized dashboard where you can monitor your progress, plus organizes lessons into complete modules. This lets you learn an entire language without needing to pick the next course manually.

The Po Man's Guide to Breaking the Poverty Cycle

Chapter 3: The Credit Game

I was going to skip over all this information and get right into the meat of the subject, but now I see the need to include this information in the book. I'm going to use some of the excerpts from the FTC Federal Trade Commission website and include links. Besides, they explain it a lot better than I can and I see no reason to rewrite what has already been written. I will, however, give you my thoughts on the matter after you have read the articles and have a good understanding of the subject matter included below.

DISCLAIMER: The following pages are excerpts from the FTC Federal Trade Commission website. I have added the links.

Credit Scores
https://www.consumer.ftc.gov/articles/0152creditscores

Ever wonder how a lender decides whether to grant you credit? For years, creditors have been using credit scoring systems to determine if you'd be a good risk for credit cards, auto loans and mortgages. These days, other types of businesses including auto and homeowners' insurance companies and phone companies are using credit scores to decide whether to issue you a policy or provide you with a service and on what terms. A higher credit score is taken to mean you are less of a risk, which, in turn, means you are more likely to get credit or insurance or pay less for it.
The Federal Trade Commission (FTC), the nation's consumer protection agency, wants you to know how credit scoring works.

What is credit scoring?

Credit scoring is system creditors use to help determine whether to give you credit. It also may be used to help decide the terms you are offered or the rate you will pay for the loan.

Information about you and your credit experiences, like your bill paying history, the number and type of accounts you have, whether you pay your bills by the date they're due, collection actions, outstanding debt and the age of your accounts is collected from your credit report. Using a statistical program, creditors compare this information to the loan repayment history of consumers with similar profiles. For example, a credit scoring system awards points for each factor to predict who is most likely to repay a debt. A total number of points a credit score helps predict how creditworthy you are: how likely it is you will repay a loan and make the payments when they're due.

The Po Man's Guide to Breaking the Poverty Cycle

Some insurance companies also use credit report information, along with other factors, to help predict your likelihood of filing an insurance claim and the amount of the claim. They may consider this information when they decide whether to grant you insurance and the amount of the premium they charge. The credit scores insurance companies use sometimes are called "insurance scores" or "credit-based insurance scores".

Credit scores and credit reports

Your credit report is a key part of many credit scoring systems. That's why it is critical to make sure your credit report is accurate. Federal law gives you the right to get a free copy of your credit reports from each of the three national credit reporting companies once every 12 months.

The Fair Credit Reporting Act (FCRA) also gives you the right to get your credit score from the national credit reporting companies. They are allowed to charge a reasonable fee for the score. When you buy your score, you often get information on how you can improve it.

To order your free annual credit report from one or all the national credit reporting companies and to purchase your credit score, visit www.annualcreditreport.com, call toll-free 8773228228, or complete the Annual Credit Report Request Form and mail it to:

Annual Credit Report Request Service
P. O. Box 105281
Atlanta, GA 303485281

How is a credit scoring system developed?

To develop a credit scoring system or model, a creditor or insurance company selects a random sample of customers and analyzes it statistically to identify characteristics related to risk. Each of the characteristics then is assigned a weight based on how strong a predictor of who is would be a good risk. Each company may use its scoring model, different scoring models for different types of credit or insurance, or a generic model developed by a scoring company.

Under the Equal Credit Opportunity Act (ECOA), a creditor's scoring system may not use certain characteristics that for example, race, sex, marital status, national origin, or religion as factors. The law allows creditors to use age, but any credit scoring system that includes age must give equal treatment to applicants who are elderly.

The Po Man's Guide to Breaking the Poverty Cycle

What can you do to improve your score?

Credit scoring systems are complex and vary among creditors or insurance companies and for different types of credit or insurance. If one factor changes, your score may change but improvement generally depends on how that factor relates to others the system considers. Only the business using the system knows what might improve your score under the particular model they use to evaluate your application.

Nevertheless, scoring models usually consider the following types of information in your credit report to help compute your credit score:

Have you paid your bills on time? You can count on payment history to be a significant factor. If your credit report indicates that you have paid bills late, had an account referred to collections, or declared bankruptcy, it is likely to affect your score negatively.

Are you maxed out? Many scoring systems evaluate the amount of debt you have compared to your credit limits. If the amount you owe is close to your credit limit, it's likely to harm your score.

How long have you had credit? Generally, scoring systems consider your credit track record. Insufficient credit history may affect your score negatively, but factors like timely payments and low balances can offset that.

Have you applied for new credit lately? Many scoring systems consider whether you have applied for credit recently by looking at "inquiries" on your credit report. If you have applied for too many new accounts recently, it could harm your score. Every inquiry isn't counted: for example, inquiries by creditors who are monitoring your account or looking at credit reports to make "prescreened" credit offers are not considered liabilities.

How many credit accounts do you have and what kinds of accounts are they? Although it is generally considered a plus to have established credit accounts, too many credit card accounts may harm your score. In addition, many scoring systems consider the type of credit accounts you have. For example, under some scoring models, loans from finance companies may harm your credit score.

Scoring models may be based on more than the information in your credit report. When you are applying for a mortgage loan, for example, the system may consider the amount of your down payment, your total debt and your income, among other things.

Improving your score significantly is likely to take some time, but it can be done. To improve your credit score under most systems, focus on paying your bills in a timely way, paying down any outstanding balances and staying away from new debt.

The Po Man's Guide to Breaking the Poverty Cycle

Are credit scoring systems reliable?

Credit scoring systems enable creditors or insurance companies to evaluate millions of applicants consistently on many different characteristics. To be statistically valid, these systems must be based on a big enough sample. They generally vary among businesses that use them.

Properly designed, credit scoring systems generally enable faster, more accurate and more impartial decisions than individual people can make. And some creditors design their systems so some applicants, those with scores not high enough to pass easily or low enough to fail absolutely are referred to a credit manager who decides whether the company or lender will extend credit. Referrals can result in discussion and negotiation between the credit manager and the would-be borrower.

What if I am denied credit or insurance, or don't get the terms I want?

If you are denied credit, the ECOA requires that the creditor give you a notice with the specific reasons your application was rejected or the news that you have the right to learn the reasons if you ask within 60 days. Ask the creditor to be specific: Indefinite and vague reasons for the denial are illegal. Acceptable reasons might be "your income was low" or "you haven't been employed long enough." Unacceptable reasons include "you didn't meet our minimum standards" or "you didn't receive enough points on our credit scoring system."

Sometimes you can be denied credit or insurance or offered less favorable terms because of information in your credit report. In case, the FCRA requires the creditor or insurance company to give you a notice that includes, among other things, the name, address and phone number of the credit reporting company that supplied the information. If a credit score was a factor in the decision to deny you credit or to offer you terms less favorable than most other customers receive, the notice also will include that credit score. If you receive one of these notices, you are entitled to a free copy of your credit report. Contact the company to find out what your report said. The credit reporting company can tell you what's in your report, but only the creditor or insurance company can tell you why your application was denied.

If a creditor or insurance company says you were denied credit or insurance because you are too near your credit limits on your credit cards, you may want to reapply after paying down your balances. Because credit scores are based on credit report information, a score often changes when the information in the credit report changes.

If you've been denied credit or insurance or didn't get the rate or terms you want, ask questions:

The Po Man's Guide to Breaking the Poverty Cycle

Ask the creditor or insurance company if a credit scoring system was used. If it was, ask what characteristics or factors were used in the system and how you can improve your application.

If you receive a notice explaining that you are being offered less favorable credit terms than those offered to most other consumers, ask the creditor or insurance company why you aren't getting its best offer.

If you are denied credit or not offered the best rate available because of inaccuracies in your credit report, be sure to dispute the inaccurate information with the credit reporting company. To learn more about this right, see Disputing Errors on Credit Reports.

Disputing Errors on Credit Reports
https://www.consumer.ftc.gov/articles/0151disputingerrorscreditreports

Your credit report contains information about where you live, how you pay your bills and whether you've been sued or arrested, or have filed for bankruptcy. Credit reporting companies sell the information in your report to creditors, insurers, employers and other businesses and use it to evaluate your applications for credit, insurance, employment, or renting a home. The federal Fair Credit Reporting Act (FCRA) promotes the accuracy and privacy of information in the files of the nation's credit reporting companies.

Some financial advisors and consumer advocates suggest you review your credit report periodically. Why?
Because the information it contains affects whether you can get a loan and how much you will have to pay to borrow money.
To make sure the information is accurate, complete and Up-to-date before you apply for a loan for a major purchase like a house or car, buy insurance, or apply for a job.
To help guard against identity theft. That's when someone uses your personal information like your name, your Social Security number, or your credit card number to commit fraud. Identity thieves may use your information to open a new credit card account in your name. Then, when they don't pay the bills, the delinquent account is reported on your credit report. Inaccurate information could affect your ability to get credit, insurance, or even a job.

The Po Man's Guide to Breaking the Poverty Cycle

How to Order Your Free Report

An amendment to the FCRA requires each of the nationwide credit reporting companies Equifax, Experian and TransUnion to provide you with a free copy of your credit report, at your request, once every 12 months.

Do not contact the three nationwide credit reporting companies individually.
You may order your reports from each of the three nationwide credit reporting companies at the same time, or you can order from only one or two. The FCRA allows you to order one free copy from each of the nationwide credit reporting companies every 12 months.

You need to provide your name, address, Social Security number and date of birth. If you have moved in the last two years, you may have to provide your previous address. To maintain the security of your file, each nationwide credit reporting company may ask you for some information that only you would know, like the amount of your monthly mortgage payment. Each company may ask you for different information because the information each has in your file may come from different sources.

Other situations where you might be eligible for a free report
You're also entitled to a free report if a company takes adverse action against you, such as denying your application for credit, insurance, or employment, based on information in your report. You must ask for your report within 60 days of receiving notice of the action. The notice will give you the name, address and phone number of the credit reporting company.

You're also entitled to one free report a year if you're unemployed and plan to look for a job within 60 days; if you're on welfare; or if your report is inaccurate because of fraud, including identity theft.

Otherwise, a credit reporting company may charge you a reasonable amount for another copy of your report within 12 months. To buy a copy of your report, contact the three credit report companies:

Experian 1 888 397 3742
www.experian.com

TransUnion 1 800 916 8800
www.transunion.com

Equifax 1 800 685 1111
www.equifax.com
Correcting Errors

The Po Man's Guide to Breaking the Poverty Cycle

Under the FCRA, both the credit reporting company and the information provider (That is, the person, company, or organization provides information about you to a credit reporting company) are responsible for correcting inaccurate or incomplete information in your report. To take advantage of all your rights under this law, contact the credit reporting company and the information provider.

Step One
Tell the credit reporting company, in writing, what information you think is inaccurate. Use our sample dispute letter. Include copies (NOT originals) of documents to support your position. In addition to providing your complete name and address, your letter should identify each item in your report you dispute, state the facts and explain why you dispute the information and request it be removed or corrected. You may want to enclose a copy of your report with the items in question circled. Send your letter by certified mail, "return receipt requested", so you can document what the credit reporting company received. Keep copies of your dispute letter and enclosures.

Credit reporting companies must investigate the items in question usually within 30 days unless they consider your dispute frivolous. They also must forward all the relevant data you provide about the inaccuracy to the organization provided the information. After the information provider receives notice of a dispute from the credit reporting company, it must investigate, review the relevant information and report the results back to the credit reporting company. If the information provider finds the disputed information is inaccurate, it must notify all three nationwide credit reporting companies so they can correct the information in your file.

When the investigation is complete, the credit reporting company must give you the results in writing and a free copy of your report if the dispute results in a change. This free report does not count as your annual free report. If an item is changed or deleted, the credit reporting company cannot put the disputed information back in your file unless the information provider verifies it is accurate and complete. The credit reporting company also must send you a written notice that includes the name, address and phone number of the information provider.

If you ask, the credit reporting company must send notices of any corrections to anyone who received your report in the past six months. You can have a corrected copy of your report sent to anyone who received a copy during the past two years for employment purposes.

If an investigation doesn't resolve your dispute with the credit reporting company, you can ask that a statement of the dispute be included in your file and future reports. You also can ask the credit reporting company to provide your statement to anyone who received a copy of your report in the recent past. You can expect to pay a fee for this service.

The Po Man's Guide to Breaking the Poverty Cycle

Step Two
Tell the information provider (That is, the person, company, or organization provides information about you to a credit reporting company), in writing, you dispute an item in your credit report. Use this sample dispute letter. Include copies (NOT originals) of documents that support your position. If the provider listed an address on your credit report, send your letter to that address. If no address is listed, contact the provider and ask for the correct address to send your letter. If the information provider does not give you an address, you can send your letter to any business address for that provider.

If the provider continues to report the item you disputed to a credit reporting company, it must let the credit reporting company know about your dispute. And if you are correct that is, if the information you dispute is found to be inaccurate or incomplete then the information provider must tell the credit reporting company to update or delete the item.

About Your File
Your credit file may not reflect all your credit accounts. Although most national department stores and all-purpose bank credit card accounts will be included in your file, not all creditors supply information to credit reporting companies: some local retailers, credit unions, travel, entertainment and gasoline card companies are among the creditors that don't.

When negative information in your report is accurate, only the passage of time can assure its removal. A credit reporting company can report the most accurate negative information for seven years and bankruptcy information for 10 years. Information about an unpaid judgment against you can be reported for seven years or until the statute of limitations runs out, whichever is longer. There is no time limit on reporting: information about criminal convictions; information reported in response to your application for a job that pays more than $75,000 a year; and information reported because you've applied for more than $150,000 worth of credit or life insurance. There is a standard method for calculating the seven-year reporting period. Generally, the period runs from the date that the event took place.

The Po Man's Guide to Breaking the Poverty Cycle

Sample Letter for Disputing Errors on Your Credit Report

Use this sample to draft a letter disputing errors on your credit report.

Your letter should identify each item in your report you dispute, state the facts and explain why you dispute the information and request that it be removed or corrected. You may want to enclose a copy of your report with the items in question circled.

Send your letter by certified mail, "return receipt requested", so you can document what the credit reporting company received. Remember to include copies of the applicable enclosures and save copies for your files.

[Your Name]
[Your Address]
[Your City, State, Zip Code]

[Date]

Complaint Department
[Company Name]
[Street Address]
[City, State, Zip Code]

Dear Sir or Madam:

I am writing to dispute the following information in my file. I have circled the items I dispute on the attached copy of the report I received.

This item [identify the item(s) disputed by name of the source, such as creditors or tax court and identify the type of item, such as credit account, judgment, etc.] is [inaccurate or incomplete] because [describe what is inaccurate or incomplete and why]. I am requesting that the item be removed [or request another specific change] to correct the information.

Enclosed are copies of [use this sentence if applicable and describe any enclosed documentation, such as payment records and court documents] supporting my position. Please reinvestigate this [these] matter[s] and [delete or correct] the disputed item[s] as soon as possible.

Sincerely,
Your name

The Po Man's Guide to Breaking the Poverty Cycle

Sample Letter for Disputing Errors on Your Credit Report with Businesses that Provided the Information

[Your Name] [Your Address]
[Your City, State, Zip Code] [Date]

Complaint Department

[Company Name] [Street Address]
[City, State, Zip Code]

I am writing to dispute the following information that your business provided to [give the name of the credit bureau whose report has incorrect information]. I have circled the item[s] I dispute on the attached copy of the credit report I received.

This [These] item[s] [identify the item(s) disputed by type of item, such as credit account, judgment, etc. and your account number or another method for the business to locate your account] is [inaccurate or incomplete] because [describe what is inaccurate or incomplete and why]. I am requesting that [name of company] have the item[s] removed [or request another specific change] to correct the information.

Enclosed are copies of [use this sentence if applicable and describe any enclosed documents, such as payment records and court documents] supporting my position. Please reinvestigate this [these] matter[s] and contact the national credit bureaus to which you provided this information to have them [delete or correct] the disputed item[s] as soon as possible.

Sincerely, Your name

The Po Man's Guide to Breaking the Poverty Cycle

Fixing Your Credit
https://www.consumer.ftc.gov/articles/fixingyourcredit#Credit%20Reports

Are you wondering how to fix your credit? No one can legally remove negative information from your credit report if it's accurate and current. But there are steps you can take to fix errors and improve your credit.

Maybe you've heard about credit repair companies and are wondering if they can help? Be careful: many are scams. Here's what you need to know about how to fix your credit.

Credit Reports
What makes my credit good or bad?
Your credit report has information about:

- whether you pay your bills on time
- what loans and credit cards do you have and what you owe on them
- whether you've been sued or arrested or have filed for bankruptcy
- The more positive information you have in your credit report, the better your credit will be.

What happens if there's negative information in my credit report?
Credit bureaus sell the information in your credit report to creditors, insurers, employers and other businesses that use it to make decisions about you. If there's a lot of negative information in your report, you could have trouble getting a loan, or might have to pay more in interest. You also could be turned down for a job, insurance, or some services.

Can I get negative information removed from my credit report if it's true?
Only time can make it go away. Most negative information will stay in your report for seven years and bankruptcy information will stay on for 10 years. Unpaid judgments against you will stay on your report for seven years or until the statute of limitations runs out, whichever is longer.

There are exceptions. In certain situations, like when you seek a job paying more than $75,000 a year, or a loan or insurance valued at more than $150,000 a credit bureau will include older negative information on your report that wouldn't show up otherwise.

Each of the nationwide credit bureaus Equifax, Experian and TransUnion is required to provide you with a free copy of your credit report once every 12 months if you ask for it. Go to annualcreditreport.com and call 18773228228. Otherwise, a credit bureau may charge you a reasonable amount for another copy of your report within 12 months.

The Po Man's Guide to Breaking the Poverty Cycle

How do I know what's in my credit report?
You can order free reports from each of the three credit bureaus from annualcreditreport.com at the same time, or you can stagger your requests throughout the year. Some financial advisors say staggering your requests during 12 months may be a good way to keep an eye on the accuracy and completeness of the information in your reports. Because each credit bureau gets its information from different sources, the information in your report from one credit bureau may not reflect all or the same information in your reports from the other two credit bureaus.

What happens if a company takes a negative action against me because of something in my credit report?
When a company takes "adverse action" against you, you're entitled to another free credit report if you ask for it within 60 days of getting notified about the action. The company has to send you a notice that includes the name, address and phone number of the credit bureau that provided your report.

You're also entitled to another free report each year if:

- you're unemployed and plan to look for a job within 60 days
- you're on welfare
- your report is inaccurate because of fraud, including identity theft
- If you think someone might be using your personal information to open accounts, file taxes, or make purchases, go to IdentityTheft.gov to report it and get a personalized recovery plan.

What if I see a mistake on my credit report?
You can dispute mistakes or outdated items on your credit report for free. Both the credit bureau and the business that provided the information about you to a credit bureau that is responsible for correcting inaccurate or incomplete information in your report.

Make sure the information in your report is accurate, complete and up to date before you apply for a loan for a major purchase like a house or car, buy insurance, or apply for a job.

How do I dispute mistakes on my credit report?
To take advantage of all your rights, contact the credit bureau and the business that reported the information.

The Po Man's Guide to Breaking the Poverty Cycle

Send a letter to the credit bureau.
Use our sample letter for disputing errors with credit bureaus to help write your own (see below). Your letter should include:

- your complete name and address
- each item you're disputing and why
- copies (not originals) of documents that support your position
- a request that the mistake(s) be removed or corrected
- You might want to enclose a copy of your report and circle the items in question. Send your letter by certified mail and pay for a "return receipt" so you have a record the credit bureau got it. Keep copies of everything that you sent.

Send a letter to the business that provided the information.
Use our sample letter to dispute errors with businesses (see below). Say that you're disputing an item and include the same information. Again, include copies (not originals) of documents that support your position. Many businesses specify an address for disputes. If the business reports the item to a credit bureau, it must include a notice of your dispute.

How soon will I hear back from the credit bureau?
Credit bureaus have to investigate the items you question within 30 days unless they reasonably determine that your dispute is frivolous. The credit bureau will forward all the relevant information you gave about the error to the business that reported the information. After the business is notified, it must investigate, review the relevant information and report the results back to the credit bureau.

What happens if the investigation finds there's a mistake?
If the investigation finds there was a mistake, the business has to notify all three credit bureaus so they can correct it in your file. The credit bureaus have to give you the results in writing and a free copy of your report if the dispute results in a change.

If the information on your report is changed or deleted, the credit bureau can't put the disputed information back in your file (unless the business that provided the information certifies that it's accurate and complete). The credit bureau also has to:

- send you a notice that includes the name, address and phone number of the business that provided the information
- send notices of the correction(s) to anyone who got your report in the past six months, if you ask
- send a corrected copy of your report to anyone who got a copy during the past two years for employment purposes, if you ask

The Po Man's Guide to Breaking the Poverty Cycle

What can I do if the investigation doesn't find there's a mistake?

If the investigation doesn't resolve your dispute with the credit bureau, you can ask that a statement of the dispute be included in your file and future reports. You also can ask the credit bureau to give your statement to anyone who got a copy of your report in the recent past. You'll probably have to pay for the credit bureau to do it.

Credit Repair

What is a credit repair company?
People hire credit repair companies to help them investigate mistakes in their credit reports. Credit repair companies can't remove negative information that's accurate and timely from your credit report.

Is using a credit repair company a good idea?
Anything a credit repair company can do legally; you can do for yourself at little or no cost.

Only time and a personal debt repayment plan will improve your credit.

What does a credit repair company have to tell me?
It's illegal for credit repair companies to lie about what they can do for you, or charge you before they help you. Credit repair companies also must explain:

- your legal rights in a written contract that also details the services they'll perform
- your three-day right to cancel without any charge and provide a written cancellation form
- how long it will take to get results
- the total cost you'll pay
- any guarantees

What if I pay a credit repair company and it doesn't live up to its promises?

You can: sue the company in federal court for your actual losses or what you paid the company, whichever is more seek punitive damages, money to punish the company for violating the law join other people in a class action lawsuit against the company

The Po Man's Guide to Breaking the Poverty Cycle

How do I know if I'm dealing with a credit repair scam?
You know you're dealing with a credit repair scam if a company:

- insists you pay it before it helps you
- tells you not to contact the credit bureaus directly
- tells you to dispute information in your credit report you know is accurate
- tells you to lie on your applications for credit or a loan
- doesn't explain your legal rights when it tells you what it can do for you
- These are all bad ideas and they'll hurt your credit.

If a company promises to create a new credit identity or hide your bad credit history or bankruptcy, it's also a scam. These companies often use stolen Social Security numbers or get people to apply for Employer Identifications Numbers from the IRS under pretenses to create new credit reports. If you use a number other than your own to apply for credit, you won't get it and you could face fines or prison.

Where do I report a credit repair scam?
If you have a problem with a credit repair company, report it to:

- your state attorney general or local consumer affairs office. Many states have laws covering credit repair companies.

- the FTC at ftc.gov/complaint or 1877FTCHELP. The FTC can't resolve individual credit disputes, but it can take action against a company for breaking the law.

Is there anything else I can do to improve my credit?

It takes time to improve your credit, but you can rebuild your credit by paying your bills by the due date, paying off debt especially on your credit cards and not taking on new debt.

If you're in debt and need help, a reputable credit counseling organization might be able to help. Good credit counselors spend time discussing your entire financial situation with you before coming up with a personalized plan to solve your money problems. They won't promise to fix all your problems or ask you to pay a lot of money before doing anything.
You often can find nonprofit credit counseling programs offered through credit unions universities, military bases and U.S. Cooperative Extension Service branches.

The Po Man's Guide to Breaking the Poverty Cycle

How to read credit reports
https://www.youtube.com/watch?v=cNgQil3upYw
https://www.bing.com/search?q=how+to+read+a+credit+report&FORM=QSRE5

How to Use a Credit Card to Build Credit
https://www.thebalance.com/creditcardbuildcredit2385756
https://www.youtube.com/watch?v=74pIfAOVuEA

Building a Better Credit Report
https://www.consumer.ftc.gov/articles/pdf0032buildingabettercreditreport.pdf

Cash Crisis Money Traps that Keep You Broke very important link
https://www.uaex.edu/healthliving/personalfinance/lifestagesandevents/Money%20Traps.pdf

HARD Inquires
https://www.preventloanscams.org/creditinquiryremovalletter/ READ ONLY
https://www.creditinfocenter.com/community/topic/320899toomanyhardinquiriesbycardealer/

The Po Man's Guide to Breaking the Poverty Cycle

Money Traps that Keep You Broke

Advance Fee Loans
https://www.consumer.ftc.gov/articles/0078advancefeeloans
Looking for a loan or credit card but don't think you'll qualify? Have you been turned down by a bank because of your poor credit history? You may be tempted by ads and websites that guarantee loans or credit cards, regardless of your credit history. Rule number one: Legitimate lenders never "guarantee" or say that you are likely to get a loan or a credit card before you apply, especially if you have bad credit, no credit, or a bankruptcy.

Six Sure Signs of an Advance Fee Loan Scam
Dealing with Debt
Six Sure Signs of an Advance Fee Loan Scam
Some red flags can tip you off to scam artists' tricks. For example:

A lender who isn't interested in your credit history. A lender may offer loans or credit cards for many purposes, for example, so you can start a business or consolidate your bills. But one who doesn't care about your credit record should worry you. Ads that say "Bad credit? No problem" or "We don't care about your past. You deserve a loan" or "Get money fast" or even "No hassle guaranteed" often indicate a scam.
Banks and other legitimate lenders generally evaluate creditworthiness and confirm the information in an application before they grant firm offers of credit to anyone.

Fees that aren't disclosed clearly or prominently. Scam lenders may say you've been approved for a loan, then call or email demanding a fee before you can get the money. Any upfront fee that the lender wants to collect before granting the loan is a cue to walk away, especially if you're told it's for "insurance", "processing", or just "paperwork". Legitimate lenders often charge application, appraisal, or credit report fees. The differences? They disclose their fees clearly and prominently; they take their fees from the amount you borrow; the fees usually are paid to the lender or broker after the loan is approved.

And if a lender says they won't check your credit history, but wants your personal information, like your Social Security number or bank account number? Go somewhere else. They may use your information to debit your bank account to pay a fee they're hiding.

A loan that is offered by phone. It is illegal for companies doing business by phone in the U.S. to promise you a loan or credit card and ask you to pay for it before they deliver.
A lender who uses a copycat or want-to-be name. Crooks give their companies names that sound like well-known or respected organizations and create websites that look professional. Some scam artists have pretended to be the Better Business Bureau, a

The Po Man's Guide to Breaking the Poverty Cycle

major bank, or another reputable organization; some even produce forged paperwork or pay people to pretend to be referenced. Always get a company's phone number from the phone book or directory assistance and call to check they are who they say they are. Get a physical address, too: a company that advertises a PO Box as its address is one to check out with the appropriate authorities.

A lender who is not registered in your state. Lenders and loan brokers are required to register in the states where they do business. To check registration, call your state Attorney General's office or your state's Department of Banking or Financial Regulation. Checking registration does not guarantee that you will be happy with a lender, but it helps weed out the crooks...a lender who asks you to wire money or pay an individual. Don't make a payment for a loan or credit card directly to an individual; legitimate lenders don't ask anyone to do that. In addition, don't use a wire transfer service or send money orders for a loan. You have little recourse if there's a problem with a wire transaction and legitimate lenders don't pressure their customers to wire money.

Finally, just because you've received a slick promotion, seen an ad for a loan or credit card in a prominent place in your neighborhood or your newspaper, on television or the Internet, or heard one on the radio, don't assume it's a good deal or even legitimate. Scam artists work hard to make you think they're legitimate, so it's really important to do your homework.

Dealing with Debt

If you have debt problems, try to solve them with your creditors as soon as you realize you won't be able to make your payments. If you can't resolve the problems yourself or you need help to do it, you may want to contact a credit counseling service. Nonprofit organizations in every state counsel and educate people and families on debt problems, budgeting and using credit wisely. Often, these services are free or low-cost. Universities, military bases, credit unions and housing authorities also may offer low or no cost credit counseling programs.

The Po Man's Guide to Breaking the Poverty Cycle

Payday Loans
https://www.consumer.ftc.gov/articles/0097paydayloans
Why You Should Avoid Payday Loans at All Costs
Written by Susan Lahey

Published February 8, 2019

Why you should avoid payday loans why you should avoid payday loans
If you are stranded at sea and have little or no water, you may be tempted to drink seawater. Unfortunately, the salt in the seawater will dehydrate you and kill you even faster than you would have died without any water. That's the metaphor for payday loans. When you're in dire financial circumstances, someone offering you a "quick and easy" loan seems so tempting. However, it's like seawater and can rapidly land you in much worse financial trouble than you were in originally. That's why you should never use payday loans to get out of a financial jam.

Payday Loans: The Terms

•Bottom line, with a payday loan you pay roughly 400% interest on the money you borrow, compared to an average of 12%to30% interest on normal loans.

•Most payday loans are for less than $500 and lenders charge between 10% and 30% for every $100 borrowed. So, if the payday lender lent $500 for two weeks at 15%, a borrower would have to repay the loan on their next payday plus $75.

•Borrowers frequently lack the money to pay the loan back with interest when it comes due, so they roll the loan over into a new loan and they wind up even more indebted to the payday lender.
•Lenders may require the borrower to leave a signed check for the amount or may get permission to draft money from the borrower's account on the agreed upon date. This has several times led to massive fraud.

The Not So Fine Print

In one case the Federal Trade Commission (FTC) was able to find payday lender AMG more than $500 million for extra fines and illegal withdrawals from customers' banks. One customer had agreed to pay AMG $390 for a $300 loan, for example. The payday company helped itself to $975. This is only one of several such schemes the FTC has had to prosecute in recent years.

In other cases, the company took out monthly payments for interest on loans already paid back and even used customers' bank accounts for money laundering. The FTC was able to prosecute those cases, but it can only prosecute a fraction of the cases filed. In other words, the fact that you were defrauded may or may not ever result in your money being returned to you.

A Better Solution

There are better solutions for people in a financial pinch. Among those proposed by the FTC include talking to your credit union about a short-term loan. Credit unions work in favor of their members and often offer the best loan rates and terms.

Customers should also consider talking to creditors about their situations. Creditors usually have programs to help customers who are having a difficult time financially. Especially if you're a customer with a good record, they may defer payment, make catchup arrangements, or offer other remedies. Usually, the cost of being a bit late on a payment is much lower than the cost of a payday loan.

Finances can be challenging and most people find themselves in a money pinch from time to time. However, if it becomes a habit, it's time to get a handle on spending by having an expert help you figure out either how to make ends meet on your current income or look for other solutions. Some companies that offer assistance will make things worse while others are there to help.

Just try to get help early in the game, before you wreck your credit, or somebody does it for you. We love to help our members get and stay on top of their finances for their sense of security and wellbeing. If we can help you out, contact us today! I don't get me started with this one a payday loan is borrowing from Peter to pay Paul you're trying to anticipate having a future job you may get fired tomorrow how do you pay a payday loan? So now you have another market guess your credit that you cannot pay

Pawn Shop Loans (Author)

If you are anything like I am. Then you'll know: anything you put in the pawnshop you will lose! I don't know why it happens; but for some reason: people go into a pawn shop with the best of intentions and they always end up losing whatever they hock or get a loan for…. Now I will admit some people do get lucky and they manage to get their items out right away! If you must. You must. But there are other ways! If you can find no other way, ask for the smallest loan possible! You know something you can always come up with in a bind. If you have nowhere else to turn then do what you have got to do!

Tax Refund Anticipation Loan
https://www.consumerreports.org/taxes/taxrefundadvanceshouldyouapply/

The Po Man's Guide to Breaking the Poverty Cycle

Car Title Loans
https://www.consumer.ftc.gov/articles/0514cartitleloans

"Get Cash for a Car Title Loan Today!"

"Keep Your Vehicle No Credit Checks Easy Online Form Get Cash in 15 Minutes!"

"No Proof of Employment or Income Required!"

You've probably seen or heard ads like these. If you need cash quickly and you've had problems getting a loan from a traditional lender like a bank, you may think a car title loan is an answer. The Federal Trade Commission (FTC), the nation's consumer protection agency, advises you to put on the brakes and understand the costs of a car title loan. You may want to consider other options. A car title loan will put your car at risk: you may lose one of your most valuable possessions and your transportation.

- Applying for a Loan
- Title Loans are Expensive
- Payment Options
- The "Roll Over"
- Repossession

Applying for a Loan

Car title lenders operate out of storefronts and online. Whether you apply in person or online, you'll be asked to complete a loan application. Online applicants are given a list of title loan stores near them. You'll need to present your car, the clear title, a photo ID and proof of insurance to complete the transaction. Many lenders also require a duplicate set of car keys.

If you apply for a car title loan, it's important to:

Review the loan terms. Car title lenders must give you the terms of the loan in writing before you sign for the loan. The federal Truth in Lending Act treats car title loans like other types of credit: lenders must disclose the cost of the loan. Specifically, lenders must give you the finance charge (a dollar amount) and the APR (the cost of credit yearly). The APR is based on several things, including the amount you borrow, the interest rate and credit costs you're being charged and the length of your loan. In addition to the finance charge, car title loans also may include charges, like processing fees, document fees, late fees, loan origination fees, title charges and lien fees.

Beware of "add-ons" that can increase the cost of the loan. In addition to your loan, you may have to buy add-ons like a vehicle roadside service plan. The cost of the plan may depend on the value of the loan. If add-ons are required, they become part of the finance charge/APR, making the costs of credit even higher. In addition, add-ons themselves can be expensive and add significant payment amounts to your loan.

Once your loan is approved, you get your money and the lender gets your title. You will not get your title back until you pay off the loan.

Title Loans are Expensive

Lenders often charge an average of 25 percent per month to finance the loan. Translates to an APR of at least 300 percent. It could be higher, depending on the additional fees that the lenders may require. For example, if you borrow $500 for 30 days, you could have to pay, on average, $125 plus the original $500 loan amount $625 plus additional fees within 30 days of taking out the loan.

Payment Options

You generally have three options to pay: in person, through an online system, or an automated repayment system.

An automated repayment plan is when you authorize a lender to make regular payments directly from your bank or debit card when a payment is due. Lenders cannot make recurring automatic debits unless you agree in advance to these transfers from your bank account and then, only after you get a clear disclosure of the terms of the transaction. The lender must give you a copy of your authorization for the recurring automatic debits. In addition, it is illegal for a company to require credit to be repaid through pre-authorized automatic transfers.

The "Rollover"

If you cannot pay off the loan in the typical 30-day period, the lender may offer to "roll over" the loan into a new loan. But the rollover process always adds fees and interest to the amount you originally borrowed. Say you take a loan of $500 for 30 days. But you can't pay back the full $625 plus other fees at the end of 30 days. You can pay only $125. If the remaining amount is rolled over into a new loan, it would add more fees and interest to the amount you already owe. This may result in a dangerous cycle of borrowing and rolling over the loan amount. You may end up paying more in fees than the amount you originally borrowed and you may find it impossible to pay off the full debt. If you don't pay what you owe, the lender may decide to repossess your vehicle.

The Po Man's Guide to Breaking the Poverty Cycle

Repossession

If your car is repossessed, you lose not only your transportation to work, school and other places you need to go, but also the money your car was worth. Some lenders require the installation of a Global Positioning System (GPS) or starter interrupt devices on the vehicles for repossession, among other purposes.

GPS devices track the location of your vehicle, giving the lender quick access to it.

Starter interrupt devices impair your ability to start the ignition. Sometimes, they're used for repossession. Other times, they're used with a system that reminds you to make your payment. Then, you get another code to restart the car.

Some states have laws that force lenders who have repossessed and sold your car to pay you the difference between the sale price and the loan amount. Other states allow lenders to keep the full amount from the sale.

Alternatives to Car Title Loans

Before you decide to take out a car title loan, think about some other choices:

Take a small loan from a bank. Consider a small loan from your bank, credit union, or a small loan company. Some banks may offer short-term loans for small amounts of money at competitive rates. Some community-based organizations may make small loans to people, too. A cash advance on a credit card also may be possible, but it may have a higher interest rate than other sources of funds. Find out the terms before you decide. Always shop first and compare all available offers before signing any papers.

Shop for credit. Whether you're looking for a car title loan or another form of credit, always shop for the best offer. When you're looking at lending products, compare the APR and the finance charge, which includes the loan fees, interest and other credit costs. You are looking for the lowest APR. Military personnel have special protections against super high fees or rates and some states and the District of Columbia impose limits on rates for title and certain other loans. Even with these protections, though, car title loans can be particularly expensive, especially if you rollover the loan and are responsible for paying additional fees. Offers for other types of credit may come with lower rates and costs.

Contact your creditor if you fall behind on payments. If you're considering a car title loan because you're having trouble paying your bills, contact your creditors or loan servicer as quickly as possible and ask for more time. Many may be willing to work with you if they believe you're acting in good faith. They may offer an extension on your

The Po Man's Guide to Breaking the Poverty Cycle

bills, in which case you should make sure to find out the charges for that service, such as a late charge, an additional finance charge, or a higher interest rate.

Find a credit counseling service. Contact your local nonprofit consumer credit counseling service if you need help working out a debt repayment plan with creditors or developing a budget. These groups offer credit guidance in every state for no or low cost.

Make a budget. Make a realistic budget, including your monthly and daily expenditures and plan, plan, plan. Try to avoid unnecessary purchases: the costs of small, everyday items like a cup of coffee add up. At the same time, try to build some savings: small deposits do help. A savings plan, even a modest one, can help you avoid borrowing for emergencies. Saving the fee on a $500 car title loan for three months, for example, can help you create a buffer against some financial emergencies.

Enroll in overdraft protection. Find out if you have it or if your bank offers overdraft protection on your checking account. If you are using most or all the funds in your account regularly and you make a mistake in your account records, overdraft protection might help protect you from additional credit problems. But this service also can have fees and limits. Find out the terms of the overdraft protection available to you, what it costs and what it covers.

Protections for Military Consumers

Car title loans and certain other financing that are offered to service members and their dependents must include special protections under federal law and a Department of Defense rule. For example, the military APR for car title loans offered since Oct. 1, 2007 with a term of 181 days or less cannot exceed 36 percent. Most fees, with few exceptions, are included in the rate. Creditors also may not require the use of a check or access to a bank account for the loan, mandatory arbitration and unreasonable legal notices. Military consumers also must be given certain disclosures about the loan costs and their rights as borrowers. Credit agreements that violate the protections are void. Creditors that offer car title loans may ask loan applicants to sign a statement about their military affiliation.

Even with these protections, car title loans can be particularly expensive, especially if you rollover the loan. So, you may want to check out financial assistance from military aid societies, including the Army Emergency Relief, Navy and Marine Corps Relief Society, Air Force Aid Society, or Coast Guard Mutual Aid. You may be able to borrow from family or friends or get an advance on your paycheck from your employer. If you still need credit, loans from a credit union, bank, or a small loan company may offer you lower rates and costs than car title loans. They may have special offers for military applicants and may help you start a savings account.

The Po Man's Guide to Breaking the Poverty Cycle

A cash advance on your credit card may be possible, but it could be costly, too. Find out the terms for any credit before you sign. You may ask for free legal advice about a credit application from a service legal assistance office, or financial counseling from a consumer credit counselor, including advice about deferring your payments. Military consumers can contact the Department of Defense, toll-free, 24 hours a day, 7 days a week, at 180034 9647, or www.militaryonesource.mil. Information on the Department of Defense rule, alternatives to car title and payday loans, financial planning and other guidance is available.

Unless you have two or three cars in the driveway you don't mind losing this is the dumbest thing you possibly do but just for the sake of objectivity say you managed to somehow make all your payments on time and you only have a little left to go what happens if you lose your job what happens if you have a medical bill does more important and you have to pay it right away now you are in breach of contract they can come and they will come and take away your vehicle they didn't pay for they did not but now they're going to get your vehicle for pennies on the dollar so now it's on your credit report as a collection you no longer have a vehicle so now you can get back and forth your walking totally bad deal no matter how you look at why would you take such a chance nephew on your vehicle I understand it's an asset but is not an asset if you allow any type of lean on it a give anyone else access to it's what a car title loan those it gives them the legal right to come and take possession of your vehicle is no longer yours they've taken you have nothing

The Po Man's Guide to Breaking the Poverty Cycle

Using a Credit Card
https://www.consumer.ftc.gov/articles/0205usingcreditcard

Regardless of whether you're using your credit card to buy a laptop or laundry soap, you have rights and responsibilities under the law. Getting a good grip on the safe use of credit cards can help you avoid a credit calamity.

- Pay By the Due Date
- Refunds, Errors, Disputes and Unauthorized Charges
- Security Tips and More Information
- Pay By the Due Date

It's important to pay your bill on time. If you don't, count on paying late fees and additional finance charges.

When you make a payment, your card issuer generally must credit your account the day they receive it, but there are exceptions.

Your issuer can specify reasonable requirements for payment. For example, your issuer can set a reasonable cutoff hour for your payment to be received for crediting on that day, but generally, it can't be before 5 p.m. on the due date at the location the issuer specifies.

Your issuer can require that you include an account number or payment stub with your payment. Your issuer doesn't have to credit your account the day your payment is received if a delay won't result in a charge to you. To help avoid additional charges, follow your issuer's payment instructions. Sending your payment to the wrong address that even if the payment is received and accepted at some other office of the issuer that could delay crediting your account for up to five days. If you pay by mail and misplace your payment envelope, look for the payment address on your billing statement or call the issuer for the correct address for payments. If you pay your bill online, set up a reminder a week or so before the bill is due to be sure you pay on time and to the proper electronic address. Set up a return electronic notice showing the company received your online payment. No matter what method you use, check your billing statement to be sure you have the right due date and location for each account.

Automatic debiting to your bank account can be a convenient way to pay bills, but there are factors to consider. For example, the amount due each month could vary and you would need sufficient funds in your bank account to pay it. Otherwise, you could overdraw your account, be charged for insufficient funds and damage your credit rating. Under federal law, you can't be required to use automatic debits from your bank account to repay an extension of credit.

The Po Man's Guide to Breaking the Poverty Cycle

If you decide to set up automatic debits, the creditor must:

- disclose the terms of the transfers.
- get your written or electronic authorization;
- give you a copy of the authorization disclosing the terms.
- Refunds, Errors, Disputes and Unauthorized Charges
- Refunds. If you have a credit balance on your account, you can keep it or write to your issuer for a refund if the amount is more than one dollar. Your card issuer must send you a refund within seven business days of getting your request. If you don't ask for a refund and you don't make any other purchases for more than six months, the issuer must make a good faith effort to send you a refund.

Errors. Card issuers must follow rules for correcting billing errors promptly. They must send you a statement outlining these rules when you open an account and then, at least once a year while your account is open. Many creditors routinely include a summary of your rights with your billing statements.

If you find a mistake on your bill, you can dispute the charge and withhold payment of that amount while the charge is being investigated. The error might be a charge for the wrong amount, for something you didn't accept, or for an item that wasn't delivered as agreed. You still have to pay any part of the bill that's not in dispute, including finance and other charges not related to the disputed amount.

To dispute a charge:

Write to the issuer at the address indicated on your statement for "billing inquiries." Include your name, address, account number and a description of the error.
Send your letter as soon as possible. It must reach the issuer within 60 days after the issuer mailed you the first bill with the error.

The issuer must acknowledge your complaint in writing within 30 days of getting it unless they've resolved the problem. The issuer must resolve your dispute within two billing cycles or 90 days, whichever is later.

Disputes about Merchandise or Services. You generally can dispute charges for unsatisfactory goods or services (including issues about the quality of an item) if you made a good faith effort to resolve the dispute with the seller, if the charge is for more than $50, or if you made the purchase in your home state or within 100 miles of your current billing address. In addition to disputing the charge with the issuer, you may want to consider filing an action against the merchant in small claims court.

The Po Man's Guide to Breaking the Poverty Cycle

Unauthorized Charges. If your credit card is lost, stolen, or used without your permission, you can be responsible for up to $50. If you report the loss before the card is used, you're not responsible for any unauthorized charges. But if a thief uses your card before you report it missing, the most you will owe for unauthorized charges is $50. If the thief uses your card number but not your card you are not responsible for the unauthorized charges.

To minimize your liability, report a loss as soon as possible. Some issuers have 24-hour toll-free telephone numbers to accept emergency information. It's a good idea to follow up with a letter: include your account number, the date you noticed your card missing and the date you reported the loss. Keep a copy of the letter for your files.

Security Tips and More Information

- Never lend your card to anyone.
- Never sign a blank charge slip. Draw lines through blank spaces on the charge slip above the total so the amount can't be changed.
- Never put your account number on the outside of an envelope or a postcard.
- Always be cautious about disclosing your account number on the telephone, online, or on other communication devices unless you know the person that you're dealing with represents a reputable company.
- Keep your receipts and print out online receipts so you can reconcile the charges on your bill.
- Carry only the cards you expect to use to minimize the damage of a potential loss or theft.
- Keep a record in a safe place separate from your cards of your account numbers, expiration dates and phone numbers of each creditor to report a loss quickly.

Cosigning a Loan
https://www.consumer.ftc.gov/articles/0215cosigningloan

What do you do if a friend or relative asks you to cosign a loan? Before you say yes, think about the obligations involved and how they may affect your finances and creditworthiness. When you agree to cosign a loan, you're taking a risk a lender won't take the Cosigner's Notice Before You Cosign a Cosigner Notice.

When you cosign a loan, the lender (known as the "creditor") must spell out your obligations in a cosigner notice, which says:

- You are being asked to **guarantee this debt**. Think carefully before you do. If the borrower does not pay the debt, you will have to. Be sure you can afford to pay if you have to and you want to accept this responsibility.

- You may have to pay up to the full amount of the debt if the borrower does not pay. You may also have to pay late fees or collection costs, which increases this amount.

- The creditor can collect this debt from you without first trying to collect it from the borrower. * The creditor can use the same collection methods against you can be used against the borrower, including suing you or garnishing your wages. If this debt is ever in default, that fact may become a part of your credit record.

- This notice is not the contract that makes you liable for the debt.

- *Depending on the laws in your state, this may not apply. If state law forbids a creditor from collecting from a cosigner without first trying to collect from the primary debtor, this sentence may be crossed out or omitted.

Before You Cosign

Despite the risks, there may be times when you want to cosign. Your child may need a first loan, or a close friend may need help. Before you cosign, consider how it might affect your financial wellbeing.

- Can you afford to pay the loan? If you're asked to pay and can't, you could be sued, or your credit rating could be damaged.

The Po Man's Guide to Breaking the Poverty Cycle

- Even if you're not asked to repay the debt, your liability for the loan may keep you from getting other credit. Creditors will consider the cosigned loan as one of your obligations.

- Before you pledge property to secure the loan, like your car, furniture, or jewelry, make sure you understand the consequences. If the borrower defaults, you could lose these items.

- Ask the creditor to calculate the amount you might owe. The creditor doesn't have to do this, but might if you ask. You also may be able to negotiate specific terms of your obligation. For example, you may want to limit your liability to the principal on the loan and not include late charges, court costs, or attorneys' fees. In this case, ask the creditor to include a statement in the contract like "The cosigner will be responsible only for the principal balance on this loan at the time of default." before you cosign.

- Ask the creditor to agree, in writing, to notify you if the borrower misses a payment or the terms on the loan change. Will give you time to deal with the problem or make back payments without having to repay the entire amount immediately.

- If you're cosigning for a purchase, make sure you get copies of all important papers, like the loan contract, the Truth in Lending Disclosure Statement and warranties. These documents may come in handy if there's a dispute between the borrower and the seller. The creditor doesn't have to give you these papers; you may have to get copies from the borrower.

- Check your state law for additional cosigner rights.

The Po Man's Guide to Breaking the Poverty Cycle

The "Real Deal" About Your Credit (Author)

So, then friends, let's discuss credit: how to build, maintain and improve your credit. If you are poor like the rest of us you need only remember one thing: Get your bills in order! You can't focus on rebuilding credit; if you are still doing all those irresponsible things you did to destroy your credit.

The Credit Scam

The only way to win in the credit game is not to play the game! Naivety normally gets people into trouble and sets them on the wrong path. **Good credit is not what you think!** The average Joe believes the key to good credit is a simple matter: open an account and pay your bills on time. If we were still in the 1800's you'd be correct! But we are not in the 1800s anymore and antiquated thinking is the main reason most of us have bad credit. Credit is a racket, only you're not in on it! You are the mark!

Back in the 1800s, everybody knew everybody, so you simply had to go to a merchant or business and ask them to extend you a line of credit. The merchant would look you up and down and decide on the spot. If they thought you were shady looking, they'd ask for some form of collateral. If you were known to be decent and upstanding, they would start you off small and increase the amount of your credit limit based on your ability to pay on your account on time. This worked out all right for a while, but America was still growing and everybody was a risk-taker. People began to lose their land, their livestock could be wiped out overnight, so the merchants got together and made lists of the people who they considered to be credit risks. If you were new to town and no one would or could vouch for you, you were going to need collateral of some sort to get started.

Enter the bankers, the fathers of Corporate America stage left. These moguls came in and set up shop, they owned huge department stores and BIG and small banks. Layaway transactions originated during the period of The Great Depression when a lot of people did not have enough cash to make full payments for their merchandise. The retailers, aware of the cash crunch, allowed customers to make payments bit by bit and pick up the items when they completed paying the purchase amount in full. The transactions went on until the 1980s and 1990s during the advent of credit cards. The inventor of the first bank issued credit card was John Biggins of the Flatbush National Bank of Brooklyn in New York. In 1946, Biggins invented the "Charge It" program between bank customers and local merchants.

The Po Man's Guide to Breaking the Poverty Cycle

These aren't the good ole days! Now, credit is designed to keep you in debt. The system is a circle designed to lock you into an endless cycle of debt that feeds and perpetuates itself until you are slowly overwhelmed and penniless. The bankers want you to be in debt! Look around you! I challenge you to buy a house or car and not pay 3 times its value! There are many little tricks and/or solutions to getting around this and you are expected to know them all. Yeah, I know! If you knew everything that you should do or shouldn't do, you wouldn't be reading this book!

FREE information is everywhere, it's not the bankers' fault **poor people don't read!** It's not the bankers' fault you don't know you are expected to keep up with all new laws and regulations! I added the excerpts from the FTC Federal Trade Commission website to drive my point home! I even added the links.

What now? Now I will begin to cover most if not all the typical mistakes we make! In most cases, people are destroying their credit in an attempt to build or rebuild it!

Auto Loans (If you can master buying a car you can master buying a house)!

Always find yourself a good bank or credit union. Establish a good history. And use them when you want to buy a vehicle! Never, under any circumstances, use the car dealer's fly-by-night credit advertisements! Remember if it sounds too good to be true, it is too good to be true! People don't understand they're buying into the advertisement, not the actual product. The advertisement had absolutely nothing to do with the product! The purpose of the advertisement is to get you, the willing victim, to walk through the door.

The higher your down payment the lower your car payment. The higher your credit score, the lower your interest rate. Friends, this is the secret to auto loans! Anything else is simply total smoke! So, if I the banker can set up a system where you mess up your credit score when you apply for a loan, I can charge you the highest interest rate. Means you will pay up to 3 times the value of anything you buy when you apply for a loan at my bank!

Most car dealers know their customers are barely getting by, so why do they always try to place you in the most expensive vehicle on the lot? Commission they don't care about you! You represent a sale! A commission! The bigger the idiot or more naïve the buyer the better! They can keep selling cars even if you default on the loan. The lender owns the vehicle and they have your signature on a contract promising to repay the full balance of the loan. So, if you fall on hard times, they will repo the vehicle, auction it off for half its value and demand payment for the outstanding balance. Your goal should be to buy a vehicle as close to the base retail price as possible and at the lowest interest rate! Now you have an outstanding loan, no vehicle and bad credit. The goal of this guide is to teach you the reader to make smart choices. To cause you to think outside the box!

The Po Man's Guide to Breaking the Poverty Cycle

REALITY CHECK: If you have a decent income, job security and stability, you will most likely get ahead in life. If you lack one, you must compensate. If you lack two, you are considered to be struggling. If you lack all three. Yup! You guessed it! YOU ARE POOR!

We didn't create the box. They did! But their actions are designed to affect everything we do here! Every commercial you see is designed to intimidate, regulate and take away any semblance of choice you may think you have. These nameless entities don't want to see you prosper! They're not concerned about your wellbeing. What you need! What you want! They are vultures waiting to pick apart all the little delicious morsels that are left over after your financial death. You play the game according to the rules they have created and you will get burned! So how do you spot these vultures? One simple rule of thumb is never to answer advertisements. Never answer cold calls. Never allow some fast-talking salesman to sell you anything you neither want nor need!

Throughout this process (you are learning and growing) and most of the revelations I will be sharing throughout this guide, **I must get you to understand your financial future is in your own hands!** From this day forward, never allow yourself to be swindled, manipulated, intimidated, or fooled into giving up your financial freedom!

Get angry, suitably upset. Go outside and scream if you must to get it out of your system! Do whatever you need to do to get motivated. Just don't go back to sleep!

Everything out there is designed to take you for what you have! You have been lied to about everything! No one is there to help and nothing is free! There are no good companies, just good products! Go to any so-called good company and work for them, you won't have to wait exceptionally long before you see the truth! There is no such thing as a respectable job, only a decent one.

But, for the sake of argument, go and apply to a so-called good company. They will screen you and reject you if all your ducks are not in a row! You can't have a decent life if all your ducks are not in a row! My job is to cause you to take an honest look at yourself! To assist you in learning how to properly exercise your fiduciary rights and responsibilities so that you may overcome and learn to work a system that is designed to take us for everything we have! In short. My job is to wake you the hell up!

Let's get back on topic.

CAR LOAN HARD INQUIRIES

Do not shop around for vehicles if you are NOT seriously considering a purchase. Do your research! Any time you give your social security number to a potential lender, there will be a **HARD** inquiry added to your credit report (This may cost you 35 points for each inquiry). If you do buy from a lender, the inquiry will not be deleted when an account is activated. And don't believe the hype if an account is not activated; the inquiry will still be on your credit report for two years. And too many **HARD** inquiries are just as bad as not paying your existing accounts on time or defaulting on your bills. **WARNING: Most dealerships will still place HARD inquiries on your credit even if you have told them, you already have a lender. They will tell you it's standard practice. You may have to dispute these inquiries and produce proof you did not give your permission.**

NEVER use a company that offers to reduce your monthly payments or combine all your bills into one lump sum monthly payment. It's all B.S. Sometimes they won't even make the payments on time or worse they take your money and do nothing. Don't fall for the scam, a lot of these fly-by-night credit assistance agencies charge hundreds of dollars to help you fix your credit. In truth, they don't do jack squat. If you have collections, they will still be there! Yeah, they might dispute an item here and there and even get an item removed from your credit report; but they are not worth the money. You can make disputes on your own and it won't cost you anything. You can get items removed and then buy yourself a cake.

REALITY CHECK:
A hard truth to swallow, most of those mistakes you made WILL remain on your credit report for the next 7 years and there isn't a damn thing you can do about it! Except wait for them to fall off!

Collections: The Truth
If your bills fall into arrears, it is more than likely your account will be turned over to a collection's agency. It's nothing to be ashamed of, it happens to the best of us. Now I'm not going to waste your time teaching you how to duck or avoid collections agents. I'm sure you're already a Pro! Instead, we are going to discuss paying these collections off if you are able. If you are not able then more than likely you can continue to duck and do your best to avoid these agencies until the seven years run out. **If you are able to pay these people!** The best thing you can do is open a separate savings account and start adding as much money as you can every month to it until you can pay off the smallest collection amount. And after one has been paid off and it falls off your credit report go to the next one and pay it off as well. **It's not like the old days when you could duck them for seven years and hope it'll go away. Nowadays these people are more than willing to take you to court to get their money and charge for the legal fees. You're better off doing whatever you can. Instead of going to buy some stuff, you don't need to pay off the debt at income tax time.**

Let's say for the sake of argument, that it's not your fault and somehow this collection was added to your report and you can prove it. You should have already read the helpful articles on the FTC Federal Trade Commission website. Below are links to dispute those erroneous entries that somehow found their way onto your credit report:

The Po Man's Guide to Breaking the Poverty Cycle

https://www.transunion.com/creditdisputes/disputesnewd
https://www.equifax.com/personal/creditreportservices/creditdispute/
https://www.experian.com/disputes/main.html

Collections: Debtors Prisons (They are bringing them back)!

Library of Congress in the United States, debtors' prisons were banned under federal law in 1833. A century and a half later, in 1983, the Supreme Court affirmed incarcerating indigent debtors was unconstitutional under the Fourteenth Amendment's Equal Protection clause.

What happens to unpaid credit card debt after 7 years?

After seven years, most negative items will simply fall off your credit report... You still owe your creditor even when the debt is no longer listed on your credit report. Creditors, lenders and debt collectors can still use the proper legal channels to collect the debt from you. Don't believe me, take a look at the articles below:

https://www.nbcnews.com/news/usnews/debtorsprisonaclureportdetailscriminalizationprivatedebtn849996

https://www.thenation.com/article/archive/prosecutorsandjudgeshavebroughtbackdebtorsprisons/

The Po Man's Guide to Breaking the Poverty Cycle

Using Credit Cards - How to Build Your Credit

Credit cards? This may seem crazy to some people, but bear with me, you never want to get a credit card from a credit card company. What you will want to do is open maybe three or four accounts with really good credit unions or banks. You want at least $10,000 in available credit.

Now you will want to apply for credit cards from your banks or credit unions. Most credit card companies will decline your request for a larger credit line if you are not spending money. You want to stay away from credit card companies, they will close your account if you don't spend enough money. Banks and credit unions don't seem to mind, they're just offering an additional service and as long as your money is with them, they're fine.

The goal is to never buy anything on credit! What you are going to do is budget out your money, allocate the appropriate funds for whatever purchases you need to make and use these credit cards to make the payment. The idea is you pay off each debt as soon as they post.

This method will affect you in 3 ways:

1. You will have no actual debt.

2. It will cause your credit score to go higher if you pay off everything in less than 30 days or before the reporting date.

3. Your spending habits will cause these banks or credit unions to automatically extend a higher line of credit (after evaluation).

Credit card companies make money off the interest that accrues when you make changes. The idea is to get you to over extend, only be able to meet the minimum payment amounts and pay large amounts of usury which is high interest. Once caught in this cycle of hell digging yourself out becomes next to impossible! I say again. Avoid using credit card companies at all costs! Stick with the banks and credit unions! So, when you get those congratulatory cards in the mail stating that you've been preapproved tear them up and throw them in the trash where they belong. If you didn't ask for it never take it. Take out a small loan from your 401(k) if you need money. **You can also use PayPal as a lay-away program.** Six months the same as cash on purchases over $100.

The Po Man's Guide to Breaking the Poverty Cycle

Credit card companies are the new loan sharks they will take away everything you have, only they won't send actual goons to break your legs when you don't pay them back on time. Now, they will have the power to throw you into a debtor's prison. Never allow yourself to be put in a position where you're borrowing from tomorrow to satisfy your needs today!

Using Credit Cards: How to RAISE Your Score
When it comes to using credit cards to build your credit, there is more than one way to skin a cat. The pre-approved offers you get in the mail are a no-go. Don't even consider applying for one of them! And only use secured cards if you are willing to lose your initial investment. You also have to make sure you are already financially stable before even thinking about using this method.
There is lots of advice out there about raising your credit limit. The simple truth of the matter is that you're better off getting your credit cards from banks that will automatically check your credit once a year and raise your credit limit without doing a hard inquiry. They don't usually penalize you for inactivity and are more concerned about your debt-to-income ratio.

Some people say, maintaining a small balance on your credit cards is a good thing, maybe they are right, but I wouldn't advise following their advice. The average Joe doesn't have 1000s in the bank just in case they make a mistake. Out here in the REAL WORLD we are lucky enough to have the money we need to pay our bills in full. I would suggest using your credit cards to pay off monthly bills and then simply paying the balance out of your banking account before any interest can be accrued. If you find yourself in a position where you have to have a balance on one of your cards at the end of the month it should be no more than 71% of your available credit; having a balance of 5% or less is even better. The more available credit you have the better. I tend to make sure I pay all of my bills in full before the end of the credit reporting cycle.

On some of my cards, the **reporting date** is the 25th of the month, so I will make sure I pay off any bills before the 25th of the next month. Always pay your bills off before the reporting date, not after! If you are like me and use Credit Karma, look at the date reported on your summary for each card, it will give you your monthly cycle.

I try to use each one of my credit cards at least once per monthly reporting cycle and if at all possible, I pay off 100% of the debt. This kept my credit score growing a little higher each month. A good rule to follow is not to use the card unless you have the money in the bank at the time you use the card. That way, when the bill comes due, you will always be able to pay it off. I'm not a credit guru nor will I ever claim to be, but I only use methods I know will work for anyone. Don't believe the hype and start trying to follow one of those super complicated methods where the math is endless and your confusion will only grow. Keep it simple. If you have a balance on your cards when the reporting date comes around your score will go down! It's simple people. If you pay the

The Po Man's Guide to Breaking the Poverty Cycle

minimum amount due your score will go down and won't come back up until a month after the reporting date you paid off the balance of the account.

The more you keep your card balances at $0 the better your credit score will be. Simple! You are **only** using these cards to keep them from closing your account! Simple! The GOAL is to build your credit. NOT USE IT!

The best way to improve your score is to use the cards for buying groceries, gas and paying for your dry cleaning. All of these funds should be in your bank account **when** you make the charge! You should know that the money is in your account because you have accounted for these expenses in your budget. All you have to do is pay the bill as soon as the account lets you make a payment, usually 2 days after the initial purchase. You don't have to carry a balance month to month, and you don't ever have to pay any interest.
You are **only** using these cards to keep them from closing your account!

Increase Your Credit Limit: Raise Your Score
Every year you should attempt to get your credit limit increased; but only if you can apply for an increase without them doing a HARD INQUIRY.
If your credit limit is $500, which might be considered on the low side, a balance of $250 will drop your score. A balance of 10% would be $50 and will drop your score. Just remember any balance other than zero will result in a drop in your credit score if the balance is not paid off before the reporting date on the card you are using. I never wait to get a bill nor do I ever wait for the payment due date. I always check online and wait for the purchase to be posted. Once the charge is no longer pending and has been posted you will be able to make a payment. I ALWAYS pay in full unless there has been an issue and I have no choice but to make payments. Then I pay as much as I can above the minimum due amount. It is not rocket science to keep your balance at $0. Make your payments before the reporting date each month so you keep your card in service and you should have no problems. You will have plenty of transactions and your account will always show a $0 balance.

HARD Inquiries

NOTE: It seems like I'm repeating what I said earlier, I am. But there is a slight difference between cars and other purchases.

Any time you apply for any kind of credit, a **HARD** Inquiry will appear on your credit report. Expect your score to drop 35 points every time you apply for credit. Any time you apply for any kind of credit, a HARD Inquiry will appear on your credit report. Expect your score to drop 35 points every time you apply for credit. If you get the loan, the inquiry will remain on your credit report and won't wall off for at least 2 years. Some people will tell you they fall off when you get the account or the loan, but that's not true. Some of the gurus out there say too many HARD Inquiries will cause your score to

The Po Man's Guide to Breaking the Poverty Cycle

plummet, and that's true. But I've safely had four and saw my score drop maybe 10 points. It's best to have none, but I don't see that happening. Keep them reigning in under six points, and you should be fine.

Follow these buying tips:

- **If you can't make this payment twice a month don't get it!** In the case of an automobile or a home mortgage, you can't get around this rule; but if you can afford to, you should always follow it.

- **If you don't need it don't get it!** This requires discipline and is one of the most important rules

- **If you feel pressured walk away!** Don't allow a fast-talking salesman to talk you into buying something you don't want! Take your time. Do your research. And find the best deal for you. Don't allow yourself to feel intimidated by anyone trying to sell you anything! They're only after your money and it's your job to spend your money wisely

- **If you don't understand the terms and or you are not getting what you want never sign your name.**

- **Debt is not an asset Period!** Car is not yours until it is paid off. House isn't yours until it is paid off. And if possible, stay away from homeowners' associations! One little slipup and they can take away your home.

- **Never allow a car dealer to come and pick you up!** It makes it easier for them to pressure you into a sale. Always ride with someone else or drive yourself. You need to always be free to get up and walk away.

Get educated about private prisons!

https://www.youtube.com/results?search_query=PROOF++The+Music+Industry+%26+Private+Prisons+

REALITY CHECK:
A hard truth to swallow, most of those mistakes you made WILL remain on your credit report for the next 7 years and there isn't a damn thing you can do about it! Except wait for them to fall off!

The Po Man's Guide to Breaking the Poverty Cycle

Chapter 4: Why You Need a Computer

NOTE: If you have no choice, I can see using your phone, but don't get into the habit. You can't see everything on those little screens. Below are 10 reasons why you need a computer at home:

1. Job search - Having a computer at home while conducting a job search can be invaluable. When it's time to respond, you can do it faster than the people using someone else's computer. It will save you a lot of time, energy and effort, money, heartache, and rejection! Most companies don't want you to show up at their door asking for an application! They will direct you to their website and ask you to apply online. There are workforce commission annexes set up so anyone can show up and use their computers, if you have one, in your city or town. All you have to do is sign in and then you can utilize one of their computers for hours. But when they are really busy, you are going to have to wait in line. And if you have to wait, it can be for hours at a time. It is going to cost you gas to get there depending on the size of your city or town.

2. Information storage - I have seen a lot of people lose all of their files because their data was stored on a flash drive. Sometimes the flash drive gets broken and becomes unusable. Most people lose them. Same result! All of your files are gone! With a PC you can store thousands of documents, movies, videos, books and music.

3. Entertainment - You can play games on the computer whether they be simple games or the more complex variety of role-playing games. With a little practice, you could even download ROM and learn how to use the many different emulators to play them. There are so many choices out there. You can play Super Nintendo, Play Station One, Sega Nintendo64 and most of the old arcade games that were around when you were a kid. Heck! Even some of the old games were around when your mom and dad were young depending on your age.

4. Budgeting - Let us face facts! It is considerably easier to maintain your budget on a computer using Microsoft Excel rather than writing it down on paper. For starters, you can make changes a second after you have made a purchase and you don't have to rewrite the entire thing or wait to update your budget. You can run multiple scenarios and develop many courses of action in minutes. You can price almost anything online and plan out how to pay for said item in moments. All without ever having to pick up a pen.

5. Music - I have thousands of songs stored on my hard drive in Music folders. I load all of my music onto my computer. Long ago, I took all of my old CDs and loaded them onto my hard drive! Because once a CD gets scratched and it can no longer play you have just lost your money! And the only way to get your music back is to buy another

The Po Man's Guide to Breaking the Poverty Cycle

CD. With a computer, you can load your music and save your CDs to your hard drive in its pristine state. You can then burn a new CD once your old copy gets scratched. You can also download music for a couple of bucks! You can have a new song you like without having to buy the entire album as we did back in the old days. There are too many music sites to count! You can visit them and hear your music for free no matter where you are in the world! You can even buy mixing software and become the DJ you've always wanted to be minus the turn tables.

6. Cable replacement - With everyone's cable bill climbing higher and higher, lots of us have opted to get a digital antenna for most of the Network stations and signed up for streaming services. I was paying $170 a month for cable and internet. I dropped the cable and kept the internet. I had already signed up for Netflix, so I joined Amazon Prime as well. Now I only pay for internet, so my bill is $75 plus $14 for Netflix and $14 for Amazon Prime. I'm still saving $67 a month! There are new streaming sites popping up all the time, such as DC universe. Even YouTube is getting into the act. Who needs cable when you can watch anything you want with no commercial interruptions? You can watch all your favorite shows on full screen just like on normal cable. Why be limited to reruns you don't even like when you can watch shows On Demand and stream thousands of movies? I can scarcely remember the last time I saw a DVD.

7. Software - This little section might be the hardest for me to explain. You are going to need special software for special needs. Microsoft Office is a must-have! Almost any company you work for is going to demand you know how to use Word, Excel and in some cases PowerPoint. It is a good idea to have them at home so you can practice. In a worst-case scenario if you are running late and need more time, you can always take the file home and finish it. I recently acquired Microsoft Project so I could use it for my Project Management courses. Designers use Autodesk AutoCAD and many more software programs. Most places are integrating SAP into their businesses. QuickBooks may be a name you have heard before. At almost every turn there are software programs out there that can make your life a lot easier! And you can use them on your computer at home. There are software programs out there that scan and repair your computer. You have a little home-based business, no problem! There is software specifically designed for small businesses. Software for almost anything you could think of...!

8. Online classes - I have enrolled in ninety online classes. I've already paid for most of them so at my leisure, I can take them on my computer anytime I like. I want to learn any and everything I possibly can. With online classes, your time is your only limiting factor! There isn't much you can't find online! You can learn anything! You can even buy a welder, watch How-to videos on YouTube and then start welding. Don't even get me starting on how many things I've learned in the last few years by looking them up on YouTube. You should take every opportunity you are given to use your computer to learn new stuff! And you can learn at home. Let's be real. No one is expecting you to earn a nuclear physics degree while sitting at home on your computer. But you should expect to learn or master minor skills in your own time.

9. Online shopping - Gives you the ability to find items from all over the world. Anything you can imagine is out there and at the same time right at your fingertips for making or buying. You never have to leave your home to go shopping at a store in New York, or a cute little place you heard of in Paris if they are online. I have personally shopped for clothing, vehicles, houses, boats and motorcycle parts. You name it, the sky is the limit. **Why waste your gas money going there when you can go online** and take a virtual tour of almost anything! See exactly how it looks in real-time without ever leaving the comfort of your favorite chair. And best of all, you can get online discounts and most of your purchases will be tax-free!

10. Hands-on experience - As I mentioned earlier in the skills chapter, you are going to need a computer to learn and practice on to gain experience.   Are you still thinking a cellphone is going to cut it? We both know a small screen is not going to give you legitimate practice! **And when you get to work, they will put you behind a desk where there is a real computer. You will be completely lost.** I have watched people who are phone masters, you know the thumb wrestling champions can't sit at a real computer and answer an email. Let's be honest about this. It's going to take you a while to get used to navigating pages, sites and programs you've never used before! There is no substitute for playing around with the system or software until you get the hang of what you're doing. These days you can go online and get quick tips! YouTube is one of those places! You can also take cheap or free college courses from places such as Udemy and Allison. Don't just sit there on your derrière thumb wrestling your phone! Sit at your computer desk and learn something useful and practical. You know, something you'll be able to take to the outside world and it will be known as a skill.

The Po Man's Guide to Breaking the Poverty Cycle

Get a Starter System

Buying a computer can be scary if you don't know where to begin. I will now attempt to help take some of the mystery out of the computer buying process. If you never had a computer before and you're working with a limited budget, you shouldn't be spending anything over $250.

Right now, at this very moment, you can go on eBay and buy a Seller refurbished Fast Dell Desktop Computer PC Core 2 Duo, 1TB hard drive, 8GB Ram, Windows 10 operating system, a Wi-Fi adapter, MS OFFICE 2016 installed and a 19" monitor for $216 shipped to your home. **Unless you need mobility, never go with a laptop!** You can always buy a laptop later when you're more successful and have the money to throw away. But for the naysayers, let's compare some of the pros and cons.

I don't know if you are anything like me, but I only wanted a laptop because it was the hip thing to have at the time. But I began to notice how much processing speed and RAM I was losing so I switched back to a desktop. You get a more powerful computer for your money with a desktop. I would only get a laptop if you **needed** mobility.
You have more upgrade options with a desktop. Most laptops will allow you to easily add RAM and swap out the hard drive. But your average desktop can take more RAM than your average laptop. And with a desktop's multiple bays, your drive options are greater. For instance, you don't have to choose between an SSD and a hard drive on a desktop; you can have both without paying more. Upgrading a CPU or graphics card reasonably easy tasks on a desktop. These same tasks for a beginner are difficult and next to impossible on a laptop.

If this is going to be your first computer don't go all out! And don't try to keep up with the Joneses and go and buy a supercomputer you cannot afford! A computer that will take you two years to pay off! The idea is to make one simple purchase and get a reliable efficient computer to suit all of your present needs! As you learn and become more proficient you can update your system and update your system until you are satisfied! Your choice of software can add many bells and whistles to your system if that's your thing, but I suggest you keep your spending to a minimum.
There is reasonable software out there don't go and spend $380 on the software programs that you can get for $10! Do a little research, bide your time and make a good purchase. Ask around. Ask your friends. Ask **anyone who knows what they are doing**. As I said before, you can get a decent computer on eBay for $250. No problem. So don't go looking at QVC and buy a new computer for $1500. Don't go to some rental center and sign a two-year contract to buy a $3000 computer when you can easily buy a refurbished computer that will perform the same functions and use the same software for $250!

The Po Man's Guide to Breaking the Poverty Cycle

Let's talk about protecting your computer

Now don't get me wrong, I'm not talking to the people who know what they're doing the experienced gamers and guys who have been working on computers for years. This next section is not going to do you any good! You already know these things so skip ahead.

As for the rest of you slugs, this information is going to be helpful. I hope. Taking care of your computer if you never had one there are so many small little things you can do to protect your investment.   Again, I'm not calling myself an expert or anything but I can say, I have done these things for years and they seem to work well for me. I have had to repair computers for friends and family on many occasions throughout the years! I rarely get viruses or malware my software can't handle. In my humble opinion, buying good software can keep you up and running for years without an issue.

Knowing how to set up your software, now that's a different story. So, it is a small matter of knowing which software to use. Why you're using it. And what effect if any is it going to have on your machine. There's no point in spending a lot of money on a computer you break every two days and then you send out because you don't know what you're doing! And haven't taken the time to figure out what you are doing wrong. You're going to have to know your machine! You're going to have to know how to fix it! And you will need to put yourself in a position where you can fix it quickly and not need to send it off to the shop. There are too many places online you can go to learn this stuff. And if I can learn all of these tips and tricks on my own, so can you!

Rule # 1: Stay away from Administrator passwords!

If you are a normal person, which means normally you are too busy to pay attention to everyone who uses your computer, you'll live to regret it. But, if you must use an Administrator password, write the password down in several different places only you know.   I say several; because, things get moved and papers get lost. Trust me, I know! I've had to reset so many passwords and reload Windows Operating Systems too many times over the years because people forgot their passwords.   People tend to devise the most elaborate passwords in a vain attempt to come up with a random combination of words and numbers no one would ever figure out.   And they, if given enough time, are prone to forget. I have a fairly new computer, donated by some rich "genius", who forgot their password after a long vacation and could no longer access their files. Thanks mate!

In the good ole days, on the older systems, you could simply remove the battery on the motherboard reboot and presto, you were back in business. Not so nowadays, you could remove a hundred batteries with no such luck! There is an old saying using the acronym K.I.S.S. which stands for Keep It Simple Stupid! So, in the writing of this book I intend to do just that.... Keep It Simple!

We are going to operate under the pretense or assumption, no one, reading this: Po Man's Guide has the money to throw away by putting their computer in the repair shop.

114

The Po Man's Guide to Breaking the Poverty Cycle

One little uh oh can cost you about $200 easily. This isn't going to be one of those longwinded overly complicated manuals that leave you more dazed than you were before you picked it up. Most people don't want long dissertations on the inner workings of their computers. They want to be told what to do to fix the problem not be lectured to death.

If you know nothing about computers, keep reading!
Most of the people I've encountered knew next to little about protecting their computers and knew even less about how they functioned. I would ask question after question about their operating systems and they would always reply, "I don't know". Ignorance is only bliss when it costs you nothing to remain ignorant. The simple truth is what you don't know will cost you! Maybe not today, but someday, you will have to pay for what you could have learned and yet choose not to learn. Look, people there are no getting around having to learn new things! A lot of my friends are older than I am and they seem to revel in their computer illiteracy until they have a problem. Then there is this panicked scramble to make some sense of what happened to their computer. If you are not part of the solution, you are the problem! You are the weakest link. Goodbye. No money, no glory, just an overwhelming sense of helplessness. Now if you have the funds to just throw away you've just wasted your money, time, energy and effort on this book. Po Man's Guide, remember.

The Po Man's Guide to Breaking the Poverty Cycle

System Information: Things YOU NEED to KNOW!

Rule # 2: You NEED to KNOW your System!

Click on the Start Button scroll over until you see the Control Panel icon app or folder and click. Click the System icon.

- What's your operating system? (Windows Vista, 7, 8, or Windows 10)
- How big is your hard drive? (How many Gigs)
- How much ram do you have? (How many Megabytes or Gigs)
- Is your system an older ATX or SATA?
- How fast is your Processor?
- Do you have a 32 or 64Bit Operating System?
- When do you defragment your hard drive?
- Do you have an updated virus program? If so, which one is currently protecting your system?
- Is your hard drive over half full?
- Do you have Microsoft Office?
- How much music do you have? (How many Terabytes or Gigs)
- How many videos do you have? (How many Terabytes or Gigs)

Important tools you will need

You must have an Antivirus program. I can't afford one, you'll say. I say you can't afford to have one. There once was a time I knew next to nothing about computers. But I hate not knowing! And when I could afford one, I bought an old used 386 computer. Yeah, long ago sometime in 1996. Intel 486's was the new thing, but I was broke. So, I bought a used 386, using the classifieds, had Windows 3.1 loaded onto it and paid $300 for the whole shebang. At the time Windows 95 was dominant. But I knew: I needed to learn with the system I had; before, I could even think about an upgrade. I crashed the system so many times I lost count! But I learned what I needed to know! The first time I loaded a Monkey B virus onto my system I paid $100 for DOS and Windows 3.1 disks so I would never have to take my computer to the shop again. Thus, began my journey and every time thereafter when my system crashed it was because of a virus. But I was always able to fix it!
Before we get into virus scans, let's talk about free browsers. Browsers are not important you say? But I had a friend who had a Mac and I noticed I would always get viruses and he never had any. We did a little research and decided the only reason must be my browser. He was not better at using his computer, but I had the wrong browser! Most often, I'd find myself on the wrong site trying to find CRACKS or some other form of software I knew I shouldn't have been using. Usually, I'd be on some hacker site and bang! So, one day, he looked at the browsers that came with his Mac and told me those were the ones I should look into. I did. And I have never had another virus problem

The Po Man's Guide to Breaking the Poverty Cycle

concerning my browser again. There are many out there to choose from. I prefer opera. Opera takes a little getting used to in the beginning; but after a while, you could never imagine using any other browser. I set up opera so it automatically blocks popups and prevents intrusions. I've never had my homepage changed without my wanting it changed again. And to be honest, every time I ever had a virus get into my system it came through my browser! I don't think hackers spend as much time learning to hack Opera or the other browsers as they do the browsers that come from Microsoft. So, for safety's sake, I will continue to use Opera.

Warning: Do not go to free movie sites if you do not have good antivirus software or some sort of malware remover! I bought my little sister the same computer listed above and where do you think she went first? That's just asking for trouble! If you don't know what you're doing don't go there! Anytime you see something too good to be true because it is too good to be true! Most free movie sites will introduce your system to their friend Trojan! Trojans, PUP, or any other type of malware can destroy hardware or crash your system and even hijack your desktop! You can solve a lot of problems by only going to pages with site certificates! Yeah, I know you can't fix stupid! Someone is always going to go there! Someone is always going to click on the wrong link and get their system corrupted and have to start all over! So, if you are going to go there anyway, **we both know you will** take the necessary precautions! Your computer is your gateway to the entire world. Would you like somebody to set up a roadblock and stop you from freely traveling?

Notifications
Notifications can be just as bad as viruses or malware! You may think: It's a good thing you're notified when something new comes up you'll be the first to know. That's fine in theory! What happens when all of those sites you **allow instead of denying** all start sending you notifications at the same time, cluttering up your system, devouring your RAM so you can't even look up an Internet page? You will find out quickly notifications can be a bad thing! I would advise you against it. But, just in case you don't believe me…go ahead and press ALLOW! And give it a couple of days and you'll be searching for this: How to Disable Notifications on Windows 10.

Free **Antivirus Programs**

I recommend buying Malwarebytes! (There I said it. But you saw the word **FREE**)!

Free Antivirus Programs are usually offered by your internet provider, such as AT&T and Comcast, (Time Warner Cable) Spectrum. There are 30-day trial versions and some freeware. The best freeware Antivirus software out there (in my opinion) is AVG. https://www.avg.com/enus/freeantivirusdownload that's their website or you can find it on Cnet. Type AVG into your search bar. You can always trust Cnet. These days everything is cheaper and easier. You can usually find a Malwarebytes license online for less than $20 for a Lifetime Subscription using Bonanza or eBay.

The Po Man's Guide to Breaking the Poverty Cycle

What is an update?
As new viruses are emerging every day, the most important feature of an update is to add definitions of new viruses to the internal virus database stored on your local disk. Also, an update can contain various program changes and improvements, new features, language files, etc. To distinguish between updates of different importance, Update Levels have been defined. If a virus database is outdated, it means your antivirus program does not contain definitions of the latest threats that are currently spreading and cannot give you full protection!
To ensure your antivirus installation gets updated on the recommended daily basis, there are several manufacturers' preset update schedules, so normally you will not need to worry about updating at all.
However, you might want to know how to:
Updates are extremely important for the full functionality of your antivirus software; therefore, it is necessary to update regularly; for most users, it is advisable to perform an update once a day.
The Update Manager component administrates your Internet connection and settings for correct and timely updating. Start automatic updates uncheck to turn off regular automatic updates of the virus database. We strongly recommend not doing this unless you have a real reason!

- Periodically choose this option if you wish to check for updates more than once a day. You can then enter the preferred value (check for updates every x hours/minutes).

- At a specific interval choose this option to check for updates once a day and specify the interval by setting the desired time in the first box. Please note for server capacity reasons, the update will be performed at a random time between the hours set in the first box (by you) and the second box (which is not editable).

Manual Update
By default, your AVG updates automatically daily, but there might be situations when you need to make sure you do have the latest updates. To do so and update instantly, right click the AVG icon in the system tray and select Update now. Alternatively, Highlight and click the Update now shortcut button.

When to Run a Scan
When in doubt scan! A friend brings you a CD or DVD they burned. Scan it before you open it! A coworker allows you to borrow some information on their USB flash drive. Scan it before you open it! This is called a manual scan, my method of choice. You can manually scan a drive, directory, or external drives by right clicking on them and clicking scan with whatever Antivirus software you are using. If you wish to practice, go to your

The Po Man's Guide to Breaking the Poverty Cycle

desktop and right click any icon or you can go to My Computer and right click on any drive letter you see: C D E F G H I.

An automatic scan is called a scheduled scan and is something you have to set up. Setting up an automatic scheduled scan can be either: easy or hard, it depends on the user and the software. Usually, the schedules are easy enough to figure out, but if you run into a problem, click on the help button, which should give you step-by-step instructions. I generally like my scans to be run once a week, usually around the time I should be sleeping like 2:00 am but that's my preference you are going to have to find your own.

Redundancies

The purpose of the redundancy is filtration, I've found this to be the case with most software. One will catch what the other misses. Think of it in terms of oil filters. At 20 microns most of the large particles are caught in the first line of defense, but still smaller particles make it through. At 10 microns, even more, particles are caught in the second line of defense, but still smaller particles make it through. On your computer this equates to tracking cookies and mainly spyware.

I had internet service provided by both Comcast and AT&T both offered FREE antivirus software, yet most people fail to take advantage of this service. As soon as I found out this was available, I was in the security section of their customer service sites and downloading the antivirus software. My last internet service provider was Comcast and I was downloading the FREE Norton 360 before the installation technician had even left my apartment. Before, I was using the FREE Malware Sweeper. I suppose you could call me paranoid, but as I said before, every time my system crashed it was because of a virus. After Norton 360, I went to Cnet and downloaded the FREE AVG Antivirus software. When it was time to tackle spyware, I went to Lavasoft and downloaded FREE Adaware. This rounded out my collection of Antivirus software. Now don't go thinking, I'm advocating you should only use free software! I'm only putting this out there in case you cannot afford to buy software! It is better to have something running on your system. But at the end of the day, you are going to have to decide what works best for you.

Next, I had to do something about slowdowns and registry errors. PC Tuneup will cost you about $20/year but it's worth it for the amount of bang you get for your buck. But like I said, I believe in redundancy. I also downloaded Netgate Registry Cleaner for FREE to catch anything the PC Tuneup Registry Cleaner component might miss. I'm not saying you'll need all of the software I use, but you should at least fork over a little money to cover all your bases.

My final redundancy: CCleaner Professional costs about $18 and it's also definitely worth it. The more space you can free up on your hard disk, the faster your PC will run. CCleaner is a 3-part program:

    1. The Cleaner button allows you to scan for and delete useless files.

    2. The Issues button allows you to scan for and fix registry issues.

3. The Uninstall button allows you to locate and uninstall unneeded software.

PC Tuneup

PC Tuneup, I'm an avid believer in "If It Isn't Broke Don't Fix It!" There are newer versions out of course, but PC Tuneup works just fine for my needs and will cost me nothing to update.   You already know how an Antivirus program can protect you online. PC Tuneup is your one stop shop to help you get the most out of your PC. The latest version of a PC Tuneup program will cost about $30 a year, but it's worth it. You may also be able to find the program online for less than $10. You don't always need to have the latest and greatest .

Disk Maintenance

I would not use the Defragment to defrag, it seemed a bit too fast for me instead, I'd use the Disk Defragmenter supplied by Windows. Disk Defragmenter optimizes your file system to get the most out of your hard drive. Enjoy a faster hard disk and a more stable and smooth-running computer. Monitor your hard drive health and space usage. I would generally set up my automatic scan so my disk defragmenter will run at least once a week.

Free Up Space

Clean up old files and remove duplicates. I would not use Explorer to locate and remove programs instead I'd use the Uninstall Software or Programs and Features supplied by Windows 10,7, Vista, or remove software or go into Control Panel to uninstall programs and features I no longer want.   Don't go deleting files if you don't know what they do or how it will affect your system after those files have been deleted. You could cause your system to crash! Follow this one simple rule: **If you don't know what you're doing, don't do it.**

Software Control

Remove Startup items that are slowing down your boot sequence, or you simply no longer need. Remove installed software is no longer Up-to-date or you simply no longer need it.

System Tweaks

If you are a novice stay out! Most of these tweaks add little REAL noticeable speed to your system.

Disaster Recovery

Windows comes fully equipped with a File Recovery tool so you can recover files that have been damaged or accidentally deleted within Windows.
You can use the Rescue Center to Undo changes made to your system by other programs, just remember it has to be periodically cleaned out like the Virus Vault of the AVG Antivirus. Now I know most of these programs say they have a really good file recovery system but I've never found it to be true. The best thing you could do is have a

The Po Man's Guide to Breaking the Poverty Cycle

backup external hard drive! Copy all of the important data from your present hard drive and keep it somewhere safe, cool and dry. You should expect your system to crash like people looking for the rain! You know it's going to come. You don't know what day it's going to be, but eventually, it's going to rain!

Registry Maintenance
Registry cleaners make your PC more stable by removing or repairing broken registry links to get the most out of your PC.
Registry defrag optimizes your file system to get the most out of your hard drive. Enjoy a faster boot up and a more stable and smooth-running computer. You must reboot to make changes.

Privacy

Track Eraser Protect your privacy
Lots of information about your activities is recorded on your PC. Track eraser will help you protect your privacy by removing this personal information from your computer. Deleting files or folders removes references to them, but doesn't remove the actual data stored within the file. This means files you think you've deleted can easily be retrieved.

- Permanently delete files and wipe disks
- File shredder and disk wiper

Netgate Registry Cleaner
As I said, I also downloaded Netgate Registry Cleaner to catch anything the PC Tuneup Registry Cleaner component might miss.
NETGATE Registry Cleaner cleans and defragment your registry, speedup your PC, removes unneeded files on disks and removes activity traces. It includes a Startup manager to manage programs started at Windows startup and Uninstall manager for handy applications uninstall. Supports scheduling of scans and backup options for better security.

Features:

- Registry Defragmentation
- Registry Backup and Restore
- Startup Manager manages all applications that start at Windows startup
- Uninstall Manager a handy tool for quick uninstalling of applications from your system
- Backup all removed items are stored in backup until permanent deletion; they can be restored anytime
- Registry Cleanup
- Disk Cleanup

The Po Man's Guide to Breaking the Poverty Cycle

- Traces Removal
- Scheduling support
- Multilanguage translation support
- Skin support
- Premium technical support
- Registry Shield Protection

Requirements: Windows 107 (32bit and 64bit), Windows Vista (32bit and 64bit), XP (32bit), 2000 (32bit)
website: https://www.netgate.sk/content/view/19/43/

I would run the registry cleaner at least once a week or any time you notice your computer slowing down, your system files crashing, the page is not loading properly, or eating just seems weird to you or not normal when in doubt run a scan.

AdAware Free
https://www.adaware.com

AdAware
Spyware can be a lot of things. In general, it's software some Web sites and viruses install on your computer without your knowledge so some person or company can track your online movements, or even record your keystrokes with a key logger also mentioned earlier in this chapter under "Strange computer behavior". If it doesn't bother you someone you don't know knows where you go on the Internet, then you don't need to know any more about spyware.

CC Cleaner
CC Cleaner is pretty straightforward and is a system optimization, privacy and cleaning tool. It removes unused files from your system allowing Windows to run faster and freeing up valuable hard disk space. It also cleans traces of your online activities such as your Internet history. Additionally, it contains a fully featured registry cleaner. But the best part is its fast (normally taking less than a second to run) and contains NO Spyware or Adware!

- The issues blank allows you to scan for and fix issues.
- The tools section allows you to uninstall remotely.

When you use Microsoft Security Essentials, it's important to have Up-to-date definitions. Definitions are files that act like an ever-growing encyclopedia of potential software threats. Microsoft Security Essentials uses definitions to detect if a file or program is spyware, malware, or other potentially unwanted software. You will get an alert if the program is a potential risk. It also alerts you when programs attempt to

The Po Man's Guide to Breaking the Poverty Cycle

change important Windows settings and when: spyware or potentially unwanted software attempts to install itself or run on your computer.

This is by no means a comprehensive list, there is far too much information out there and way too many programs to list here! Doing your research might take you some time; but in the end, you will know what you are doing.

I hope this information will get you off to a good start! If nothing else, you should already have a good idea of where you want to start. Sometimes knowing where to start is the most important thing there is....

REPEATING MYSELF!
The idea is you are going to need a computer. Learn how to use the computer. Safeguard the data on your computer and keep it running smoothly!

The Po Man's Guide to Breaking the Poverty Cycle

Chapter 5: Dealing with Self Destructive Behaviors

WORDS OF THE WISE - Bad Company Corrupts Good Character!

Breaking bad habits is as simple as thinking before you act! If you can't do well then come up with your preventative countermeasures. What? You read correctly. Preventative countermeasures: practiced reactions to known problems. Practice reacting to things you know will cause you to stumble. Think of it as putting on a play. **Go back into your memory and relive the incident**, except this time react the way you should have. It's a Brain Hack! Your brain won't be able to tell the difference so the next time you find yourself in that situation, your brain will generate an automatic response. Practice makes perfect. Do it seven times for each circumstance or reaction you want to change.

Learn To Take a Joke
Throughout the years, I have watched a great many people fail to achieve their goals because they take themselves too seriously way too seriously! This is a harsh and brutal world and anyone who thinks differently is just deluding themselves. If it wasn't for my sense of humor, I could never have made it this far! You're going to have to learn to be able to take a joke and how to make fun of yourself. If you can't, you're not going to make it very far in today's work environment. Think about it. How many jokes do you hear throughout the day at work? Revelation: you can't escape wisecrackers at home or anywhere else. When you turn on the TV and watch commercials, most employ some form of comedy. Many of the most famous people we know started as comedians. Now, why is that? Because comedy lightens the mood! Comedy causes the day to go by faster! So, I hope you are not one of these newfangled idiots who is a wannabe gangster, who believes you have to appear to be super hard at all times! And people should fear you. If so, you are going to have to take it down a notch. In this new politically correct society, you're not going to make it very far in life if you don't learn to shrug things off. You're going to have to do a major rewrite of your personality! Nobody wants to feel threatened at work! Nobody wants to feel insecure in their person when they are working alongside someone else! You may think you're the man or whatever but, in most cases, it just makes you seem like a bully nobody else wants to be around.
There is a reason why those guys used to be the class clown in high school seem to make it farther in life than those of ill temperament. Those guys make excellent salesman and great diplomats because they know how to deal with people! They know how to broach sensitive subjects, using their sense of humor cracking jokes with the intent to lighten the mood or lessen the impact of anything negative.
Always try to find a non-threatening way to break the bad news to people. Do it with a joke or make fun of yourself as a distraction. Most people will appreciate the attempt,

The Po Man's Guide to Breaking the Poverty Cycle

even if you're not funny. Guys with a good sense of humor are usually the ones to diffuse conflict in the workplace and outside of work. They know the situation and/or circumstances leading up to an offense don't matter. The idea is to get the person to bounce back quickly and get back to work. They will find it very hard to stay angry or stuck in a rut when someone is making them laugh.   If you have a good sense of humor, people will want to be around you, they will find it easier to speak with a funny approachable guy.

And while we are on the subject of cracking or making jokes don't dish it out if you can't take it. I have known so many supervisors, who love to crack jokes and shame the people who work for them. I don't know if this stems from some sort of inferiority complex or not, but they use their position to belittle people. Knowing the other guy can't fight back without getting written up or in trouble for insubordination. I have a serious problem with that ilk.

Forgiveness: The Key Unlocks the Doors to Progress

Definitions:
 Sorry
Feeling or expressing sympathy or regret.
Poor or wretched
Grievous or sad

Apology
A statement expressing regret or asking for pardon for a fault or offense.
A formal justification or defense
An inferior substitute

Forgive
To excuse for a fault or offense, pardon
To give up anger or resentment against or the desire to punish
To absolve from payment of.

No. I'm not going to get all biblical on you, there would be no point. I am simply sharing what I have noticed. People are going to make mistakes, it's not a matter of will they make mistakes, it is a matter of when. We learn by making mistakes. So, forgiveness is crucial! Coworker is going to forget what you told him. Your boss is going to forget what he promised you. You are going to forget what you told someone else, so there is no point in holding grudges. It's counterproductive and will get you nowhere fast! If you're the type of person who holds onto a grudge, you are going to quickly run out of people who are willing to deal with you and want to deal with you. Nobody wants to work with somebody or for someone who has unrealistic expectations! Yes, you can demand the best from your people. Your boss can demand the best from you! But there is no such thing as perfection when you're dealing with people! So, once they make a mistake, walk them through the process of admitting to and acknowledging how or why

The Po Man's Guide to Breaking the Poverty Cycle

the mistake was made. What are we going to do in the future to prevent this mistake from happening again? And allow them to move forward once they have shown the mistake was unintentional. Confirm there was no malice involved. Once you know there was no malice move on. Forgiveness is your way of saying, Okay I understand. It was a mistake. You didn't mean any harm by it let's move forward. If there was malice involved you would still forgive! Let it go! And move on. But now, you are going to need to do these three things:

1. If at all possible, you don't want to work with this person anymore or deal with this person anymore. You simply say hello and goodbye if you speak to them at all. Now for someone whom you are forced to work with you speak only about work and nothing else. Show **no emotion.**

2. Never allow them to engage you in any way that is not job-related.

3. If they ask for your opinion, you don't have one. You want to limit your interaction with this individual as much as possible. Never allow them to escalate any situation. If you can walk away. If you aren't able to walk away, limit your responses to yes or no. If unable, keep them as short as possible with **no emotion.** They will soon get tired of trying to get a reaction out of you and leave you alone.

Yes, I know: some people go around seeking to be offended they are looking for trouble. And they will find it. Just make sure you are not involved. If you know a person who is a drama king or queen, give them a wide berth. Don't engage! Nobody is going to be perfect! Nobody is going to anticipate everything. And if you are a drama king or queen, give people a break! Life is stressful enough without you walking around attempting to be Lord Corrector!

The NEVERS at work

Always be aware of your surroundings.

NEVER LET YOUR GUARD DOWN when you are at work.

AS I have noticed over the years: the unlearned always attempt to establish and maintain who they are at home at work. This is ALWAYS a BIG mistake! The "you" at work, is the silent assassin! You knock out your work and move on to the next assignment! This isn't high school or your neighborhood! Check your ego and pride at the door!

Even if your boss is cool, NEVER CONSIDER THEM AS YOUR FRIEND!! They WILL betray your trust! Sometimes, they will have to let you go because you are too close. If management sees your boss's weakness is you, they will target you. When you become

The Po Man's Guide to Breaking the Poverty Cycle

the boss, it's the opposite. Never fully trust your employees and never let them get too close. They will betray your trust! Sorry, but if you are the only honest person there, that's just how it is.

NEVER put yourself in a position where your boss can't help you! If you screwed up, admit it quickly without being asked! Never try to hide your mistakes! Be the first one to point them out.

NEVER RETALIATE!!! Although the urge may be overpowering, push it down. Forgive, forget and move on. Never carry bitterness around with you because of something that happened at work. You are your greatest enemy. Your big fat mouth will get you in trouble, keep it closed. Vent when you get home.

Never call out your boss as a liar! Although the urge may be overpowering, push it down. Forgive, forget and move on. Always go with your gut when they speak to you and you don't believe them. Don't be so eager to argue the point!

Never take advice from someone who is jealous of you! Never advise someone who you "know" is jealous of you. They will twist your words, try to imply that you are a bad guy and not to be trusted.

Life Rule:
Only Make Friends with People who want to See You Succeed!

Cut Slings: A military slang term for getting rid of a person or ending a relationship with a person. As air crewmember on a CH47 D Model Helicopter, we were required to call Sling Loads. A Sling Load is an external load, suspended below a helicopter for transport during flight. Sling load operations are complex and involve training and certification courses. If a load becomes unstable or threatens to do damage to the aircraft, we were required to Cut Slings! Meaning to drop the load.

Toxic Friends
This is one of the hardest things to discuss, not because of the actual subject; but because people vary so differently. A toxic friend is one of those people who clings to you. They are always around. You didn't call for them. You didn't ask them to be there, but they show up like clockwork, whenever you don't want to be bothered with them. They always want to know what you're up to. Have you made any progress on the problem you needed to solve? And they are always there to give you unwelcome advice! You can tell by their actions that they don't like you, but for some reason, they can't stay away from you. They smile quickly anytime you fail. And they can't take a hint when you attempt to ask them to leave subtly when you are trying not to hurt their feelings!

The Po Man's Guide to Breaking the Poverty Cycle

Toxic friends appear to have one agenda: somehow keeping you stuck in a rut with them. They never seem to want to see you get ahead. They never want to see you have anything! And no matter what it is you come up with, they will always be the first to tell you it won't work. It won't do you any good. You should be happy where you are. They don't see why you need to change. You are fine the way you are! Stop letting other people fill your head with nonsense! You need to get those crazy ideas out of your head about making more money or getting a better job. Why do you need a house that big? You're dreaming. Stuff like that never happens to people like us! Before you go too far and get your heart broken, you should just accept that your dreams will never come true. They always imply or attempt to tell you how you should think! They practice groupthink.

Groupthink [ˈgro͞op,THiNGk]

NOUN
The practice of thinking or making decisions as a group in a way that discourages creativity or individual responsibility.

You're the only one of us who keeps trying to buck the system. Often, they use small actions to gain control over you. They get upset when you don't always want to agree with them! They tell you how you should spend your money! I could beat this dead horse all day, but I think you get the message.

What's the difference between a leech and a fair-weather friend? Not much! Both are only around when you have money. If you want to party, they're good to go. You want to hang out, sure, no problem. Not one of them would ever go out of their way to do anything for you! But like you, they just want some company so that they're not alone. Maybe they are broke, so they will gladly help you spend your money! If you're not sure, test them! When you are out with so-called friends, only buy what you can afford! And when you say you can't go, they'll just shrug and say, "Okay" and they're on their way to having fun without you! If you are the needy one, why go with them? Why spend your money? More than likely, you don't even really like these people! You just don't want to go somewhere alone!

There are also those real leeches who will nickel and dime you to death! Five dollars here! Ten dollars there! Three dollars here! Twelve, then maybe even twenty. And in your time of need, they have nothing to give! They also never pay you back! They always have some excuse. I have a rule If I loan you money and you start ducking me, it's cool. I consider whatever small amount of money I have loaned you to be an investment. I will Cut Slings! If a person starts ducking you over $20, it's the greatest thing in the world! It only cost you $20 to find out the truth about them! That's a deal! I don't care who you are! For $20 I got rid of you and that's a steal! If they get up the courage to ask you for something else, simply ask for your money. Tell them, "You don't

The Po Man's Guide to Breaking the Poverty Cycle

keep your word, so I don't trust you". After anything they ask for, even if it's a stick of gum the answer is always NO! Cut Slings!

Proverbs 30:15 "The horseleach hath two daughters, crying, Give, give. Three things are never satisfied, yea fore everything say not, It is enough:"

Let me repeat if you normally hang out with leeches cut slings! There is more than one type of leech. You also have the kind of people who need and want you to do everything for them. Things they can and should be able to do themselves. And don't fall for "But you do it so much better than me crap!" Knowing when to say no. This particular life skill was pretty hard for me to master. But it is something that needs to be done more than we would like to admit. A life skill you must master!

Have you ever found yourself knee-deep in someone else's problem and you think I should have just said, NO!? Somehow, you allowed yourself to be talked into doing something which had absolutely nothing to do with you! Now, this guy is sitting back, taking it easy and you are doing all the work and getting nothing in return other than a thank you with a stupid smile. He's smiling because he just duped you and you let him! How are you ever going to get anything done for yourself if you are always doing something for someone else who could and should be doing it for themselves?

Don't get me wrong, there are times when people actually will need your help and you know they can't do it themselves. Those are the times when you should perform your good deed for the day, asking for nothing in return. I have met plenty of people who simply needed me to teach them to fish. And they have been able to feed themselves for a lifetime. But if you're doing someone a simple favor and then it somehow balloons into a full-blown project. And they expect you to do it all for free, even come out of your pocket. What have you gained? You're not paying it forward! You are just feeding a leech!

When someone asks for a favor and they say it requires your skill, offer to teach them how to do it. If they start giving you excuses and you can tell they don't want to learn, cut slings! There are users out there! Instead of doing it for themselves, they want you to do it! They don't want to have to lift a finger! They won't do the work, but they expect you to do it! And they dare to want you to do it for free! They will use and abuse you for as long as you allow it! And get upset with you when you stop being a there little whipping boy! "Not happening" or "Nope", always works for me.

The Po Man's Guide to Breaking the Poverty Cycle

Associates
What are associates? Associates are people you don't mind being around at work or sometimes at home. You are not real friends and you know you are never going to be close. You simply have shared interests. If you're going to have an associate, choose wisely. Bad company corrupts good character! Don't try to make an associate out of the neighborhood drug dealer! When the time comes for you to choose an associate, pick someone good with money. Choose someone who has a plan for their life! Pick a guy who has things figured out. Someone who won't mind you asking questions. They will enjoy having you around, so they can review their options, bounce thoughts off you and get a logical response. Choose an associate who makes you think! One who will force you to speak, think, and act responsibly. Sometimes, this associate will become a mentor. Remember, hanging buddies or associates are fine as long as you call them what they are, associates. Know them for who and what they are and expect nothing more or less from them. Don't go getting all clingy, like a lost puppy.

Your associate must be someone you want to emulate! Someone you can look up to, a person who won't mind helping you elevate yourself! A person who knows how to get you pumped up and motivated. Someone who will have no problem giving you constructive criticism. You may not like it, but you need to have a guy who can give you constructive criticism without trying to put you down or belittle you! Who knows: maybe one day this person will become your best friend, somebody who is worth holding onto.

THE BREAKDOWN: Only make friends with people who want to see you succeed! No one is going to have over 2 or 3 real friends! Most individuals are self-involved users. You want to have a conversation; they offer no response, or you can tell they are disinterested when you try to engage with them, cut slings! Yes, I know, people get lonely. But no one's that lonely! You don't need more frenemies! And don't go getting all depressed cause nobody wants to play with you! Learn to be comfortable spending quality time with YOU! If you hate being alone, you are admitting that you hate being you! You need to be distracted so you get anxious when you find no one who wants to hang around with you. Fix you first! If you have issues, you know you need to work on, to become a better person, take time out and fix your shortcomings! And then you'll find you can't keep other people away.

Too Much Information TMI Separation of Professional and Personal.

In making these changes, you're going to have to learn to separate personal issues from professional ones. Keep your personal life away from work! Stay off the phone! And only receive personal phone calls if there is an emergency! I have watched so many people get fired or get written up because they COULD NOT stay off their cell

The Po Man's Guide to Breaking the Poverty Cycle

phones. These are those people who bring their problems onto the job and they expect the people at work to understand what they're going through! Newsflash! The people at work don't care about your personal life! No one cares about what's going on with your parents! They don't care about that "A" your son got in history. Your love life is of no concern to them. It's your love life. They don't care about your girlfriend leaving you for another guy. No one at work cares about what you do at home, period. Keep what you do at home at home! Never mix the two, they don't mix! Keep your political opinions to yourself! If people suddenly want to know what you think, they are probably trying to find something to use against you. Don't get caught up in useless conversations where you have nothing to gain. Oh yeah! And if you are gay, leave it at home! No one cares! If you make an issue out of it, you are saying you want attention! Special treatment! No one cares about YOUR sexuality at work! Leave it at home!

Are You LAZY?
I have explained this a thousand times, and it seems as though it never really gets easier. But the impact is always the same!

Now, I'm no expert, but this is what I have seen laziness usually comes in two different forms:
   1. We have the mentally lazy people: the ones who never want to read or learn.

   2. We have physically lazy people: who never want to do any work.

How do you overcome laziness? You can't! You can, however, change your outlook! You will still be lazy, whether it be mentally or physically, but my response will still be the same. **<u>If you hate doing it, get it done and out of the way!</u>** The main thing the two types of lazy people have in common is procrastination. It doesn't seem to matter if the issue is physical or mental, putting it off till tomorrow seems to be the norm.

You can only overcome this character flaw little by little. You are going to have to train yourself to become a lazy workaholic, whether it be mental or physical. The first thing you have to do when you find out you have a problem is admit you have a problem. But I say, admit and resolve in the same breath. So don't call yourself lazy. Call yourself a lazy workaholic, it's what you're going to have to become to solve your problem. I don't know why, but most people seem to like the idea when I explain it this way!?

Overcoming Lazy. Get it done quickly so you can go back to being lazy.
Overcoming Lazy. Get it done quickly so you can go back to being lazy.
Overcoming Lazy. Get it done quickly so you can go back to being lazy.
Overcoming Lazy. Get it done quickly so you can go back to being lazy.

The Po Man's Guide to Breaking the Poverty Cycle

The Character Hack for Physical Laziness

Initiative   noun: initiative; plural noun: initiatives; noun: the initiative

1. *the ability to assess and start things independently. "Use your initiative, imagination and common sense"*
   synonyms: enterprise, inventiveness, resourcefulness, capability.
   antonyms: unimaginativeness

2. *the power or opportunity to act or take charge before others do.*
   "We have lost the initiative and allowed our opponents to dictate the subject"
   synonyms: advantage, upper hand, edge, lead, whip hand, trump card; More

Energy [ĕn'ərjē] the capacity or power to do work, such as the capacity to move an object (of a given mass) by the application of force. Energy can exist in a variety of forms, such as electrical, mechanical, chemical, thermal, or nuclear and can be transformed from one form to another.

Before I get into what I would call "the mental aspect of physical laziness" let's consider for a moment that you may have a medical condition or something wrong with your body that robs you of your energy. If you believe this to be the case and you don't weigh 300 lbs. Go see a doctor and have them determine whether there is something wrong with you physically. You could take vitamins, apple cider vinegar and inosine. Eat more vegetables! Start juicing fruits and vegetables all to get your energy up.
Now, if there is nothing wrong with you, medically speaking, then we're going to have to assume your issue is mental. Now there are ways to correct the mental aspect of physical laziness.

Overcoming Lazy. Get it done quickly so you can go back to being lazy.

This is an example of what I mean:
Your boss comes up to you and wants you to complete a task. It's a really hard job, and it is going to take you hours to finish it. A lazy person will try to put it off and make sorry excuses explaining why you can't get it done. An hour has passed and you have done nothing. Your boss is getting ticked off! Now he wants to grind you into the dirt. More than likely, this is a test. He has had his eye on you for a while and is deciding whether or not to fire you! He has already decided this project is your last chance! You already have one foot out the door and he is about to hurl your sorry ass into the unemployment line! Sorry to say it, but this is the norm. **Anticipate your boss's tasks** and begin planning your approach before he's finished giving instructions. **The easiest**

The Po Man's Guide to Breaking the Poverty Cycle

thing to do is come up with a plan which will allow you to get the job done the fastest and easiest way possible! And then hammer and hammer at it until it's done. Now, you look like an ambitious person and when you complete a task the easiest way possible, that's always a bonus.

Now let's say your boss wants to put you in charge of a task and you have other workers aiding you with the assignment. If you believe you are going to need more help, ask for more help or ask your boss how he would do it or ask him how he wants it done. Sometimes they don't know either, so they'll bark, "I don't care what you do, just get it done! Figure it out!" Use your imagination coupled with your experience. When in doubt, ask your teammates for their input, brainstorm, and come up with a plan of action. Consider everything you are going to need to get the job done and just get it done! The harder you work, the faster the day goes by and vice versa. Once you are done, you can go back to shamming, as we say in the military, putting the shine on making yourself look busy. The harder the job, the quicker you need to get it done.

Let's Talk About Initiative

If you're like everyone else on this planet and I'm sure you are, you lack initiative! You wait to be told what to do! Even if you already know "what" you should be doing. Should this be the case, you will need to change your thinking. If you're at work and you can see certain things need to be done, depending on your level of freedom at work, you don't have to ask your boss if it's ok to tackle those small minor tasks, just do them. If your boss is a control freak, **inform him of your intention, tell him why it needs to be done, and then ask if it's all right for you to proceed.** Bosses love this 90% of the time. They will simply tell you to go ahead with a strange smile on their face. You are going to have to start retraining your mind to employ your eyes when you see something that needs to be done. You must remember you are here to break a cycle of poverty; this means you are going to have to put in the work! You are going to have to do things you wouldn't normally do. You are going to have to get used to doing a lot of things you never would've thought of doing. And showing initiative is one of those things. You're going to have to become an analytical person at work and home. If you have to you can make up a schedule so you spend your time wisely. **Your goal is to get things done! And then you can go back to slacking off.** Always take the hardest jobs!

The biggest mistake a lazy person can make is to destroy his time! There is nothing on this earth a man can't get back except his time! You can't go back to being young again. You cannot return to your former naivete. It's impossible to regain your virginity. I'm sure you have heard tales of men who have lost everything and get it all back, with one exception: time. You can never get your time back! So, I'll give you tidbits of advice I have gleaned from others. Use your allotted time wisely!

I have seen many older men suffering; because they didn't want to put in the time, energy and effort to do what they needed to do to make the latter portions of their life easier. **People, you're going to have to burn off some of your youth so that when you are older, you are not struggling!** Men don't seem to get the idea that age will overtake

The Po Man's Guide to Breaking the Poverty Cycle

them. They know it's coming, but they make no adjustments to their behaviors or goals. I have seen people screw off while they were young. And like the grasshopper, they regret it in the end. But instead of winter, old age is coming! You do not want to spend your old age suffering, having to work HARD jobs, forced to compete with younger men while your body gets hammered year after year with no end in sight. The object is to work hard while you are young and strong! To get things done and set things in motion, so when you are older, you are not crippling yourself way ahead of time. How many older guys do you see out there collaborating with young guys, trying to find a better way to get things done? They should be the ones giving the orders! Yet they are not! They can barely keep up! Why? Because they had no plans! No achievable dreams!

No one can tell you what goes on in the mind of another person! I can say, they had dreams and somewhere along the way they lost HOPE! I can say they didn't believe they could act on them. I could be right. And I could also be wrong! But the result is the same: they didn't act upon their ability to create options! Time and chance happen to all men! Now, because they couldn't or wouldn't make their dreams into reality, they're forced to work in a young man's world and it is getting harder and harder for them to compete! Who is going to help some old guy with many injuries land a good position? To them, he is just some fool who allowed opportunity to pass him by! The time my friends wait for no man! So, when I say, "Show initiative! Plan out your future! Figure out what you want to do with the rest of your life!" It's the entire purpose of this book! My goal is to stop you from becoming the older guy I just mentioned!

Mental Laziness You Hate To READ!!
If you don't read so well or you hate reading, there is only one solution: read all the time, until you do! If your reading ability is subpar, then practice until you read well. Find an author you like and get to where you can read a 300 or 400-page book in a day. The books can be science fiction, fantasy, home improvement, whatever floats your boat. But you're going to have to read! At first you will fall asleep but keep at it and little by little, you will stay awake longer and longer. Grind it out! You will get better and better until finally you find yourself reading books for hours and hours without stopping. The next thing you know, you will start absorbing information incredibly fast. You are going to realize you just created a habit that will serve you for the rest of your life! Instead of having someone tell you about a book, you will want to read it for yourself. You won't just scan it, you will read every single word to make sure you miss nothing! That's how it works!

The Po Man's Guide to Breaking the Poverty Cycle

Avoid Grouping!
Allow no one to place you in a group of people or clique: having a negative connotation! Your job is to be an individual judged solely for your work performance! Perception matters if you want to get ahead! Once others view you as a troublemaker, it's over! You know one of those guys who is always late. One of those sensitive individuals! And sensitive is just another way of saying you can't control your emotions! You are volatile! No one knows what to expect from you! If you get labeled as a sensitive person, their next step is to find a way to get rid of you! You might also find yourself blacklisted quickly! Nobody likes whiners or tattletales.

You are who you hang around! You do not want to be branded by your association with unsavory individuals! If you know your group is known for illegal activities! Stay far away from them at work! Do not allow anyone to group you in with them! Avoid situations where your group's actions could reflect badly on you. If they're going to go and hang out somewhere at work, you stay far away. If they invite you to go, always say no! NEVER allow the slightest possibility that someone else's actions can or could have any impact on your life or reputation! So, if you have a friend who is always looking for trouble, stay away! Stay away! Trouble is easy to get into, hard as hell to get out of! You don't have to listen to me now, but later on you will wish you had! Only it will be too late! Once you get labeled, it's over! Even the police officers go looking for KNOWN associates when a crime has been committed! They round up the usual suspects. Don't get caught in the crowd! Back in the army almost everybody rolled in a clique. I rolled ALONE!

The Po Man's Guide to Breaking the Poverty Cycle

Chapter 6: Knowing How and When to Ditch that Dead-end Job!

If you bothered to buy this book, chances are you are indeed working at a dead-end job. People have been trained to get a job, not the one best suited for their aptitude, a job! Often, men passively accept circumstances and unexpectedly find themselves trapped in a job they never wanted but had to take out of necessity. If your job is labor intensive and does not require any actual skills, get a clue. Do you have the ability to progress? Can you be easily replaced? Sometimes it's all about you, not the job. If your thoughts often drift to updating your resume, you already know you have outgrown your present job. Once you have outgrown your job, it's time to move on. The first step in moving on is admitting you have a problem: fear of the unknown. No one achieves anything in life without taking risks!

Below is a checklist designed to get your brain gears a turning.

1. You **hate going to work:**
You are in a dead-end job when you feel no joy at the thought of heading off to work each morning. You allow yourself to be distracted by outside forces because you want to be anywhere else. Over the years, you have grown apathetic.

When people love their jobs, they look forward to each new day. Each new challenge is an opportunity to put their best foot forward. If your heart is just not into your job, then it stands to reason it shows in your work. Your work quality has declined and doesn't reflect your best efforts.

2. There **is no job satisfaction:**
When an individual is exceptionally enthusiastic about something, this passion shines through when the person delivers a presentation or works on a particular project.

If your job fails to interest you or provide you with any sort of satisfaction, then it is a sure sign you are in a dead-end job. Job satisfaction is an important aspect of having a happy and productive professional life.

3. The **work is boring and a trained monkey could do it:**
Ideally, your job shouldn't feel like a job. It should be fun sometimes. Frequently, the satisfaction derived from challenging or stimulating work outweighs the lack of high earnings, resulting in a sense of fulfillment and happiness. If you feel your work is not exciting enough or challenging, it is surely a sign of a dead-end job. Different things excite or challenge different people! Monotony destroys the soul!

4. You **have achieved everything you possibly can:**

The Po Man's Guide to Breaking the Poverty Cycle

People with certain academic qualifications or experience can only reach a particular plateau and their career flat lines. If that is the case with you and you feel like there is nothing new for you to achieve in a particular company, it's normal. Stagnation breeds discontentment! A career death can be dreadfully dull and completely mind-numbing. No matter how old you are, your job should always continue to enthrall you! You should never feel you are wasting your time.

5. You **have been stuck in the same position for years:**
The primary reason people work so hard is to get promoted and prove their dedication. Your employer might bypass you for promotion once or twice in your career. Although this occurs often, multiple occurrences might point to a problem with your work environment rather than your job performance. In some workplaces, excelling in a certain field can hinder your career progression. Sure, this is great for the company, but they have just put the last nail in your career's coffin! That amazing work of yours has trapped you in a dead-end job you thought would help you advance.

6. There **is no work life balance:**
No one can honestly say he or she would not like to climb the ladder of success. But we all know this success should not come at the sacrifice of your personal life! Who wants a job which demands you ALWAYS miss important social or family gatherings? I am not Japanese and I have no desire to work myself to death!

7. You **are not given credit when it is due to you:**
Some companies' management teams are like slave drivers; they don't give their workers credit, even when deserved. No matter how well you perform or how hard you work to help the company succeed, someone else always gets the credit for your hard work. You never even get a pat on the back!

8. Being **overworked and underpaid:**
When companies demand work from their employees and refuse to pay them accordingly. This tends to demoralize the employees and create a feeling of being cheated. A dead-end job is neither rewarding metaphorically nor financially. No one should have to feel this way. And if you find out others in the same position at different companies are getting paid much higher wages than you, then you know you are being wronged.

9. You **know you deserve better:**
If you have a strong feeling you won't be at your job in five years, it's a sign. Just imagining it makes you furious, and you see no future. You're stuck in a rut, feeling this job is holding you back from achieving your full potential. Time to go.

10. The entire list above can be summarized in a single word! If you're feeling the urge to move on and find better opportunities, the word that encapsulates this feeling is

The Po Man's Guide to Breaking the Poverty Cycle

frustration. Serious frustration makes everything listed above twice as bad. Any little thing can set you off! "Get in where you fit in" is a cliché, but it's also a humorous truth.

You have decided you need to look for a better job. Now what?

WARNING!! THIS IS THE WHEN:
Never quit your present job until you have a new one already in place! And ALL YOU HAVE TO DO IS SHOW UP AT THE NEW JOB AND START WORKING!!!

JOB HUNTING TIP:
To land your desired job, sign up for accounts on job boards like CareerBuilder and Monster to boost your visibility to employers. Using these sites, you can manage your job search entirely from home: post resumes, receive job alerts, and apply. I almost forgot about ZipRecruiter, LinkedIn, and Indeed.

The Po Man's Guide to Breaking the Poverty Cycle

Dealing with Employment Agencies

Nowadays, people are not interested in having you come to their office looking for a job. Typically, companies need a copy of your resume or require you to complete an online application. There's that annoying computer thing again! Today's modern job search is done online. You will need to sign up for ZipRecruiter, LinkedIn, Indeed and any other site that has the potential to allow you to land that job you have been training so hard to land. Your resume should catch their attention. When in doubt details, details, details. Ignore the useless bullet point stuff they taught you in school. "You will be able to explain further in the interview", they told you. AN! *NK!!! Wrong answer! Today's boss prefers a comprehensive resume, like mine, to one that's short and simple. Your resume is comparable to a handshake, and if you write like you speak, you're in serious trouble!

This is where those old job descriptions come in handy. You don't have to make up stuff when you already have the information at hand. I can't count the number of people I've seen panic and give up rather than update their resumes. Writing a resume is not rocket science. You can always look up their old job descriptions online.

I'm going to include resumes I have written. I have blacked out the names to protect the innocent. These examples should get the ole gears a turning and hopefully help you come up with some ideas of your own.

Your only loyalty is to YOU!
I remember when I first got out of the military; I was loyal to any company that hired me and thought less of anyone who didn't share my philosophy. But one day I saw an older guy getting harassed and berated and I asked one of the older guys what was going on. "They are messing with him, so he will quit!" He answered. "He is close to retirement and they don't want to have to pay him. If they can find a reason to fire him, they will. Right now, they are trying to get him to quit. He can sue them and win," he finished. "Why would they do that to someone who has been loyal for twenty years?" I asked. "Greed, I guess," he replied. He was loyal to them and this is how they repay him, I thought. Never be loyal to a company; unless you know: they will be loyal to you in the end. (Good luck with that pipe dream!)

Resume Samples look them over carefully. You may get ideas of your own.

NOTE: Always keep your old job descriptions! They pretty much spell out everything for you. It's one of the best tricks no one ever tells you. You are going to want to keep your

The Po Man's Guide to Breaking the Poverty Cycle

resume backed up so you can't lose it. You can always go back to make changes. I intentionally left the mistakes.   If you don't speak in perfect English, your resume should be better than you speak and not as bad as you sound.
EXAMPLE #1

John Doe
14303 Your Street
Houston, TX 77020
Cell (281) 602xxxx
Email: **whatever@live.com**

Objective: To obtain a permanent Supervisory position will allow me to employ the Administrative and technical experience I've gained.

Education:
FEMA Disaster Inspectors Course 2005
Houston Community College (4 credit hrs. remaining: **Air Conditioning Repair Certificate) Mar** 2000 Apr 2001
Swagelok Certificate of Completion for Swagelok Tube Bending Course 1997
Basic Noncommissioned Officers Course (Technical Inspector's Course) (67U20) 1994
North Central Jr. College Clarksville, TN (Aviation Maintenance Technology 36 credit hrs.) 19931994
US Army Medium Helicopter (Chinook) **Repairman Course AIT** (67U10) 1986
Roswell Job Corps (Training: Electrical Apprentice) 1985
High School Diploma received from New Mexico Board of Education 1985

Qualifications: *25 years in Maintenance.*
Successful at building and leading Maintenance PM and procedural programs. Effective at making sense out of a complicated array of dissimilar production departments and relationships and then bringing them together into a cohesive and focused team. Task oriented, realistic and considerate in approach. A good sounding board for ideas and a strong advocate for useful change. Strong problem-solving insight with the ability to execute a wide range of practical, technological and operational strategies.
Proficient in reading: Schematics, Wiring Diagrams, PNID and Blueprints.
Software: Microsoft Vista, XP, Excel, Works, Word, Outlook and somewhat familiar with PowerPoint.

Employment:

ar 2013   Present
Maintenance Manager Supervises 7 personnel. Familiar with LEAN manufacturing.   Participated in daily supervisor Production Meetings to exchange information about work, safety, work windows and resources. Required within the first 30 days to generate a detailed written assessment of Maintenance Policies, Procedures, Personnel and established task deadlines for completion. Implementation of proposed changes to reduce waste within the department. Generated Operator TPM worksheets for all areas. Implemented a new PM program using FastMaint software. Purchases all materials needed for work project execution.

The Po Man's Guide to Breaking the Poverty Cycle

Manages employee work hours and overtime using E-supervisor software. Conducts plant walkdowns to identify and analyze opportunities for continuous improvement to use the maintenance department to greater effect. Using FastMaint(CMMS) software to create alpha-numeric parts finding lists within a given area and enhance inventory control.

Aug 2011 Feb 2013

Maintenance Coordinator Familiar with LEAN manufacturing. Participated in daily supervisor Production Meetings to exchange information about work, safety, work windows and resources. Volunteered to be a Kaizen team member to streamline the 5S Sort and Set a portion of LEAN and implement a new PM schedule i.e., Standard Work instructions provide direction to the Maintenance Department to Sustain ground gained and minimize machine downtime. Used Project Tracker and 30day newspapers to create a sense of urgency within the maintenance department to create a "Let's get it done!" atmosphere. Purchased all materials needed for work project execution. Conducted plant walkdowns to identify and analyze opportunities for continuous improvement to use the maintenance department to greater effect. Implementation of proposed changes to reduce waste within the department.

Performed maintenance on (5) Gribetz Border Quilters and Panel Cutters, Bale Openers, Gribetz and WBSCO Mattress Baggers, Lift Tables, Vertical Compactors, Auto Tacker, Burgess built Border Measure Cut Machines, Hotmelt Guns, Simalfa Spray Glue guns, Overhead Doors, Dock Levelers, Pacemaker Cloth Spreader and multiple minor Conveyor systems and belts. Troubleshoots and repairs: Synergy 1 and Orion Shrink Wrap Machines. Rebuilt and repaired: Vertex, Upholstery guns, Pro stick Long Nose Staplers, Flared Staple guns, Nail down guns, Nail down guns, Nailers and air motors. Worked with Accounting Department using Audit GLT to track and keep Maintenance spending within a budget. Researched, selected, developed and maintained adequate sources of supply ensuring equipment and services needed were filled in a prompt efficient manner at the lowest cost, to catch it fast and fix it fast. Used **Benchmate** (CMMS) software to create alphanumeric parts finding lists within a given area and enhance inventory control. Conducted multiple experiments which identified Takt time and reduced Cycle time within the maintenance department and other departments. A strong advocate of training.

Aug 2008 Jun 2009   (Injured in 2009 and not cleared for work until Late 2010)

Industrial Electrician/Mechanic Quietflex makes insulation glass and A.C. flex ducts.
- Hired because Maintenance Department needed multifaceted individuals: could and would design and implement troubleshooting procedures for multiple machines in the plant as needed.

Works with 3 phase 480/220 volts electric equipment, installs and programsVariable Frequency Drives(VFDs), AC inverters DC drives, DC boards, PLC Installation and testing. Performs PMs on (7) Atlas Copco, Champion and Sull Air Compressors. Troubleshoots and repairs: (8) Wulftec and Lantek Automatic & Robotic Shrink Wrap Machines.
- In**Duct Department:** Performs PMs, troubleshoots and repairs on (13) Inhouse Fabricated Duct Lines consisting of two

The Po Man's Guide to Breaking the Poverty Cycle

Pushers/Compression Assemblies, (1) Puller Line, (1) Jacket Feeder, (1) Cutter and, (1) Winding Machine.
- In **Core & Jacket Department:** Performs PMs, troubleshoots and repairs on (5) Inhouse Fabricated Jacket Fabricating Lines and (10) Core Fabricating Lines.
- In **Glass Plant:** Performs PMs, troubleshoots and repairs on MAT Line 1 & 2: these lines consist of 5 Maxxon Gas Burner Systems, hydraulic Chopper assemblies, (1) Forming Section, (1) Slicing Section, (1) Resin System, (1) Blending Section and (1) Dyken Section. (2)Regenerative Temperature Oxidizers (RTOs) and (6) Dust Collection Systems. With one exception: MAT Line 1 has (2) Hammermills, (2) Chillers, (5) Bailers, (4) Glass Feeder Lines with Choppers and (2) Scrap Openers.

Apr 2006 Aug 2008

Sr. Maintenance Technician/ Maintenance Planner, & Parts Coordinator
Planned, prepared and implemented work instructions provide direction to the Maintenance Department for corrective maintenance repairs and the performance of preventive maintenance using **Maintain It** (CMMS) software and the implementation of modifications. Created machine troubleshooting & training database. Made procurement recommendations to management for all materials needed for work project execution. Conducted plant walkdowns to identify and analyze corrective and preventive maintenance issues. Prepared and/or sent welding/grinding permits and fire impairments to ensure safety, high quality and technical rigor. Researched, selected, developed and kept adequate sources of supply ensuring equipment and services needed were filled promptly and efficiently at the lowest cost. Performed regular analysis of inventory and buying. Participated in weekly Production/Safety Committee Meetings to exchange information about work, safety, work windows and resources. Schedules outside contract work for Facility and Material Handling Equipment. Supervised 3 (& 1 nightshift) technicians performing mechanical and electrical maintenance on Autoclave, Vacuum Pumps, Bystronic XYZ F89 Cutting Machine, 2 96" Washers, 72" and 60" Washers, Bavelloni Glass Polishing and Beveling Machines, TGL 96" and 60" Furnaces, Forvetd CNC Milling Machine, 2 PIB Extruders, Infrared Heat Press and multiple Conveyor systems. On call 24/7.

Jun 2005 Apr 2006 Arch

Maintenance Supervisor & Parts Coordinator Developed MSDS Chemical Listing, Lockout Tagout Procedures, Respiratory Program, Hazcom Program and Evacuation Maps for Facility. Also Implemented HMIS labeling procedures. Researched, selected, developed and kept adequate sources of supply ensuring equipment and services needed were filled in a prompt efficient manner at the lowest cost. Performed regular analysis of inventory and buying. Participated in weekly Production/Safety Committee Meetings to exchange information about work, safety, work windows and resources. Supervises and can perform mechanical and electrical maintenance and calibration on Billco CNC Cutting Machine, Forvet CNC Milling machine, 2 84" Glass Washers, one 72" and 44" Glass Washers, Seaming Machines, HHH Furnace, Lisec Butyl Extruder, Silicone Gun, Glass Edging and Polishing Machines, Atlas Copco, Inger Soll Rand and Speedaire Compressors. Troubleshooting hydraulic and pneumatic systems vital to machine functions. Conduit bending and installation

The Po Man's Guide to Breaking the Poverty Cycle

of Control Panels, Disconnects, Receptacles, Switches and lights. On call 24/7.

Feb 2005   Jun 2005

Maintenance Mechanic Performed mechanical maintenance on equipment used in the fabrication of underground fiberglass pipes. Had to learn **MP2** (CMMS) software.

April 2004   Feb 2005

Maintenance Lead & Parts Coordinator - Designed and implemented PM schedule for Siemans' Rapid Sort Conveyor System, WheelLoks, DokLoks and Dock Levelers using Product Manuals and **MicroMain** (CMMS) software. Designed Error Code Status Sheets, Emergency shutdown and AIMS logical Spur Reference Sheets. Established Maintenance procedures for Emergencies and Preventive Maintenance concerning minimal conveyor downtime. Purchased parts and tools for conveyor maintenance and general plant usage, also setting up new vendor accounts when needed. Schedules outside contract work for Facility and Material Handling Equipment. Researched, selected, developed and kept adequate sources of supply ensuring equipment and services needed were filled in a prompt efficient manner at the lowest cost. Performed regular analysis of inventory and buying. Conducts minor and electrical repairs to Trash Compactors and Motorized Entry Gates. Assists IT professional with minor repairs of LXE and MXE RF radios connected to AIMS system, Zebra Printers and minor maintenance of AIMS Server. On call 24/7.

Jun 2002   Apr 2004

Lead Millwright/(Unofficial) Maintenance Planner & Supervisor - Designed and implemented PM schedule using **Maintain It** (CMMS) software. Developed multiple machine troubleshooting procedures as needed. Responsible for parts ordering for machine maintenance and general plant usage also setting up new vendor accounts when needed. Schedules outside contract work for Facility and Material Handling Equipment. Participated in weekly Production/Safety Committee Meetings to exchange information about work, safety, work windows and resources. Performs mechanical and electrical maintenance on Autoclave, Bystronics Cutting Machine, three 84" Washers, 72" and 64" Washers, Toritt Seaming Machines, Mroczek Furnace, TGL Furnace, Forvet CNC Milling Machine, Lisec Butyl Extruder, Infrared Heat Press, Besten Press, Silicone Gun, Hotmelt Gun and multiple Conveyor systems. Conduit bending and installation of Circuit Breaker Boxes, Receptacles, Switches and lights. Familiar with MCC Switchgear. Performed monthly inspections on Overhead Cranes and ran Atlas Copco and Sull Air Compressors. On call 24/7.

Applicable Military Skills:

- **Medium Helicopter Repairman (67U) Feb 86   Jan 95**. Five years' experience as Maintenance Team Leader of a nine-man Phase Team. Two years' experience as a Maintenance Team Member for scheduled and unscheduled inspections and Phase Maintenance. Two years' experience as an aircraft crewmember for inflight operations (Crew Chief: i.e., Loadmaster).

The Po Man's Guide to Breaking the Poverty Cycle

- **Tool Room Supervisor** Responsible for A92 tool sets and ground support equipment for four aviation companies. Organized a new Tool Room Storage Facility to enhance unit readiness. Maintained 100% accountability for over $2 million worth of equipment. A chart designed to track the flow of torque wrenches, power dynes and other equipment due for calibration. Maintained all equipment in a high state of repair, while assuring all damaged or displaced tools were replaced promptly.

- **Hydraulic Training** Almost nine years of experience with aircraft hydraulic systems. Trained in Aviation Ground Power Unit (AGPU) operations, proficient with reading tubing diagrams and operating swedge equipment.

The Po Man's Guide to Breaking the Poverty Cycle

EXAMPLE #2

John Doe
14303 Your Street
Houston, TX 77020
Cell: (281) 602xxxx
Email: **whatever@live.com**

Objective: To obtain a permanent and challenging position using the skills I've learned over the years.

Education, Awards & Certifications:
HFD Fire Extinguisher Class 2016
Held Forklift license for 10 years Renewed annually.
High School Diploma received from Evan E. Worthing High School 1975

Applicable skills:
Seven years of experience in warehouse operations supporting shipping/material handling functions
4 years of experience in a team leader role
Experience in Hazardous Material compliance
Proficiency in Outlook, Excel and Word
Knowledge of UPS, FedEx and other carriers' software, policies and procedures

Employment:
Jun 2012   PRESENT ███████████. **Lockhart, TX**
Shipping Lead - Applies knowledge and company policies to complete a wide range of assignments. Demonstrates expert understanding of all levels of the job family and has a thorough knowledge of jobs outside area of responsibility. Takes the lead in effectively applying new processes and skills in accomplishing assignments. May supply technical guidance and training to others. Maintains proper licenses, training and certifications. Works on complex problems require independent action and a high degree of initiative to resolve the issue. Makes recommendations for new or revised processes and has a role in the implementation. Adheres to all quality guidelines. Works with a minimal degree of supervision. Has latitude to make decisions in exceptional circumstances within established guidelines. Has team leader responsibilities but does not formally supervise.

Jun 2009   Jun 2010 ███████████████, **TX**
Material Handler Organized fast paced environment where everyone works warehouse with dock trucks and electric pallet jacks. Most trucks had goods on skids. The more pay was hand loaded onto pallets and moved with a pallet jack to a warehouse as a team. People are always working together to solve problems. Meet customers' delivery on time.

Self Employed 2003 2009 Lawn Cutting Service (Easy work fast money...Recession killed my business).

The Po Man's Guide to Breaking the Poverty Cycle

Jun 2002   Apr 2003   ▊▊▊▊▊▊▊▊   Lockhart, TX
Cook Prepare, to order, all food items following standard recipes and procedures within a specified timeline. Responsible for prompt and quality preparation of products according to the recipe. Reviewed the grill area and master recipes for all products and procedures and reviewed the recipe cards to ensure your food items look perfect. Ensures all discarded or wasted items are recorded and the line is always stocked, neat, clean and safe.

Jun 2002   Apr 2003 7▊▊. Austin, TX
Material Handler - Load and Unload semitrailers with propane double forklift. Move product to storage areas using the proper equipment. Stack and store products in the proper area according to established sequences and procedures. Rotate floor stock by moving the oldest product first. Document all material transfers, shipments and movements electronically and/or on appropriate forms. Ensure items are stored in an orderly and accessible manner. Maintain cleanliness in the assigned area.

Jun 20002   Apr 2001 Kelly▊▊▊▊▊▊▊▊   Austin, TX
Material Handler/Warehouse Worker Planned, prepared and implemented work instructions were supplied directly to the Lamination Department for the production of architectural windows, polycarbonate

Jun 20002   Apr 2001 Dell▊▊▊▊▊▊. Austin, TX
Material Handler - Planned, prepared and implemented work instructions were supplied directly to the direction of the Lamination Department for the production of architectural windows, polycarbonate (High Security Glass) Bulletproof glass, AG (Air Graph Glass) meant to supersede Bulletproof glass. Arranged

The Po Man's Guide to Breaking the Poverty Cycle

EXAMPLE #3

John Doe
14303 Your Street
Houston, TX 77020
Cell: (281) 602xxxx
Email: **whatever@live.com**

Objective: To obtain a permanent and challenging position using the skills I've learned over the years.

Education:
Houston Community College (Electronic Technology 15 credit hrs.) Jan 1977 Jul 1980
Indiana State University Terre Haut, Indiana (Electrical Engineering 11 credit hrs.) Jan 1975 Dec 1977
High School Diploma received from New Mexico Board of Education 1985

Occupational Licenses and Certifications:
███████████████████████ Certification; E.P.A. Certification, Type I, II, III Aug 15, 2003
Class A Commercial Driver's License Endorsements N Tanker, P Passenger, X Combination of N and H

Qualifications:
Over 10 electrical experiences, all stages. HVAC Installation gas and electrical. 19 years construction, homes to high rise office bldg.
Computer Skills: PC and Notebook
Software: Microsoft Vista, XP, Excel, Works, Word and some PowerPoint.

Employment: (Temp Agency Work Listed with Client)

Jun 10, 2011 Nov 30, 2011 ███████████████████████████
10710 Telge Rd. Houston, TX
Industrial Maintenance Technician Performed preventive maintenance on Gribetz Border Quilters and Panel Cutters. Repaired and adjusted timing on Porter 401500, Porter 4000 Flange sewing machines and Atlanta Attachment Doubleserge sewing machines. Install electrical drops to move equipment. Required to troubleshoot mattress manufacturing equipment from schematics. Made repairs and adjustments on sewing machines for maximum performance. Maintained the preventive maintenance schedules as assigned. Conduit bending and installation of Control Panels, Disconnects, Receptacles, Switches and lights. Made procurement recommendations to Maintenance Coordinator for all electrical materials needed Conducted plant walkdowns to identify and

The Po Man's Guide to Breaking the Poverty Cycle

analyze corrective and preventive maintenance for corrective maintenance repairs, the performance of preventive maintenance and the implementation of modifications issues.

Apr 07, 2010 Apr 19, 2011 ▉▉▉▉▉▉▉▉▉▉▉▉▉▉▉▉▉▉▉, **Texas**
Regional Maintenance Technician Traveled back and forth to 14 facilities within a 500mile radius.
Researched, selected, developed and maintained adequate sources of supply ensuring equipment and services needed were filled in a timely efficient manner at the lowest cost. Performed regular analysis of inventory and purchasing. Purchased equipment and materials for each different facility. Assisted maintenance personnel at each facility with the installation of equipment. Responsible for equipment troubleshooting, problem diagnoses and aid with repairs. Repaired split and package A/C units. Worked with vendors and contractors to schedule equipment installations. Wrote weekly reports and the monthly budget request.

Sep 09, 2008 Jan 20, 2010 ▉▉▉▉▉▉▉▉ **Houston, Texas**
Maintenance Supervisor Purchased parts, tools and shop equipment concerning budget guidelines. Scheduled outside contract work for installation of equipment. Implemented preventive maintenance programs and schedules. Prioritized Maintenance requests. Repaired and replaced electrical system components in hydraulic presses. Maintained the hydraulic systems, for 10+ presses. Maintained air compressors and HVAC systems throughout the plant.

Jun 03, 2008 Aug 01, 2008 ▉▉▉▉▉▉▉▉, **Texas**
Maintenance Mechanic Labor Responded to trouble calls from all production departments in to supply efficient maintenance coverage while minimizing machine downtime. Painted and shipped assembled parts.

Mar 12, 2008 Jun 03, 2008 Labor▉▉▉▉▉▉▉▉▉▉▉▉▉▉, **Texas**
Maintenance Mechanic Duties included performing minor repairs at a variety of industrial job sites were contracted through the staffing service.

Sep 18, 2005 Sep 09, 2007 ▉▉▉▉▉▉▉▉▉▉▉▉▉▉▉▉▉▉▉▉▉▉▉▉ **Austin, Texas**
Maintenance Lead (Residential) Managed the vendors. Scheduled outside contract work, ordering material. Developed preventive maintenance schedule. Implemented the proposed "Attractive Curb Appeal" idea. Bridged the gap of communication between management and residents. Maintained a cost-effective budget ensured quality repairs for residents.

Jun 12, 2005 Sep 03, 2005 ▉▉▉▉▉▉▉▉▉▉▉**/**▉▉▉▉▉▉▉▉▉ **Austin, Texas**
Maintenance Technician Performed preventive maintenance on all plant equipment. Troubleshooting electrical & mechanical systems. Repaired/replaced 120v, single and 3 phase 240, & 480 AC volt motors. Fabrication of safety guards for large grinders & sanders.

Dec 18, 2002 Jun 04, 2005, ▉▉▉▉▉▉▉▉▉▉▉▉▉▉▉▉▉▉▉▉▉▉▉▉▉, **Georgia**
Certified Residential Maintenance / Service Manager Prioritized work orders, Scheduled punchouts for marketing rental units. Ordered parts

148

The Po Man's Guide to Breaking the Poverty Cycle

and materials. Residential electrical troubleshooting & repair. Light plumbing & fixture repair. Sheetrock repair: walls & ceilings. Coordinated maintenance workload with management to meet residents' needs.

Oct 01, 2002 Dec 18, 2002 On███████████████████, Georgia
Residential Maintenance Punchout & general apartment makeready maintenance. Electrical troubleshooting & repair. Light plumbing. Repairs of A/C furnace gas & electrical.
Sheetrock repair of walls & ceilings.

Jan 02, 2001 May 15, 2002 Capital███████████████████, Texas
Bus Operator Drove 40, 35 & 30 ft. Passenger Buses.

Feb 04, 1999 Jan 02, 2001, ███████████████████ Bastrop, Louisiana
Truck Driver Drove tractor trailer cross country.

Feb 01, 1998 Nov 30, 1999 ███████████████████████████, Texas
Bus Operator Drove a 40 ft. passenger bus and a 65 ft. Articulator for the city of Houston.

Feb 01, 1996 Oct 28, 1998 ███████████████████, Texas
Journeyman Electrician Duties included installing a Main Distribution Switchgear for high-rise buildings, schools, hotels, hospitals and strip centers.

Feb 01, 1993 Nov 03, 1995, ███████████████, Texas
Journeyman Electrician / Electrical Maintenance Maintained the electrical systems for a 24-story office building.

Feb 01, 1991 Sep 10, 1993 Magnum███████████████████, Texas
Journeyman Electrician / Maintenance Technician Troubleshooting low & high voltage industrial systems. Installed and repaired electronic assembly equipment. Basic electrical maintenance of commercial office complexes.

The Po Man's Guide to Breaking the Poverty Cycle

Skills Acquired Spanning 20+ Year Period:

- Possesses electrician's license or identification card to meet governmental regulations.
- Inspects and tests equipment and circuits to identify malfunction or defect, using wiring diagrams and testing devices such as ohmmeters, voltmeters, or ammeters.
- Constructs and fabricates parts, using hand tools and specifications. Diagnoses malfunctioning systems, apparatus and components, using test equipment and hand tools.
- Directs and trains workers to install, maintain, or repair electrical wiring, equipment and fixtures.
- Inspects systems and electrical parts to detect hazards, defects and needs for adjustments or repair.
- Installs electrical wiring, equipment, apparatus and fixtures, using hand tools and power tools.
- Plans layout and installation of electrical wiring, equipment and fixtures consistent with specifications and local codes.
- Prepares sketches of the location of wiring and equipment or follows blueprints to determine the location of equipment and conformance to safety codes.
- Tests electrical systems and continuity of circuits in electrical wiring, equipment and fixtures, using testing devices, such as ohmmeter, voltmeter and oscilloscope.
- Calibrates testing instruments and installs or repaired equipment to prescribed specifications.
- Determines feasibility of using standardized equipment and develops specifications for equipment required to perform additional functions.
- Enters information into computer to copy program or to draw, modify, or store schematics, applying knowledge of software package used.
- Tests faulty equipment, using test equipment and applying knowledge of the functional operation of electronic units and systems, to diagnose malfunction.
- Prepares reports of work performed.
- Tests insulators and bushings of equipment by inducing voltage across insulation, using testing apparatus and calculating insulation loss.
- Installs auxiliary components to heating cooling equipment, such as expansion and discharge valves, air ducts, pipes, blowers, dampers, flues and stokers, following blueprints.
- Measures parts to determine tolerances, using precision measuring instruments, such as micrometers, calipers and verniers.
- Positions and aligns parts, using fixtures, jigs and templates.

References are available upon request.

The Po Man's Guide to Breaking the Poverty Cycle

EXAMPLE #3

John Doe
14303 Your Street
Houston, TX 77020
Cell: (281) 602xxxx
Email: **whatever@live.com**

Objective: To obtain a permanent position that will allow me to employ the Administrative and Practical skills I've acquired over the years.

Education:
Austin College of Cosmetology 1997
Lockhart High School High School Diploma 1996
Certified Cosmetology License Current

Applicable Skills: Microsoft Windows 710, Excel, Works and Word. Product Catalogs, Vendor Notification and Product Ordering Procedures. Customer Service, Problem Resolutions and Marketing Strategies. 20 years of Managerial skills.

Employment History:

2016 Present Great███████████████.
Store Manager Supported a customer centered attitude in the salon at all times-maintained staff scheduled two weeks out. Train and develop all staff in great clips system and dress code. Responsible for salon opening clothes along with assistant manager counseling of employees verbal and written as necessary set up and kept schedule for salon cleaning. Maintained and inventoried product stock. Prepared daily cash deposits. Consulted with owners as required concerning operational, financial, staff evaluations and human resource related issues as well as updates to the K2RB policies and procedures manual. Developed staff training schedules for Great Clips courses so all staff was certified within three months. Handle all customer service-related issues along with assistant managers. Resolve any issues at a local level so that no negative reviews for corporate offices. Assign staff marketing duties during slow periods. Interviewed and hired staff is necessary with owners' approval. Conducted audits to ensure Excellence in brand delivery measures to pinpoint areas in need of improvement. Responsible for all cash expenditures under $100

2014 2016 JC███████████████████.
Hair Stylist Cosmetology License in the state of Texas. Provided professional styling services for clientele. Ensured a superior client experience by determining the client's needs and providing services including the latest cuts, the best finishing and the industry's top chemical services. Self-motivated, solved problems and made smart decisions drove sales, profit and improved customer service; executed work efficiently and effectively. Built fan base and partnered with

151

salon team members. Displayed an eagerness to participate in the learning environment.

2011 2014 ▓▓▓▓▓▓▓▓▓▓▓▓▓▓▓▓▓▓
Store Manager Cosmetology License in the state of Texas. Maintained and inventoried product stock. Prepared daily cash deposits. Consulted with owners as required concerning operational, financial, staff evaluations and human resource related issues. Recruited stylists with colorful personalities, who worked fast, with precision and attention to detail. Maintained a passion for education. Fostered the atmosphere Smart style was a salon truly understood all things hair and allows its stylists to thrive. Developed a team that was made up of some of the most educated stylists in the industry. Finetune their core skills and had them master new trends cut, clip, color, highlight, style and do facial waxing. Certified through proprietary Hair Stylist Academy training. Improved customer traffic through our partnership with the MLB. Challenged and rewarded stylists through fun competitions showcased their work.

References are available upon request.

The Po Man's Guide to Breaking the Poverty Cycle

John Doe
14303 Your Street
Houston, TX 77020
Cell: (281) 602xxxx
Email: **whatever@live.com**

Objective: To obtain a permanent and challenging position utilizing the skills I've learned over the years.

Education, Awards & Certifications:
College Grambling ▉▉▉▉▉▉▉▉▉▉▉ of Study: *Elementary Education* (42 credit hours.)
High School Diploma received from ▉▉▉▉▉▉▉▉▉▉▉▉▉▉▉▉▉▉▉
Latest CPR Certification 2010
HFD Fire Extinguisher Class 2006
Held Forklift license for 20 years Renewed annually.

Applicable skills:
Proficient with reading: Client Templates and Blueprints.
Conversant with: P.O.'s, Parts Catalogs, Vendor Notification and Parts Ordering Procedures.
Familiar with the Following Software: Microsoft Windows: 9X, NT Workstation, 2000, XP and Vista.

Employment:
▉▉▉▉▉▉▉▉▉▉▉▉▉▉▉▉▉▉ 19791988) ▉▉▉▉▉▉▉▉▉▉▉▉▉▉▉▉▉
Jun 2011 Aug 1979
Houston, TX 77043
Lamination Department Supervisor Planned, prepared and implemented work instructions provided direction to the Lamination Department for the production of architectural windows, polycarbonate (High Security Glass) Bulletproof glass and AG (Air Graph Glass) meant to supersede Bulletproof glass. Arranged glass in appropriate order according to customer specifications, washed, laid up, properly pressed and aligned on takeoff end to assure proper spacing and integrity. Supervised Autoclave operations and Monitored Chiller Cool-down times to assure the glass units adhered to specified parameters.

Conducted weekly plant walkdowns to identify and analyze corrective and preventive maintenance issues. Monitored Lamination Workroom and Cold Storage Room for proper temperature and humidity. Recorded and reported any temperature or humidity deviations from the norm. Provides manpower **when available,** to assist the maintenance department with Autoclave Burnout Rebuild. Filled out Maintenance Work Order Request Sheets, as needed; to ensure minimal downtime. Conducted Adhesion Testing, to ensure: air bubbles do not penetrate more than ¼" into glass units as per Quality Control Regulations. Made procurement recommendations for all materials needed for work project execution.

Researched, selected, developed and maintained adequate sources of supply ensuring equipment and services needed were filled in a timely and efficient manner, at the lowest cost, to fill all Lamination orders. Participated in weekly: Supervisor & Safety Committee Meetings: to exchange information about work, safety, work windows and available resources. Trained subordinates on Glass Handling Safety Equipment, MSDS Chemical Listing, Cold-room Safety Procedures, Respiratory Program, Hazcom Program and Evacuation Maps for Facility. Implemented HMIS labeling procedures throughout Lamination Department. Trained new hires, in the safe operation and usage of the following machinery: 96" Washers, 72" and 60" Washers, Toritt Seaming Machines, Casso Solar Infrared Heat Press, Rosenthal Sheet slitter, Glass Etching Machines, Edge Deleters, Overhead Cranes and Vacuum Lifting devices.

Accomplishments:

- Worked with Maintenance Supervisor to develop a plan for Bondtek Autoclave modifications due to errors in engineering plans.

- Worked with Maintenance Supervisor to develop and implement Bag Leak detection Procedures, using shutoff valves and Autoclave software, to solve: Vacuum Pump breakdown problem.

- Worked with Maintenance Supervisor to develop: Timetable for Malfunctioning Lamination Rail Cart Identification Procedures, to boost production by more than 40% and cut down on production downtime.

References Available Upon Request

The Po Man's Guide to Breaking the Poverty Cycle

Jane Doe
14303 Your Street
Houston, TX 77020
Cell: (281) 602xxxx
Email: **whatever@live.com**

MEDICAL ASSISTANT / RECEPTIONIST

I am a dependable, friendly, outgoing individual with experience in a variety of positions such as medical assistant, receptionist, cash office/bookkeeping, customer service and management. Positive attitude, adaptability to change, handling multiple tasks in a timely proficient manner and excellent working relationship with coworkers and supervisors. I am seeking employment as a diligent medical assistant or receptionist in a medical environment in which I could apply my experience and love for helping others.

HIGHLIGHTS OF QUALIFICATIONS

- CPR certified
- Certified Medical Assistant
- Medical Terminology
- Computer skills such as EMR (Prime Suite), Medisoft, Peoplesoft, PayClock, Internet Explorer, Outlook and Microsoft Word

RELATED PROFESSIONAL EXPERIENCE

Float Nurse   June 2013 October 2013

- Prepared water solution for unsanitary instruments, scopes and rods. Sterilized instruments: prepared surgical packs and kits, cleaned autoclave monthly and tested autoclave weekly with test strips for proper maintenance. Secured medicine cabinets, stocked exam rooms accordingly, placed clean instruments in the designated exam room and changed biohazard: sharps, soups and trash as needed. Triaged patients gave injections such as B12, Influenza, Dexamethasone and Rocephin. Collected nasal and throat cultures and performed proetz and pulmonary function testing. Retrieved messages from voicemails and send tasks to designated doctors, contacted pharmacies for approvals/denials, send prescriptions electronically, faxed orders for MRI and CT scans and callbacks for labs and biopsy results.

Clinical Manager/ Therapist   January 2010 August 2012

- Responsible for supervision of seven employees delegated tasks, performed annual reviews, processed payroll, charting and signed off on chart audits. I explained to patients and family members the protocol of the program and the importance of being compliant. Roomed patients, obtained vitals, placed patients into recliners to receive pneumatic compression pumping, performed treatment; (manual lymph drainage) and applied/ reapplied compression bandages on affected extremities. Assessed, measured, cleaned and applied appropriate dressings to open and/ or heal wounds. Measured patients affected extremities and ordered over-the-counter and/or custom compression wear upon discharge from the program. Attended weekly manager's meetings to stay informed on new policies and/ or procedures and held weekly meetings with staff to inform on any new changes and patient reviews.

Medical Assistant   October 2001 April 2002

•Greeted patients as they checked in and checked out, answered multiple phone lines, collected payments, scheduled appointments, follow up and appointment reminder calls. Verified insurance, copied medical records and prepared charts for new and established patients. Roomed patients took vitals, recorded medical history and answered questions or concerns to my limit of authority. Performed injections, blood draws, pregnancy testing prepared rooms for examinations and assisted the doctor as needed. Cleaned, restocked examination rooms and notified the office manager of shortages of supplies.

PROFESSIONAL EXPERIENCE

Customer Service Associate Weekday   March 2013
June 2013

•Responsible for quick, friendly customer service by answering questions, providing purchase assistance such as special orders, internet orders and out of stock merchandise and keeping shelves stocked. Assigned to Home Organization and Home Décor, but assisted in other areas as needed.

Cash Office Specialist/ Customer Service Associate
October 2012 June 2013

•Registers reconciliation, bank deposits, maintained cash office security and petty cash. Research over and short, completed and filed daily business reports and maintained an effective information storage log and retrieval system. Partnered with the store manager and loss prevention to implement all losses and assisted on the sales floor, cash register and shipping and receiving and cross trained as needed.

Customer Service Representative
July 2009 January 2010

•Explained the different types of loans, payment options available as well as the terms of services. Analyzed applicants' financial information to determine the feasibility of granting loans. If requirements were met, scanned customers' documents into the database and completed loan amount as requested or approved. Contacted customers as a courtesy call before the due date to determine a commitment date and time for collection of payment. Printed opening and closing reports and maintained collection accounts by contacting customers directly or by skip trace to set up payment arrangements.

Administrative Assistant
May 2002 March 2007

• Supervised 5 to 15cashier daily, cross trained, delegated tasks and solved customers' problems and/or complaints. The directed flow of

The Po Man's Guide to Breaking the Poverty Cycle

customers provided orderly maintenance of frontend equipment and supplies, authorized and ensured the validity of customer returns and exchanges and check authorizations and voids. Provided quality customer service by effectively answering questions or concerns and responding to semi complex complaints and disputes within a reasonable limit of authority. Prepared and processed internet based, email, postal mail, telephone and fax orders from customers and cooperate accounts; approved and processed, credit card, personnel/commercial checks purchases. Maintained files such as daily business, purchasing cards and outstanding check reports. Made adjustments due to discounts/ discrepancies and opened new consumer, business and escrow accounts. Reconciled processed work by verifying entries and comparing system reports to balances. Bank account reconciliation processed daily deposits and reported to and assisted as needed in varied accounting functions directly to the administrative manager.

The Po Man's Guide to Breaking the Poverty Cycle

John Doe
14303 Your Street
Houston, TX 77020
Cell: (281) 602xxxx
Email: **whatever@live.com**

Object: A position that utilizes my electrical/maintenance skills and provides an opportunity for growth.

Applicable Skills:

Troubleshooting: PLC Systems, Control Panel Wiring, Hydraulic Systems and Pneumatic Systems.
Fabricating: Electrical Control Panels, Conduit Bending, Wiring and Assembly.
Proficient with Reading: Schematics, Wiring Diagrams and Blueprints.

Experience

June 2006 to Present Old████████████, TX
Maintenance Technician Performs mechanical and electrical maintenance on Autoclave, Bystronic Cutting Machine, 84" 72" and 64" Washers, Toritt Seaming Machines, TGL 60" and 96" Furnaces, Forvet Milling Machine, Butyl Extruder, Casso Solar Infrared Heat Press, Besten Press, Silicone Gun, Hotmelt Gun and multiple Conveyor systems. Conduit bending and installation of Circuit Breaker Boxes, Receptacles, Switches and lights. Responsible for parts ordering for machine maintenance and general plant usage, also establishing new vendor accounts when needed.
Contact: Eric 713 464XXXX

2004 to June 2006 Builders████████████, TX
Lead Maintenance Electrician Installed and repaired Hightech Saws, Frame Corner Cleaners, Hightech Ovens and Washers. Programmed Hightech Saws and Frame Corner Washers. Installed Main Disconnects, Motor Starters and Contact Blocks.
Contact: 7138492110

2000 to 2004 Champion████████████, TX
Lead Electrical Technician Installed and wired Drive Motors. Work with PLC, Installed and programmed Variable Frequency Drives. Fabricated and wired Disconnect Boxes. Wired and installed Photo Cells. Installed Main Panel Boxes. Wired elevators and set limit switches. Assembled Hand Control and Roof Top Control Devices.

The Po Man's Guide to Breaking the Poverty Cycle

Contact: 7136408500

1999 to 2000 ███████████████████ : ███████
███████████████, **TX**
Electrical Technician Building and wiring equipment. Installed 8 & 11 Pin Relay, PLC Motor Starter, AC/DC Solar Switches, Limit Switches, Power Switches and Power Packs.
Contact: 7136904610 or 7136864331

1999 to 1999 WAG██████████████████ **Houston, TX**
Electrical Contractor Electrical rewiring of remodeled restaurants. Install Cat 5 Lines, Track Lighting, Breaker Boxes and receptacles. Bend and Install Conduit.

1989 to 1999 ████████████████████████
Houston, TX
Maintenance Electrician Technician Maintained and operated production machinery in the cement room. Installed lighting, ceiling fans and weather heads.

1997 to 1998 New█████████████████████
███████, **TX**
Electrician Installed wiring, lighting, ceiling fans, weather heads, conduit and breaker boxes.

New Dimension ██████████████████████, **TX**
Electrician Installed limit switches, solar switches, DC drivers and crane cables.

New Dimension ██████████████████████, **TX**
Electrician Worked with R.I.E. units. Rewired and installed UPS changed AC to DC breaker boxes. Installed transformers, conduit and emergency lighting.
Military Service   United States Military   3 Years
Aircraft Electrician

Education   Houston Community College   2 ½ Years
Industrial

References upon request

Fill in the fields below and build your first rough draft. Keep tweaking your resume until it looks pleasing to you!

The Po Man's Guide to Breaking the Poverty Cycle

John Doe
14303 Your Street
Houston, TX 77020
Cell: (281) 602xxxx
Email: **whatever@live.com**

Objective: To use your company as a stepping stone, which will allow me to get more experience and skills so I can pursue the job I want.

Education:
Whatever college you have goes here
High School diploma or GED
You can also list your certifications

Applicable Skills:
Whatever marketable skills you possess

Experience

June 2006 to Present Company Houston, TX
Job Title This is where keeping your old job descriptions will come in handy. You should also always add your new company to your resume as soon as you get hired, so you can start putting down the new things you learn. I tend to always keep my resume updated like my budget. You're also going to repeat this formula for each job you have had. Starting from your present job or the last job you held. Go back as far as you can or at least the last ten years. Here is where you will put the details of all the accomplishments you made while employed at this job.
Contact: Eric Nobody 713 464XXXX

May 2004 to June 2006   Company Houston, TX
Job Title If you can't remember your old job description, you can always go online and look it up as long as you have the job title. When you look up the company and the job title your search will usually give you a job description. You simply have to get in the habit of doing research.
Contact: Josh Nobody 713 523xxxx

References upon request: Back then, I always kept a sheet with all my references listed.

The Po Man's Guide to Breaking the Poverty Cycle

What to Look for in a New Job

When looking for a new job to replace the one you presently have:

1. Look for the pay you need to "make it" without counting on overtime.
2. Make sure you are going to be able to make it to work on time.
3. Look for a company with good employee retention.
4. Check the papers and listen to the news concerning the industry, there is nothing worse than getting a new job and then the company going under
5. Is this job: something you can see yourself doing for the next 5 years?
6. Does this job excite you!? If the job doesn't excite you, good luck.
7. Is this job something you want to brag about? Men brag when they love something. Mine is better than yours!

YouTube will help you. (Research)
Acing The Interview (Don't be lazy! Watch the videos!)

Let's be honest about this, I had spoken with many people and they always tell me they know how to conduct themselves during an interview. And every time, I'll say, "Okay, then let's do a mock interview." And almost every time I find out that they completely suck at interviewing. You need to sound confident and professional, most people don't! People tend to overrate themselves. The answers they give may sound great in their heads, but only in THEIR heads! When people have a much higher opinion of themselves, their word usage will often reveal their shortcomings. Practice makes perfect people. I can't stress that enough! Stop trying to reinvent the wheel and stick to proven methods that work!

I got this information on YouTube. It will help you. (Research)

The Po Man's Guide to Breaking the Poverty Cycle

How to answer the TELL ME ABOUT YOURSELF interview question
https://www.youtube.com/results?search_query=How+to+answer+the+TELL+ME+ABOUT+YOURSELF+interview+question

1} What is your philosophy towards work?
2} Tell us about a time when you had to go above and beyond the call of duty to get a job done.
3} Do you occupy any position at the moment?
4} How many hours will you be able to devote to the company daily?
5} How well do you work under pressure?
6} Have you ever worked with data entry software before?
7} How would you describe yourself including your full name and location?
8} Do you have any idea of how to use MS excel and do you know your typing speed?
9} Give me 1 genuine and specific reason why you should be hired by the company?
10} What is your highest educational diploma?
When did you receive your highest educational diploma?
11} Are you also a team player?
12} What do you understand by privacy and code of conduct in business?
13} What do you think is the greatest quality fill-in the blank should possess?
14} Have you ever been interviewed online before by a different company?
15} Rate yourself on a scale of 15 based on the following MATHEMATICAL ACCURACY, SPELLING ACCURACY, TYPING SPEED, STATISTICAL ACCURACY?
16} What would you say is your greatest weakness and what steps have been taken to correct it?
17} Do you have an issue with overtime?
18} How would you handle a disagreement between you and another employee?
19} How would you handle a disagreement between you and your supervisor?
20} what do you know about safety programs?
21} what would you do if you got hurt at work?
22} do you have any children? If so, how are you going to handle childcare while at work will it be a problem?
23} Why did you leave your last job?

The Po Man's Guide to Breaking the Poverty Cycle

I got this information on YouTube. It will help you.
How to Answer BEHAVIORAL INTERVIEW QUESTIONS Using the STAR Method (TOP 10 Behavioral Questions)
https://www.youtube.com/watch?v=uQEuo7woEEk

List of questions:

2:11 Tell us about a time when you had to go above and beyond the call of duty to get a job done?
3:38 What is the most competitive work situation you have experienced? How did you handle it? What was the result?
5:00 When you have a lot of work to do, how do you get it all done? Give me an example?
6:16 Give a specific example of a time when you had to address an angry customer. What was the problem and what was the outcome?
8:15 Can you tell me about a time when you were not able to build a successful relationship with a difficult person?
10:49 Have you ever worked in a situation where the rules and guidelines were not clear?
12:34 Describe the most significant presentation you had to give.
14:15 How do you go about explaining a complex technical problem to a person who does not understand technical jargon?
16:37 Describe a recent unpopular decision you made and what the result was.
18:28 Give an example of a time when you had to remain calm on the outside when you were upset on the inside.

Interviewing the Interviewer
Make a list of questions for you to ask during the interview. Don't get cocky and go in thinking: I'm going to remember everything and then freeze. You will only be hurting yourself. The idea is to put your best foot forward, not come off sounding like a babbling idiot! People are confident when they are prepared! But there is always some idiot trying to wing it! Winging it tells me you are lazy! It also tells me you didn't think this job was important enough for you to properly prepare for the interview! Your resume will be swiftly ushered into File 13, where it will be properly disposed of...!

The Po Man's Guide to Breaking the Poverty Cycle

Chapter 7: Research! Research! Research!

Social Research - ALWAYS BE AWARE

As I said before, this world will chew you up, spit you out and leave you with nothing, if you allow it. No job is going to help you. No job is going to save you. There is no such thing as job security! So get that idiotic thought out of your head! Your job is not your life and never allow anyone to make it your life. Consider each job you take as a training ground if you will. Your job while at work is to learn any and everything you can about how things work in that organization. Learn the unspoken rules that apply but are never written down and rarely spoken of above a whisper.

Get on the wrong side of a clique and you are history. Say the wrong thing at the wrong time and you have been marked for termination. You need to be observant at all times! Do more watching and less yapping! Never be caught by surprise! Subtle hand gestures and nervous twitches say a lot more than the lies your boss is telling you! You are going to have to learn what I call Social Research. Learn to ask unrelated questions to get the answers you want.

Like the gamblers say, everyone has a "tell." I can't lie. I completely suck at it. So, when my normally aggressive voice sounds timid you automatically know I'm lying. When people lie, they hesitate for a fraction of a second before they speak. They don't notice this because they are too busy running the lie through their mind so that it sounds like the truth. The next time you suspect someone of lying, instead of looking into their eyes, turn your ear towards them and listen. I don't know how it works, but it does….

Always be mindful of the things your bosses say, they give you little subtle glimpses of what's to come, clues and indications of the things they intend to do. Pay attention to unspoken cues or get blind-sided. While you're at work you may walk up to your supervisor speaking or maybe they are giving instructions to someone else and they use words you don't understand. Look them up! Never remain ignorant. Your supervisors and bosses are going to talk about new technologies. Pay attention! Nine times out of ten, they are talking about automation or lean. Translation: how soon it will be before they start replacing people with a machine or program. Always keep up with the latest technologies. Know what's out there! Know what's coming. You can either know what's coming and prepare yourself or you can choose to remain ignorant and allow them to trample you into the dirt as they move their shiny new machine into the position you used to stand in. This section is about paying attention to keywords and phrases people use around you so you always know what is coming. Remember your ignorance can cause you to lose everything you own. Never forget that.

The Po Man's Guide to Breaking the Poverty Cycle

Remember, the advice about **constant awareness** is a reminder to conduct social research to stay up-to-date on what's happening, so that you stay informed and never get surprised.

I'm going to go into some detail but not specifics about jobs, cars, houses, apartments and or investments, but I will use examples and scenarios so you get my meaning when I say, "Research! Research! Research!"

Let's talk about cars. Remember I'm only trying to get your gears a turning so you understand the value of research. Before you go out there and start driving around, look at vehicles online, analyze and compare different vehicles. Don't be lazy, do the math! How much can you afford to pay each month? Buy the car, you can pay off the quickest! If you bought this book, a car is a need and not a want. Will you be able to afford the maintenance on this vehicle and if so, how? What happens if you miss a scheduled maintenance checkup on your vehicle? What happens if you miss a payment? Will this vehicle pass inspection? Does it have an owner's manual? Can you perform small maintenance activities on your own? How much is the repair manual for this vehicle? Does this manual show you how to do the maintenance on your own? Are you prepared to buy a hydraulic jack? Do you know why a hydraulic jack is better than the manual jack you have? Do you have jumper cables? Why do you need thicker cables for more amperage? How long before you have to replace the battery? What's covered under the warranty? What's not quite covered under the warranty? If you're a responsible owner, you should know these things.

Getting and Giving Good Advice at Work

Always ask for advice! Always find someone who knows how to do whatever it is you're trying to do if you are not confident in your ability to pull it off. Don't be one of those proud idiots who think he knows everything. When selecting a person to ask for advice, ensure they possess the necessary skills; otherwise, the outcome will be far worse than if you'd handled it yourself. That's where the TRUST comes in. People lie all the time and profess to know how to do lots of things! **TEST THEM! TEST EVERYONE!** If I have tested you and found your words to be true, then and then only, can I trust you! And once you have found a few people you can trust, make sure you ask more than one person. If it's good advice, you should get similar answers from three or more people. Again, I stress to make sure it's someone you can trust! Don't get lazy and go to one of your idiot friends who is in the same predicament as you and doesn't know jack about anything. And above all, don't go to someone who doesn't even know what you're talking about and expect him to become Albert Einstein all of a sudden. Who in their right mind will take advice from someone who knows less than they do!? OK I'm good. I got that off my chest.

Giving good advice is simple. If it takes you more than 10 seconds to come up with an good answer, shut up and point them to someone who knows what is going on or what needs to be done. And if you do have a clue, you don't need me to explain what you already know.

For those times when you are stuck grinding it out on your own.
How should I best conduct research? Some conduct online searches. Some research their topics on YouTube for explanatory videos. We already discussed asking friends. Reading and gathering information are not the only aspects of research, but they are a good place to begin. Oh. You hate reading. Tuff nuggets! Do it anyway!

I typically look things up online. I also look for "how-to" books and gather as much information as I possibly can before I even think about making a decision. You can't be lazy. Conduct exhaustive research! You want to research to where you never want to see anything else on the subject. You can't just pick a thing and say, "Yeah. I'm going to do that" You have to ask yourself questions! What does it take to get this thing done? Who is going to help me with this? How long before I can get this done? If it's about a task, are there instructions? How many people will I need? Is it labor intensive? If you know someone who has already done it, you can talk to them? You want to get as much information as possible in order to come up with a workable plan of action. Do I need to go somewhere else? Later on, you can hop in your ride and find the place, after you have printed out the directions or added the address into the GPS app on your phone. How many miles is the drive? How much in gas will it cost me? Will I need to leave early because of the traffic?

Let's say you're looking for a new insurance company for your automobile. You're going to want multiple quotes. Which company gives you the most coverage at the best price? What happens if I have an accident in the first six months? How long before my rates go down? Type in the name of the company and look at the reviews. This is a MUST! ALWAYS READ THE REVIEWS! What does this policy cover? How do I cancel the policy? Do I have to do it in writing? How much is the deductible? What happens if your car gets stolen? Will they raise your rates? Do they have accident forgiveness?
You can't just go out there and buy coverage! You have to know what you're getting! And your task is to get more bang for your buck! Research involves asking many questions and finding their answers.

Note: This section isn't about answers. This section is to remind you that you should question everything. Your head should be full of questions at all times. Don't be mentally lazy! You should be more than willing to find the answers to those questions. Your **goal in all things** is to **be well informed and prepared**!

The Po Man's Guide to Breaking the Poverty Cycle

Research aims to gather comprehensive information on any subject, product, or task before proceeding or purchasing. Research gives you the ability to make an informed decision.

Let's say you're looking for a job. Yeah. I'm using it again! To update your resume, you might need to go online and find your old job description. Find and review multiple job descriptions related to the position you're seeking. You are going to have to know what's required of you, before you take the job and after you have landed it, you will have a general idea of what to expect before you ever get started. Wherever you find yourself working, you should look up your supervisor's job description. That way you will know the necessary skills you will need to acquire to assume the same position. And if he's cool, he may be willing to train you. Learn the procedures and execute them swiftly. Ask intelligent questions. What training should I expect to receive? What is my job title? Is it a fixed shift? What's the overtime demand? How long before I see a raise? How often will I receive employee evaluations? How many days can I miss before I get terminated? Am I allowed to talk to other employees during work? Am I allowed to use the phone? What's the turnover rate? How long before I qualify for benefits? How long before I get to keep all the money in my 401(k)? What will my medical expenses be? Do they offer medical insurance? What types of medical insurance? Do they allow alternatives? Know if the tasks you are undertaking will assist you in gaining more experience or if they are simple busy work or menial labor. Always volunteer if it will give you more experience! What you don't know, will hurt you.

Vehicles (it's unrelated but a good example!)

Get AAA it's $20 a month! Or you will wish you had!

Let's talk about cars. Remember I'm only trying to get your gears a turning so you understand the value of research. Before you go out there and start driving around, look at vehicles online, analyze and compare different vehicles. Don't be lazy, do the math! How much can you afford to pay each month? Buy the car, you can pay off the quickest! If you bought this book, a car is a need and not a want. Will you be able to afford the maintenance on this vehicle and if so, how? What happens if you miss a scheduled maintenance checkup on your vehicle? What happens if you miss a payment? Will this vehicle pass inspection? Does it have an owner's manual? Can you perform small maintenance activities on your own? How much is the repair manual for this vehicle? Does this manual show you how to do the maintenance on your own? Are you prepared to buy a hydraulic jack? Do you know why a hydraulic jack is better than the manual jack you have? Do you have jumper cables? How long before you have to replace the battery? What's covered under the warranty? What's not quite covered under the warranty? If you're a responsible owner, you should know these things.

Warning: Never under any circumstances get an Adjustable-Rate Mortgage! (it's unrelated but a good example!)

The Po Man's Guide to Breaking the Poverty Cycle

Now that you're getting into it, let's do the same thing with houses. When was this house built? Are there any structural issues I should be aware of? What do I do if there are maintenance issues with this house? Is there a homeowner's association? Where can I find the rules? What are the zoning laws regarding my property? Am I allowed to build anything in the backyard? Can I build a deck without approval? Can I be fined by the HOA? Can I lose my house if I don't pay the HOA? Do I want to live under an HOA? What's the crime rate in his neighborhood? Are your stand ground laws in effect? Do I have the right to defend my property? What are the school taxes? Do I want an escrow account? Can I pay all my taxes without an escrow account? Are there any tax exemptions? Do I have the skills to do some of the maintenance of the house myself? How old is the HVAC system? Does the electrical system meet code?

Apartments (it's unrelated but a good example!)
Before you move into an apartment there are questions, you're going to need answers to:
What's the crime rate like in this complex and the surrounding neighborhood? How often do they raise the rent? Do they conduct periodic unit inspections? Are they going to invade my privacy? Do people steal mail around here? How will I get my mail if the office is closed? How long will I have to wait for someone to come and fix a maintenance request? What are the online reviews about this complex? When does quiet time start? What's the parking situation like? Are there known drug dealers in this complex? How often do these units get broken into?

Investments
Can I afford to buy gold? Can I afford to buy silver? How much do I know about my 401(k)? Can I change the stock mix if I want? What's the rate of return on my 401(k)? How often can I increase my contribution percentage? How much do I know about bitcoin? What do I know about stocks? How much do I know about bonds? If someone gave me a hot stock tip, could I act on it? If not why? If someone offered me an ounce of gold for $200, would I take the deal?

If you haven't figured it out, I have been telling you how to conduct research throughout this book! Method to my madness!

The Po Man's Guide to Breaking the Poverty Cycle

Chapter 8: Plan! Evaluate! Make Adjustments! Plan Again!

In the process of integrating all of the things you learn about breaking your poverty cycle, you're going to have to learn how to use and master **the seven problem-solving steps:**

1. **Identify the problem**
2. **Gather information**
3. **Develop multiple courses of action**
4. **Analyze and compare courses of action**
5. **Make a decision** (Choose the course of action you are going to take).
6. **Make a plan**
7. **Implement the plan**

Step One: Identify the problem. I know this seems obvious, but some problems are harder to detect! People will most often point to a symptom, believing they have determined the root cause of a problem. Be thorough when analyzing your issues. Not every issue is the root cause of the problem. But you have to start somewhere. Sometimes you get a better idea about things only after you have written them down. So, you write down what the problem is and then the solution you intend to use to take care of the problem. Let's say you need new glasses and can only afford one pair. You add new glasses to your budget and use a question mark as a placeholder for the price. Now you are going to go to step two.

Step Two: Gather information. You're going to have to ask yourself some questions. What type of glasses do you need? Are you nearsighted or farsighted? How much are the lenses going to cost? How much are the frames going to cost? Where are you going to go to get these glasses? Do you have insurance or do you have to pay for these glasses completely out of pocket? The more information you gather the more prepared you are going to be to tackle the problem. You want to know everything you can know about these glasses, except for how you're going to pay for them.

Step Three: Develop multiple courses of action. Now you're going to have to figure out at least three ways to pay for these glasses if something goes wrong. If possible 10 different ways you can pay for them. Remember you can tackle each problem by dissecting it and coming up with as many different ways to get the job done. You may be able to take a hundred bucks from a placeholder in your budget. You may be able to sell a pair of shoes. You could sell some of your old clothes on eBay, Swap.com or Poshmark.com. You figure out workable realistic courses of action you can take to solve the problem. Never sit there and think you're powerless or you can't get this done, there is always an answer to every problem.

Step Four: Analyze and compare courses of action. Which course of action will be the easiest to accomplish? Which course of action will be the hardest to accomplish? Which courses of action will allow me to reach my goal the fastest? When is the deadline? Come up with multiple ways you can afford to pay for these glasses and make sure they're all decent ways to achieve your goal.

Step Five: Make a decision and select the best course of action available to you.

Step Six: Make a good plan, one which details how you are going to pay for these glasses. Where are you going to get them, the retailer? What day are you going to get them? How will you pay? Will you need to use a credit card or can you pay in cash?

Step Seven: Implement the plan. Once you implement the plan stick to it and keep going until it is done and your goal is accomplished.

NOTE: Every plan has setbacks! So, don't get rattled when something goes wrong. Adapt your plan. Your plan must change with your circumstances! Don't throw it away at the first sign of trouble.

Problems are never going away so stop avoiding them. Attack them head-on until you become known as a problem solver! Some of the most successful people in life are problem solvers.

How to keep those problems from coming back

Find out Who

I suppose this little detail will come up when you are gathering information. you are always going to have to find out the "Who".

- Who created this problem?
- Who allowed this problem to continue?
- Who is going to help me solve this problem?
- Who is going to try to stop me from solving this problem?

There are a great many situations where you are going to have fight to find out the "Who." You are going to have to do research, make phone calls or simply look in the mirror. This is simply a part of gathering information. It can be either a school, an agency, a company or a person.

Find out the What

- What did I do to allow this person to create the problem?
- What can I do next time so this problem never arises?
- What have I learned that will help me eliminate this problem?
- What can I do to prevent anyone from stopping me?
- What are my options?

The Po Man's Guide to Breaking the Poverty Cycle

- What do I have the power to fix right now?
- What's my first step in solving this problem?

Find out the When

- When did this problem start?
- When did this problem get out of hand?
- When did I give up my power to solve this problem?
- When did I give up?

Plan out or find the Where
- Where do I have to go to fix this problem?
- Where did this problem start
- Where do I go to get information about solving this problem

Plan out the How

- How did the problem start?
- How do I solve this problem?
- How do I get motivated?

Get The Right Person Involved

I can't recall how many times I've been at a loss for what to do next. I usually came up with the solution myself. But only after I had a conversation with the RIGHT person! I needed someone to force me to think differently. The hardest thing any man can learn is how to get out of his own way! I have spent years making trustworthy friends that I can count on. Typically, these individuals highlight my errors, suggest improvements, and often offer insightful advice that resonates with me and causes my brain to click. Clicking causes me to come up with solutions I never would've thought of on my own. Nobody makes it on their own and I mean nobody! Don't keep your thoughts bottled up.

Ask advice of someone who will challenge you to help you gain deeper understanding. Your experience isn't your only resource. You can benefit from the experiences of others. They may flag potential roadblocks in advance. A helpful sounding board will gladly share all their knowledge to prevent you from repeating their past mistakes. From my perspective, navigating life solo is already quite difficult. Past tough decisions would have been impossible for me to make alone; I needed someone to brainstorm with. Helpful feedback provides valuable perspectives. A good sounding board is essential for effective decision-making. While they can't decide for you, they'll equip you for the challenges ahead.

The Po Man's Guide to Breaking the Poverty Cycle

The Enemies of GOOD Planning and Sound Decision Making

Avoidance
Men can behave like little girls when they don't get their way. No one is going to rescue you! GRIND IT OUT! No friend is going to ride in and save the day! This is not the movies! Drugs won't help you escape your reality either, remember that! Drinking will only help you feel better while you are drinking! Once you sober up, BANG! "Hello, I'm that problem you tried to run away from last night. I'm sorry I allowed you to forget about me, so here I am to remind you that there is no escape!" This is REAL LIFE! You must learn to face all of your problems head on. Get them dealt with swiftly while they are small enough for you to handle on your own. Planning can and will serve you well. Good planning will ensure you always come out on top no matter how many times you fail! Use that imagination of yours to come up with bulletproof plans, not avoiding your problems.

Fear
I combat fear by directly confronting whatever frightens me. When I got out of the military, I was fine. Years later, I started having these panic attacks whenever I was driving and cars started boxing me in. It was worse when my wife drove the car and I had no control. She was oblivious, and I felt like the world was caving in on me! So, I would start screaming at her whenever she let us get boxed in! Once I realized it was PTSD, I came up with a plan. I got in my truck and drove down those same streets repeatedly, allowing myself to get boxed in until it no longer bothered me. Fear is like a bad ex-wife. Just when you think you have the situation under control, she finds new and inventive ways to screw with your life. And just like the ex, your fears never really go away, but their effect is greatly diminished when you face them down and refuse to be moved!

Procrastination
You get nothing done by talking about it! Hashing out your thoughts is one thing, moving on those thoughts is another. Action is everything! If you fail the first time, so what? Inaction is a child of fear. Do something! Do anything except nothing! Take small steps towards the world you want to build. Anything is better than nothing! One small victory will embolden you! Living is like walking. You can't get anywhere until you take that next step!

Wishing
 The last refuge of hope for men who lack confidence! Do you believe in magic? Neither do I! If it doesn't work or if it doesn't solve your problems, don't do it! Letting your imagination run wild is like telling your child it's ok to cross the street without looking both ways! Weak men believe in luck! Real men conquer! In order to conquer an overwhelming foe, you NEED a GOOD PLAN!

The Po Man's Guide to Breaking the Poverty Cycle

Whining
Whining is like eating Pringles once you start you can't stop! Does whining solve your problems? Does whining cause you to suddenly get what you want? Or does it simply prevent you from seeking your answer? If whining empowers you, keep going. If it prevents you from moving forward stop! Do something about it! You will be too busy solving problems instead of taking time out to whine. We both know action speaks louder than words! Whining is just a weak man's way of justifying inaction! Don't like feeling weak stop whining!

Money
Everyone always says that money is their problem. Lie! It's not true. The lack of skills is your problem. The lack of creativity is your problem. Laziness is your problem. Apathy is your problem. Good ideas make money! Implementing those ideas takes planning! Master budgeting and you will become a planner! Even if someone was willing to give you money they would never move on your plan without a budget! There is a reason why movies have budgets!

Time and Youth
Time and youth are the only two things you can never get back. Be care full of where and how you spend them! I hate to sound like your boss but time is better spent being productive! Your youth is better spent learning how to BEST spend your time!

NOTE: This is an old Facebook post, but I was told to put it here. My use of large caps isn't shouting. It means I'm placing emphasis on the words to bring greater clarity, using written inflection to drive home the point.

When you are BROKE or POOR, meaning you have no dollars, you are left with only one currency: TIME! How you spend YOUR TIME will determine YOUR FUTURE. SPEND YOUR TIME researching how to make money, honestly of course. No ill-gotten gains. SPEND YOUR TIME learning how to earn more by spending less. PAY Attention. This means WATCH EVERYTHING that happens around you. Don't just listen, HEAR "WHAT" is being said. If your memory sucks, choose to have a good one. SPEND YOUR TIME ON IMPROVING YOUR MEMORY. SPEND YOUR TIME ON IMPROVING YOUR SKILLS. SPEND YOUR TIME attacking YOUR areas of WEAKNESS!

That's the problem. What's the solution?
Everybody and their mama can come up with a thousand reasons why your plans won't work! Before you cut slings, here is a sure fired method of eliminating haters! If they have no problem bringing up problems with your plans, then they should have no problem offering workable solutions! If they only provide problems then they are a problem. Cut Slings! If they offer workable solutions then you have gained a TRUE FRIEND! It's a win—win!

The Po Man's Guide to Breaking the Poverty Cycle

Micromanaging and Micromanagers
If you hate it when someone is trying to tell you what you need to do in every aspect of your life then don't do it to others! Micromanagers can throw a monkey wrench into your well thought out plans. They say that they will teach you and train you but really, they are just there to bark orders. The only real way to deal with them is to gain their trust. Once they trust you, they will leave you alone. If you are the micromanager, then only employ the help of those you trust! **And then leave them alone!**

Take up The Hippocratic Oath for your life!
Do no harm to your plans! Once you make a plan, stick to it! Don't abandon your plan at the first sign of trouble, make adjustments! Stay on course. New problem. Make an adjustment. Not enough money. Make an adjustment! Starting to see a pattern here?

YOU are the WEAKEST LINK. Goodbye!
Acknowledgement of YOUR shortcomings is the first step in becoming the MAN YOU always wanted to be! Whatever your faults, have a plan that deals with them. Set up roadblocks against failure. If you are prone to gambling, give your money to someone you trust. Do whatever is necessary to counteract your destructive habits!

Staying Motivated! How to see things through till the END!
I have found that the best way to stay motivated is to continue to progress. As long as you can see results, you will be inspired to achieve more and more! People get apathetic when they feel like they are getting nowhere in life! Progress is the key!

MY BOSS and I came up with this Mantra How to ALWAYS WIN!

1. Piss in their Oatmeal (Speak the TRUTH NO matter HOW MUCH they LIE!) Never attack back!

2. Beat them at their OWN game (Forgive them! Never return EVIL FOR EVIL! NEVER ASSIGN BLAME EVEN WHEN YOU KNOW!)

3. Let them DIG their own GRAVE! Never attack back Let the TRUTH be revealed ALL ON its OWN! Don't defend yourself (LET OTHERS DO IT!)

4. Let them cover themselves with their DIRT! (HE never agreed to this one). (It means keep doing 1 through 3 until they destroy themselves!)

5. YOU DON"T ALWAYS HAVE TO FIGHT EVIL PEOPLE! YOU JUST HAVE TO BE SMART ENOUGH TO WAIT!

The Po Man's Guide to Breaking the Poverty Cycle

Start small and learn to Dream Bigger
You've heard the old saying, *if you're going to dream—then dream big!* I used to think that it was an awesome saying. But over the years, progressing little by little won me over! It's true. You have to crawl before you walk. Slow and steady does win the race! Pick one of those little items on your little dream list and go for it! Do your best to make it happen. Do your due diligence, meaning research. Find out everything you can and then plan so it gets done. This plan has to be reasonable and achievable. I've also learned you have to start off small. Pick a small goal and meet that goal. Then set a goal that is a little harder to accomplish. Repeat as necessary. Before you know what has happened, you'll find that you are on a whole new level. It will give you a sense of achievement; you will need that high to carry you through the hard stuff.
Your time should be spent planning out your goals, seeking new challenges until you meet the wall. When you meet a wall and you can go no further, meaning you have to wait until a new opportunity presents itself. Your time should be spent enhancing your skills, destroying your weaknesses.

What if you feel like you're getting burnt out? Take a break and seek meaningful distractions. There's nothing wrong with escape, as long as the escape has a designated purpose. This time should be spent watching or doing something completely unrelated so that your brain doesn't feel like it is back at work. Just like any other computer your brain needs to be rebooted every now and again to function properly. Grinding it out does not mean overload. Given time, your goals will grow bigger and BIGGER! Your dreams will follow the same pattern. Trying to conquer your world all at once will only lead to frustration. **Don't ever willingly set yourself up to be frustrated!**

Learn to trust your intuition. If you think something bad is going to happen keep your guard up and stay alert. We have our senses for a reason. Whenever my spider sense starts tingling, I pay attention. And I'm usually right. Learn to go with your gut instincts. Learn to trust your gut!
 if you want to make changes in your life to make everything different, is going to be very important for you whatever you put out there comes back to you in other words you reap what you sow a syllable ago ask well so you cannot reach any of your goals by stepping on anyone else your job is to do no harm why you are increasing yourself up bettering yourself you don't get to walk on other people you don't get to treat them wrong treat them how you want to be treated it doesn't matter what they're doing you are supposed to treat them right regardless of what they do when it is time for you to train someone do it would a good attitude so later on what is so modest time to train you they will do it would a good attitude do not Lord what you know of others but I have found people don't want to learn if you tick them off Dell learned just to spite you will be in the water doing it with the love you for it later

The Po Man's Guide to Breaking the Poverty Cycle

Chapter 9: Miscellaneous Topics - Things YOU NEED TO KNOW!

Auto Parts

I maintain a parts listing for my vehicles, so that I know the current prices of most of the major components I believe might go out on me. If I notice anything out of the ordinary or even if it's just a hunch, I start saving for the part I know I'm going to need. If I already have the funds, I simply set them aside and wait for the part to start going out on me or I will go and buy the part and let it sit in its box until I need it. Most people will ignore the problem and do nothing. Once the part goes out, then and only then, will they do something about the issue, because they have no choice in the matter. You have to keep your vehicle road worthy.

I have also found it very helpful to have an AAA account for emergencies. This account only cost me $15 a month for two people. If you have a significant other it's the best way to go for your peace of mind.

I like to start saving for a new set of tires six months after I bought the last set. Tires can be real pain once one blows the rest are sure to follow. And for heaven sakes buy yourself a hydraulic jack so your wife won't be stranded on the side of the road trying to figure out how to use that cheap piece of crap that came with the car. Jumper cables are another must have in times of emergency. Some people might stop to help but they never have a set of cables.

Common Parts	Cost	Where
Water Pump/with Fan Clutch	$ 120.00	AutoZone
Hood Lift Support	$ 36.00	AutoZone
Serpentine Belt	$ 43.00	AutoZone
Radiator Hose (Upper)	$ 20.00	AutoZone
Radiator Hose (Lower)	$ 20.00	AutoZone
Radiator	$ 204.00	AutoZone
Radiator/Water Pump Fan	$ 76.00	AutoZone
Fuel Pump	$ 217.00	AutoZone
Oil Pump	$ 110.00	AutoZone
Starter	$ 217.00	AutoZone
Alternator	$ 220.00	AutoZone
Sparkplugs	$ 48.00	AutoZone
Tires	$ 800.00	Walmart
Lubricants	**Cost**	**Where**
Gear and Axle Lubricant Qt	$ 24.00	Amazon
Mopar Antifreeze Gal	$ 25.00	Amazon
Brake Fluid 12oz.	$ 17.00	Amazon
Transmission Fluid Qt	$ 12.74	Amazon
Power steering Fluid Qt	$ 14.00	Amazon

The Po Man's Guide to Breaking the Poverty Cycle

Medical Flexible Spending Accounts

What is a prepaid debit card?
A prepaid debit card is a special-purpose Visa® card that gives you an easy, automatic way to pay for qualified health care/benefit expenses by electronically accessing the pre-tax amounts set aside in your Flexible Spending Account (FSA). It works like a Visa card, but has the amount of your FSA contribution stored on it. You or an eligible dependent can use your card for qualified, eligible expenses at businesses that accept Visa cards. The amount of the qualified purchases will be deducted automatically from your account, and the pre-tax dollars will be electronically transferred to the provider/merchant for immediate payment.

Where can I use my prepaid debit card?
IRS regulations allow you to use your cards in participating pharmacies, mail order pharmacies, discount stores, department stores and supermarkets that can identify FSA-eligible items at checkout. Transactions at these merchants are fully substantiated and, in most cases, no paper follow-up is needed. If pharmacies are not equipped to identify the eligible items at point of sale, but have certified that 90% of the merchandise they sell is FSA-eligible, you may use your card. However, since these pharmacies cannot identify the eligible items at the point of sale, another form of auto substantiation or paper follow-up will be required. Expenses are deducted from the account balance at the point of sale. You **cannot** use your cards at discount stores and supermarkets that do not participate. You can continue to use your cards at freestanding pharmacies and health care providers, such as hospitals, doctors, dentists, etc.

My Opinion on FSA prepaid debit cards
Flexible Spending Account (FSA) are **great if you cannot budget your money.** They will take whatever percentage you select out of your gross pay and you will not be taxed for that amount sounds great. **Here is the punchline: at the end of the year, they keep your money!** Whatever is left in the account at the end of the year goes to them. In my opinion, you are better off creating a separate checking account and making those same deposits each pay period. And at the end of the year, your money that is left over, you keep. Instead of starting from $0 at the beginning of the next year, you will have that same remaining balance to help you kick off the New Year. You will have no restrictions and if you want you can spend your remaining balance each year on anything you like. Or you can simply leave the money in the account and allow your balance to increase over time.

I usually save a predetermined amount each pay period into a checking account that I have set aside for medical expenses. My goal is to save enough money during the year to cover my deductible. I will also add money to cover the costs of Co-pays. Simple planning can save you a lot of heartache and financial stress. If it can go wrong. It will go wrong! The idea is to hold onto your money not give it away. Imagine 5,000 people that leave $20 in their account at the end of the year. That's $100,000 that the

The Po Man's Guide to Breaking the Poverty Cycle

insurance company gets to keep. It's big business. All they have to do is wait for the end of the year. Now imagine that it's 1 million people. These same companies take those millions and lobby the government, they get greedy politicians to pass new legislation that will not work out for you in the end. Why help these people take you for every penny you own?

The Po Man's Guide to Breaking the Poverty Cycle

Child Support

There is only **one right way** to deal with Child Support! Pay it off. And do whatever it takes to make sure you don't fall behind.

Sounds harsh but it's TRUE—plain and simple reality. Sometimes child support can be a blessing in disguise. Why would I say such a thing, you ask? I say this because it is true. In the beginning, it can be hard but I have found that I was giving up the same amount of money anyway. Child Support can put a dent in your pocket forcing you to realize you are going to have to find a job that will offset the child support. You have to get a better paying job so that you can afford to live your life and simultaneously support the child you brought into this world. I have watched many men wake up to this truth and I always smile when they take the appropriate steps to make it right for all parties involved, instead of doing nothing and whining about how unfair it is for them.

Most guys are under the impression that you can't quit your job if you are paying child support. Not true! I have walked away from low paying jobs so many times that the agency sent me a letter telling me to mail in my payments because they couldn't keep up with my job changes. I was still sending in payments, so there were no arrears. There were times when I got laid off and got behind on payments. As soon as I got another job, I made multiple payments until I got caught up. When I got hurt on the job and was out of work for 3 years, I sent in payments every week. I was getting worker's compensation so I had the money. No one had to tell me to do it—it was my responsibility!

Remember no cheating! No quick fixes. Pay them now or pay them later! But you will pay for them! I know, you're thinking, *that's easy for me to say—I'm not in the same position as you. I know I don't know the hell that you have been through!* True. But I do know the hell that I have been through! I remember how bad it can be. I also remember that I'm glad it's over! Get er done while you are young! So, you won't be in your 50's worrying about paying child support for a 30-year-old child who has already started a family of his own! It's HARD because it's supposed to be hard! A MAN must FIGHT to LIVE!

Don't worry gents, there is a silver lining in this storm cloud! Child support is also a double-edged sword. Once you have paid it off and the child is grown, he or she can no longer be manipulated. Your standard of living will increase while the woman's standard will decrease. Remember her standard of living depended on your timely payments and when that "free money" has been cut off, she will be on her own. Your child will be grown and hopefully off on their own. If you want to give them money it's completely up to you. No one will be exerting the "force of law" to compel you to do it. So, if your child hates you and has grown up to become someone you utterly despise you are free to disown them in their face and go your separate ways. If the love is mutual, there will be no hate-filled-lying mother to get in your way!

When my ex-wife calls and wants me to contribute for anything involving my son I always say "If he wants it tell him to ask me for it, he's grown now. Why is he asking "you" to get in the middle of "our" business?"

The Po Man's Guide to Breaking the Poverty Cycle

Let's say you're OK with paying child support. You have absolutely NO DOUBT that the child is YOURS! That's fine. If not, the first thing you're going to need is a DNA test to ensure that this is your child. It is better to cough up the money and pay for a DNA test and find out the child is not yours than to pay child support for the next 18 to 25 years and then after you have paid find out the child is not yours. Yes, I'm saying, NEVER TRUST THE WOMAN! There is a reason "why" we have the saying, "Momma's baby, Daddy's maybe!" I paid child support for two children for 22 years all the while knowing that only one of the two boys was mine! In some states you get hosed, mine is one of them. So, before you embark on this journey of monetary love make sure you are investing in YOUR bloodline!
So, let's recap once you have agreed to pay there is only one right way to deal with Child Support! Pay it off. And do whatever it takes to make sure you don't fall behind.

The Po Man's Guide to Breaking the Poverty Cycle

Prepping For Hard Times

Ah yes, the big bad "P" word. Prepper is short for preparer your job is to always be prepared. I understand prepping usually has a crazy conspiracy theory connotation to it thanks to the media. But in this case, we're not going to be discussing the end of the world or aliens taking over the earth. Nothing like that! Your goal should be to have the things you will need if you lose your job or find yourself without money for a prolonged period of time.

Let's say, you get sick and miss work, so much so, your paychecks will not be enough to cover all of your expenses. You will need to go into your reserves if you want to eat or if you need medication or something as simple as a pain pill.

Money

Gold: I'm not saying I think you are rich but if you find yourself in the position to buy gold and hold on to it, then by all means do so. Gold at the time of this writing is selling for $1,548.83 an ounce. This price is likely to go up. One ounce of gold could pay your rent during a HARD Time period.

Silver: Unlike gold, silver is way more affordable to buy and stack. It will obviously take more silver to pay your rent during a HARD Time period. Silver at the time of this writing is selling for $17.89 an ounce. This price usually fluctuates up and down more so than gold, which ironically makes it easier to stack. When the price drops, you buy. I have had to sell silver on more than one occasion.

Food

Can Goods: Canned food is not that expensive; it may not be as cheap as it once was but the prices are still manageable. You can do yourself a really big favor by taking 2 to 3 dollars a paycheck and buying canned goods.

Meat: If you find yourself financially well off enough to buy a deep freezer, go crazy and fill that thing up. Worst-case scenario you have to eat a lot of meat. Best case scenario you have food when you need it.

Beans: It will cost you more, but buy a big bag of beans set aside 10 bucks every so often and get an 8lb bag.

Rice: It will cost you more, but buy a big bag/sack of rice set aside 15 bucks every so often and get a 20lb bag. Worst-case scenario you won't have to go shopping as much.

Seasonings

Nowadays, seasonings are more expensive than the actual food items. Most people will go to the store and stock up on the small bottles, that's fine; but more expensive. I usually go here: https://nuts.com.

Flour: You can't really store flour the way you would anything else; because of the weevils. But if you take a bag of flour, place it in a large freezer bag and freeze it for 7

The Po Man's Guide to Breaking the Poverty Cycle

days, it will kill the weevils. And store it in one of those glass jars used for canning. It will last you a very long time. Or any airtight container.
Sugar: Sugar is an easy store. Place it in a large freezer bag and presto you're done.
 Pepper: People don't realize it until they go to the store, pepper is expensive. Normally I just go to the store and buy one of those $10 containers of pepper and call it done. Later I got crazy, and ordered a 5-gallon jug from Sam's.
Salt: It has always been cheap, it's always going to be cheap (I hope), there's no real point in elaborating further, just make sure you store some.
Cooking Oil: This is one of those Oh crap! I forgot to buy some items. Nobody thinks about cooking at all until of course they have none. Make sure you have at least eight bottles and you should be good.

Hygiene

Toilet Paper: This stuff is like gold, when you find yourself without money or once again on an extremely tight budget. All I can say about TP is Stock up! Stock up! Stock up!
Dish Washing Liquid: You wouldn't think so but this little everyday item is a lifesaver. All I have to say is clean dishes.
Soap: Unless we have somehow traveled back in time and it's the 1700's, I need not explain. Stock up!
Trash bags: A totally necessary item which can easily take away the last eight bucks in your wallet.
Bleach: If you don't want to get sick, and something happens and you need bleach. You need bleach.
Washing Detergent:
I usually grab 5 or 6 of those large bottles. They last for months.

First Aid

Before you go thinking I'm talking about "what" you are going to need in a combat zone…relax. These are just those 8, 9, or 10-dollar items that can break you when funds are low. They are listed below so that you can see them. So don't have a cow man.
Band Aids: I once scratched my ear at work after handling chemicals, later the small scratch got infected. I got so sick that I had to go to the emergency room, which cost me $700! Since then, I learned to use a band aid and a dab of Neosporin to kill any infection that might arise. It is the simplest things that we overlook which cost us the most money.
Sinus Medicine: A sinus infection doesn't mean much to you until you don't have the proper medication to treat it. At the first sign of getting sick before anything gets worse, I'll take Sudafed. Seems simple enough but we're talking about not having money. So how do you buy Sudafed if you are broke? If you lost your job and things get worse and if you're not a veteran, how are you going to seek treatment? You can find loads in any dollar store. Buy 3 packs and call it a day. If you use any, restock.

The Po Man's Guide to Breaking the Poverty Cycle

Antibiotics: If you get infection doctors usually give you antibiotics. It goes without saying. When you're in between jobs and have no access to a doctor I usually start off with raw garlic or onions, most people don't know: they are natural antibiotics. Also keep a bottle of amoxicillin just in case.
Neosporin: This little tube of sunshine is invaluable, it's also a triple antibiotic. If I get burned, I apply Neosporin. If I get cut, nicked or scraped I apply Neosporin.
Aleve: These pills are miracle workers, especially if you have arthritis. I will also take them if I work really hard so that I have no inflammation.
Motrin: When I was in the Army, every time anything happened to you, they gave you Motrin. It was the cure-all. End-all. Be-all for most of the little things which could affect a soldier throughout the normal performance of his/her duties.

Emergency Items

Once again, we're not talking about the apocalypse, just simple little things like a power outage.
Batteries: I used batteries for almost everything there is in my house. Keeping some available for a time of need is just smart. When you are broke, who can afford batteries?
Spare Phone Charger: How many times has your phone charger gone out on you and you had the money to replace it? Even then you screamed about the cost. So, it would only be reasonable for me to say you would need to have a spare.

The Po Man's Guide to Breaking the Poverty Cycle

Cooking like Mom or Better (Seems irrelevant until you look at how much money guys spend on fast food!)
Why of all things do you need to learn how to cook?

- Saves you money, you won't be in such a hurry to go out and buy fast food.
- It increases your health because you will be forced to make healthier choices. Cooking requires effort.
- It returns you to the good ole days when you loved the food you ate and would cause you to want more of it.
- It decreases your need for a woman because you know how to cook for yourself and won't be relying on someone else's ability.

So how do you get started? Well, that's simple enough, follow the list below:

1. Learn the names of all the dishes you like or in some cases love, you have to know what these dishes are called.
2. Go online and find all the recipes for all the dishes you want to learn how to prepare. I happen to know: you can find a "how to" video on YouTube for almost any dish you could ever want to know how to prepare.
3. Check out the list of ingredients for each meal and buy all the common spices. The spices which are listed in many of the recipes or at least the spices listed in more than five or six recipes.
4. You will also need to buy all of the silverware, pottery and/or utensils you might need. So, that's going to mean pots, pans, skillets, maybe a roasting pan or whatever you are going to need to prepare these meals.

Unlike most people, I have a tendency to cook by smell. Yeah, I know some people think that's crazy but it's what works for me. I cook by smell because of my past. I can still remember walking by the kitchen and how each individual dish smelled while it was cooking. So now that I'm doing the cooking, I rely on my memory. When a meal doesn't smell quite right, I add the appropriate seasoning.

Now, don't go thinking you become a chef Anton overnight, it takes time, lots of practice and attention to detail. And little by little, after preparing many meals you will gain mastery over each dish. Once you know what you are doing, you will be moved to add your little tweaks to make each meal your own. You will make each recipe your own.

Almost everyone in America has a phone, use it. Call your mom and find out from her exactly how she prepares everything that you love. It won't kill you to ask. More than likely, she will be thrilled to tell you exactly what she does, how she does it and why she does it. She will probably give you many of the little tips and tricks she has learned over the years so that you can use them at home. Remember kids knowledge is power.

The main thing you are going to have to do is practice. You are never going to become really good at anything if you don't practice. Not every meal is going to come out perfect. Not every meal you make is going to taste right but you are going to have to keep at it until you perfect your craft.

The Po Man's Guide to Breaking the Poverty Cycle

There is going to come a time when you will notice you're getting better and better! Without thing about it, you will begin to start experimenting, start adding your own little tweaks to the recipes. Don't get cocky write them down or just edit the recipe so that your tweaks are included. And if you're like most men, you are not going to understand season to taste. I hate those words! When in doubt, stick to the math-- measure everything that you put in the pot! And if you add anything edit your recipe! We are looking for consistency. You are going to want to be able to reproduce the same results over and over again. If you cook it right and if it tastes good you will repeat your masterpiece! Writing down your measurements will aid you in this venture. So, take detailed notes.

I treat cooking like a chemistry experiment. I observe how they prepare the meal on the video and do my best to copy each step exactly as shown or described.
Ingredients make the meal, so don't go skimping on the ingredients. Sometimes you may get lucky but most of the time it won't taste right.

Learning to cook is like learning to fight. Those head feints don't make sense until someone tags you! Cook a horrible meal, I guarantee you will start paying more attention and getting it right the next time.

The Po Man's Guide to Breaking the Poverty Cycle

Buying Good Cheap Tools

After much consideration, I have decided to add this section to the book. Not everyone gets to sit behind a desk. I have also noticed over the years people suck at buying tools. So, I will be giving tips I wish someone had given me earlier in my career. Never buy screwdrivers with the ridges on the blade tip, they will just break off when you apply too much force. You want good solid tips with sharp edges.

Screw Drivers	Where	Cost
#2 Philips 810" long	Home Depot	$10.83
Drill Adapters	eBay	$5.00
#2 Philips 6" Screwdriver Bit Set	Northern Tools	$8.70
3/8" x 8" Flat Tip	Harbor Freight	$2.05
3/8" x 17" Flat Tip	Harbor Freight	$15.00
3/16" x 6" Flat Tip	Harbor Freight	$3.00
1/4" x 6" Flat Tip	Harbor Freight	$3.00
5/16" x 8" Flat Tip	Harbor Freight	$3.00

Hammers simply need good well secured handles and a heavy head that won't bounce back when striking.

Hammers	Where	Cost
Ball Peen Set	Harbor Freight	$20.00
Large Sledge Hammer	Harbor Freight	$17.00
Dead Blow Hammer 3lb	Harbor Freight	$10.00
Dead Blow Hammer 2lb W BRASS CAP	Northern Tools	$10.83
Copper Hammer	Hard To Find	$30.00
Brass Hammer	Harbor Freight	$27.00
Small Brass Hammer	Northern Tools	$17.00

When you are buying wrenches, you want to find the ones that look and feel like the good ones. You should always know a quality wrench when you see one. They will last you a lifetime and you won't cry if and when they get stolen. They should be heavy and have crisp millwork with flat edges where the tools contact the nut or bolt head not smooth.

Wrenches	Where	Cost
Metric Combo Wrench Set 8 24mm	Harbor Freight	$20.00
SAE Combo Wrench Set 1/4 1 1/4"	Harbor Freight	$20.00
SAE Combo Wrench Set 1/4 1 1/4"	Harbor Freight	$30.30
Metric Combo Wrench Set 6 19mm	Harbor Freight	$10.83
7mm Wrench	Northern Tool	$3.50
Durabilt SAE Box end Ratchet Set	Target	$10.83
Durabilt Metric Box End Ratchet Set	Target	$10.83
Adjustable Wrench Set	Harbor Freight	$20.00
15" Adjustable Wrench	Northern Tool	$20.00

Everybody needs sockets, but I suggest you buy a thick sturdy 6point. The 12point are more expensive and look better, but they tend to strip bolt heads. You don't want to be known as a guy who strips out bolt heads on everything he works on.

The Po Man's Guide to Breaking the Poverty Cycle

You will need a set of ¼, 3/8 and ½ drive sockets, sizes ranging from ¼ inch to 1 ¼ inch in today's manufacturing world. Some sockets need to be redundant so when the job requires more than one you have them on hand. Craftsmen are great but stolen the most. If you don't want half of your new set stolen and/or missing after the first week buy according to the listings.

6point Sockets	Where	Cost
3/8" Drive 1019mm Deep	Harbor Freight	$14.00
3/8" Drive 10mm Regular	Northern Tools	$4.00
3/8" Drive 13mm Regular	Northern Tools	$4.00
3/8" Drive 18mm Regular	Northern Tools	$4.00
3/8" Drive 10mm Deep	Northern Tools	$3.50
3/8" Drive 11mm Deep	Northern Tools	$3.50
3/8" Drive 19mm Deep	Northern Tools	$4.00
1/2" Drive 15/16"	Northern Tools	$3.50
1/2" Drive 1"	Northern Tools	$3.50
1/2" Drive 11/16"	Northern Tools	$3.50
1/2" Drive 1 1/8"	Northern Tools	$3.50
1/2" Drive 1 1/4"	Northern Tools	$3.50
1/2" Drive 21mm	Northern Tools	$3.50
1/2" Drive 22mm	Northern Tools	$3.50
1/2" Drive 24mm	Northern Tools	$3.50
3/8" Drive SAE Allen Sockets	Harbor Freight	$17.00
3/8" Drive Metric Allen Sockets	Harbor Freight	$17.00
1/2" Drive 7/16" Allen Socket	Northern Tools	**Hard To Find**

Every technician needs a good reliable meter. If you want a Fluke, but don't have Fluke money, get a Craftsman; they are good meters and will last until you can afford the Fluke. When it comes to wire strippers, never skimp, always buy Klein. There is nothing worse than a cheap tool that doesn't work. Spend a little more money in the beginning, so you don't have to go back and buy a better tool later. I have never really had a problem with people stealing my electrical tools, but don't quote me on it does happen, but not often enough for you to be worried.

Electrical	Where	Cost
Multimeter	Sears	$ 34.62
Clamp Ammeter	Harbor Freight	$ 21.63
Heat gun	Harbor Freight	$ 20.00
Klein Wire Strippers	Northern Tool	$ 9.00
Kline Wire **Strippers**	Home Depot	$ 12.00
Klein Strippers w Threads	Home Depot	$ 11.84
1/8" Terminal Screwdriver	Northern	$ 6.00
Insulated Terminal Screwdriver Set	Harbor Freight	$ 8.67

The Po Man's Guide to Breaking the Poverty Cycle

Insulated Screwdrivers	Harbor Freight	$ 14.20
Insulated Dykes	Harbor Freight	$ 7.60
Insulated Linemen Pliers	Harbor Freight	$ 7.60
Insulated Needle Nose	Harbor Freight	$ 7.60
Cable Tie Gun	Harbor Freight	$ 8.65

Vise grips should always be high quality, spend the money, the cheap ones always break and don't work when you need them most. Snap Ring pliers should also cost you, better to buy one good set, rather than four bad ones. Cutters should have a good level at the jaws, if they look smooth and sleek, don't buy them chances are they will be crap. If they can't cut anything you will have just wasted your money. Never buy flashy shiny tools, it makes people want to steal them or so I have learned.

Pliers	Where	Cost
12" Channel Locks	Harbor Freight	$20.00
Vise Grip Set	AutoZone	$20.00
10" Vise Grips	Harbor Freight	$10.00
Aviation Snips	Harbor Freight	$10.00
Snap Ring Pliers	SEARS	$30.00
3" close cutters	Harbor Freight	$12.00
3" Curved Needle Nose	Harbor Freight	$3.00
3" Needle Nose	Harbor Freight	$3.00
3" long Needle Nose	Harbor Freight	$3.00
8" close cutters	Harbor Freight	$8.65
3" close cutters	Harbor Freight	$2.05
3" close cutters	Harbor Freight	$3.00

I bought a Sturdy US General rolling toolbox for less than $200 from Harbor Freight. I got it in the sale. Harbor freight has sales all the time always check their sales pages. The idea is to get more tools with your limited funds. I have stretched many a dollar by going into their stores. Below is a diagram I created to store and organize my tools.

The Po Man's Guide to Breaking the Poverty Cycle

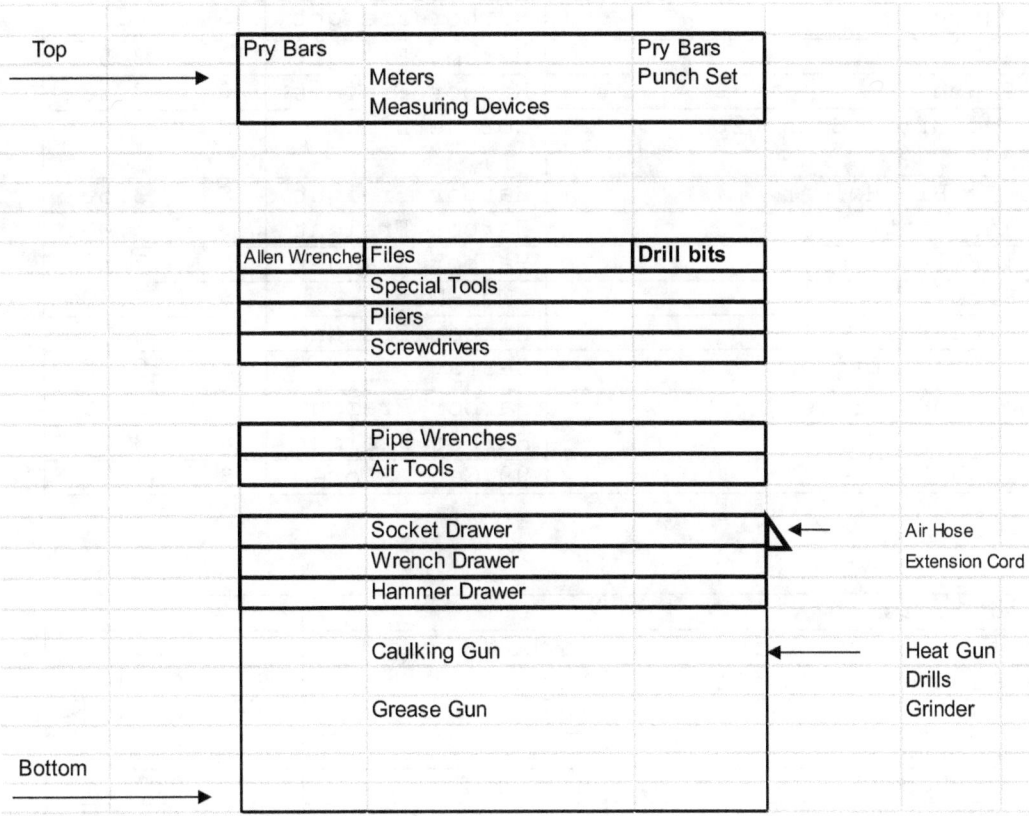

Some tools are simply throw-away! I know sounds crazy, but you will never be able to keep them on hand people will steal them just because you have them. Or you buy them when you start a new job, but at the moment your funds will allow them to buy the better-quality items. And always LOCK YOUR TOOLS AWAY!

Special Tools	Where	Cost
4way Chuck Key Lot 1745	Harbor Freight	$ 10.83
Hand Rivet Set lot 38353	Harbor Freight	$ 6.50
Industrial Scissors		$ 20.00
*18volt drill	Wal-Mart	$ 45.00
Skill *4 1/2"Grinder lot 91223	Wal-Mart	$ 30.00
Black & Decker 18 Volt Battery	Wal-Mart	$ 39.00
Black & Decker 18 Volt Battery Charger	Wal-Mart	$ 32.00
Hacksaw	AutoZone	$ 10.00
Caulking Gun	Home Depot	$ 3.00
tri square	Home Depot	$ 8.00
Measuring Tape 25'	Northern	$ 3.00
Punch & Chisel Set	Harbor Freight	$ 14.10
Pry Bars	Harbor Freight	$ 12.00
Jimmy Pry Bar	Harbor Freight	$ 7.60
Torpedo Level	Home Depot	$ 5.00
Brass Punch x 2	Harbor Freight	$ 14.00
Hole Punch Set	Harbor Freight	$ 8.65

The Po Man's Guide to Breaking the Poverty Cycle

Nail Punch Set	Harbor Freight	$	4.33
Awl	Harbor Freight	$	3.50
Auto Punch	Harbor Freight	$	3.50
Titanium Drill Bits 62pc 3319233	Northern	$	15.00
Magnetic Bit Holder	Harbor Freight	$	3.50
Mini File Set	Harbor Freight	$	5.00
4 in 1 File	Harbor Freight	$	7.50
Flat File	Wal-Mart	$	7.50
Rasp File Set	Harbor Freight	$	4.50
Speeder 1/4" Drive	Sears	$	20.00
Speeder 3/8" Drive	Harbor Freight	$	8.00
Speeder 1/2" Drive	Harbor Freight	$	8.00
Flashlight	99 Cent Store	$	3.50

Special Tools			
Inspection Mirror Large	Harbor Freight	$	8.65
Inspection Mirror Small	AutoZone	$	6.00
Magnet	AutoZone	$	6.00
Screw Starter	Sears	$	6.48
Tap Set 42pc	Harbor Freight	$	40.00
Feeler Gauge	Harbor Freight	$	4.40
*Stainless Steel Scribe Set	Harbor Freight	$	7.00
Magnifier	Harbor Freight	$	2.16
Mechanical Fingers	Harbor Freight	$	2.00

The Po Man's Guide to Breaking the Poverty Cycle

I have decided to include the next section because I have noticed that it affects a lot of people. You can't move forward if your very identity has been called into question. If you barely managed to get the job you have to get it fixed. So, you can move forward. Waiting won't help you it will only make it harder to get your issue resolved!

Birth Certificate Corrections

It is very difficult to attempt to go out and conquer the world: when your very identity is being called into question. My situation isn't so unique, my mom only made it as far as the 6th grade and she couldn't spell. She was also under the delusion you could swap letters in your name. So, my birth certificate was useless. I was going to be in for one heck of a ride later on in life. At the writing of these words, I had just turned 51 on August 11, 2019. I went to renew my driver's license just like everyone else and got a very big surprise. The state of Texas chose this year to put the hammer down on being REAL ID compliant. There is no need to feel powerless. If you have a copy of your original birth certificate or not. Don't start freaking out, there is always an answer to every problem. You will however need to read the section that follows this one.

Birth Certificate Corrections: What YOU NEED TO KNOW before you send them your money!

- **Make sure you take your time and fill in each entry correctly. Any mistake you make can lead to having your request denied and it may take them a month to notify you. You WILL lose your money and months of your time if you leave a line blank!**

- **Don't attempt to correct the misspelling of your parents' names, you will only find yourself being denied because you didn't submit the appropriate paperwork! Any mistake you make WILL result in a denial and more time wasted! You will also lose your money.**

- **When submitting your paperwork, make sure you send good copies if they can't read them, your request will be denied! If you are denied you have lost your money!**

- **Your ID must be valid. If your ID is expired, you will need to send them a copy of your social security card. Leaving out copies of the relevant ID can lead to having your request denied and it may take them a month to notify you. You will have lost time and money!**

Make sure you are on the official government site. There are a lot of businesses out there that will try to fool you. They have no affiliation with the real Vital Statistics Office in your state. Make sure you read the fine print at the bottom of their website.

The Po Man's Guide to Breaking the Poverty Cycle

O.V.U.S. (Onlinevitalus) is a privately-owned website that is not affiliated with, not owned, or operated by any government agency. O.V.U.S. (Onlinevitalus) is an independent preparer that provides vital records application preparation assistance services.

Don't get sucked in, you don't need a middleman. Look for the Vital Records or Vital Statistics Special Services Unit in your state.

The Po Man's Guide to Breaking the Poverty Cycle

Sacrificing For a Better Life

Before you get super concerned, sacrificing for a better life is and isn't exactly how it sounds. Think of it as going without now so you can have more later in life's basically it in a nutshell. Sacrificing for a better life is all about your youth and your old age. I've noticed throughout the years, or should I say I have watched the outcome of others and come to the conclusion that what you do while you're young has the greatest amount of impact on how you live when you're older. Allow me to explain that while you're young enough to sacrifice is when most of your sacrifice should be done! You're young enough to do it! Strong enough to endure it. Hopefully ambitious enough to get it done! And if you have "drive" you will be single-minded in your pursuit of that which you desire. I have watched other men scrimp and save checking out articles, deciding on what color, all in an effort to buy their dream car! And after a couple of years of suffering, they have that car sitting in their driveway, fully paid for.
Life is not the pursuit of items! Life is about fulfilling one's dreams! Nobody wants to reach their old age and have nothing. The American dream in a nutshell is sacrificing while you are young so when you're older you can live the easy life not vice versa.
There are three types of people in this world the first is the planner, the second is the dreamer and the third is the carefree. We're going to focus on these three types of people.

The planner: I've noticed that most planners have really good role models. They know what they want and even if they don't know what they want they know how to build an excellent foundation. Planners are well coached by their parents from the time they can speak. Whenever the child shows any semblance of understanding their parents would pounce, teaching, guiding and instructing them. Because of this, they know how things work and what they should do to avoid most pitfalls. These children are well taught, coached and their knowledge is tested daily. Their parents know the only way to test a child's understanding is to ask them questions and gauge their answers. Because of the diligence of their parents, they have a firm grasp on how to build their own foundation to succeed. They show this in the movies but no one pays attention. Who do you think can afford to be cub scouts and boy scouts? Poor parents can't afford this for their children! Planners will pursue those things which are fundamental to getting what they want even though they may not know what it is yet. They will most likely start off taking certain classes beginning in high school and will lay down the first stones of their foundation. If such a person wants to go into the medical field, they will focus on the science courses even in their electives. Robot Wars and technical programs for children. Spelling bees and science fairs…. Do you see the children of poor folks signing up for these events? It's all about building a foundation suitable and stable enough to support future success!

The Po Man's Guide to Breaking the Poverty Cycle

Planners are ruled by strict parents. They crave structure. They will be the first one to ask, "Who's in charge?" They get an allowance and are forced to plan out investment strategies early on in life. Their time, their energy, even their time for relaxation activities is spent in the pursuit of excellence! They are not allowed to deviate from the schedules set for them.

Planners are trained to be goal oriented and will dismiss or disregard anyone or anything that gets in the way of those goals. Planners hate distraction and are irritated by spontaneity. They have their entire lives mapped out. They live life by the numbers. They are meticulous to a fault. Failure is not an acceptable outcome! Only when a planner's parents perceive they have overloaded the child's mind will the child be given a temporary break, which is also structured to allow the parents time to step back and regroup and wait for the information to be absorbed and understood. Ever heard of summer camp? Once the child is rested and ready to proceed it all begins again.

These planners have a strong sense of self discipline, so much so in fact, they tend to unravel when life throws them a curveball. Anything out of order, anything out of place, can send them into a tizzy until the issue is resolved to their satisfaction. They will only take advice which they have researched, found proof it works or they are reasonably certain things will work out in their favor. What happens when these children rebel? Ever hear of military academies? You can't get pregnant or get pregnant when you attend an all-girls school or an all-boys school.

I sometimes use the old fables to get a point across, take into account the story of the tortoise and the hare. The planner is like the hare, supremely confident and sure of its ability to win the race. The planner will often run as far ahead as possible and leave us poor dreamers in the wakes of their dust. And just like the hare, the planner will often stop and take a designated rest. While the tortoise a.k.a. dreamer, will continue plodding along ever so slowly taking his time, while navigating through life's many obstacles. One day, while the hare is still taking its rest, the dreamer or tortoise, will awaken to a new way of thinking. A new way of doing things, a new way of getting things done, he would've found his catalyst. Now fully energized, the tortoise a.k.a. dreamer begins to take on the characteristics of the planner more and more each day. And on this day the hare will awaken and find itself no longer in a race he is destined to win but instead, this hare will find itself in for the race of his life! A slow tortoise is now another hare, running in a race he can actually win. The issue is the hare or the planner, never thought for one moment that the tortoise had the ability to become another hare. No one is stuck in any designation! You can become whatever and whoever you choose to become. There are no set rules in this life, time and chance happen to all men each according to his ability to overcome. Each according to his ability to change.

The Po Man's Guide to Breaking the Poverty Cycle

Dreamers: These people are unique. They have the ability to switch over into planning mode. Lots of dreamers had planning parents but we are not going to talk about those guys, we're going to talk about the dreamers who were born from dreamers. We are going to focus on dreamers who grew up poor. They are created by a longing to possess those things the children of planners have. A lot of these children have grown up in single parent homes, where they are not taught how to plan. Nothing was prepared for them and anything they wished to do they had to make it on their own. They are driven by the desire to possess all of the things they were denied while growing up. They have an idea of their end state but no idea of how to actually get there, or the steps they will need to take to achieve these dreams.

These dreamers are hungry and they don't know how to quit because they can't quit. If they quit all of your dreams will go up and ashes. Ever watched *An Officer and a Gentleman?* They have nowhere else to go but up! They usually have no one to run to for good advice, so they will study and do research. But this is only after an avenue has been opened unto them, which causes them to believe they might yet achieve their dreams. Once they have a catalyst, they admittedly switch over to becoming planners. These dreamers are triggered by their fears of failure or of never accomplishing anything! Never having the things, they desire or being stopped before they can achieve their goals. This group of people will sacrifice whatever it takes to ensure what they have dreamed will someday become a reality.

The Carefree: These people are usually delusional and live only for the moment. They willfully ignore the passage of time! And it would never occur to any of them there is any other way to live life. They would never allow the thought to enter into their mind their way of thinking and doing things could ever possibly be wrong. You see these people meandering about, stopping to smell the flowers, taking the time to enjoy the beautiful day the way the sun shines its rays across a beautiful meadow. They call themselves spontaneous! Life should just happen they don't like planning! They don't like being "Tied down to anything or in some cases anyone". They live in Lala land and the rent is free! The world is their oyster! Nothing bad ever happens there not to them! But, as in all cases, as it is with all men, they will despite their supercilious belief system, encounter which they propose does not exist reality.

I will ask for your indulgence, while I once again recount another fable. The story of the grasshopper and the ant. Here's my take on the story:

All throughout the summer the grasshopper hopped around dancing rubbing his back legs together to make music having a good ole time completely carefree. There was food to be had in abundance and everything was lush and green. Time to make merry! Who wants to spend their time toiling away in the hot summer sun? As time progressed the leaves started falling from the trees and the food was a little less abundant, more so as the winter approached. The Grasshopper is no longer singing and dancing, the time for frolicking in the woods has passed.

The Po Man's Guide to Breaking the Poverty Cycle

Now the grasshopper was starving and it was beginning to get cold. Now usually the story has this conversation goes on between the grasshopper and the ants but that's nonsense. Grasshoppers don't talk to ants. Ants don't talk to grasshoppers. There's a time for work and a time for dreaming. Planning is the first stage of work. Dreaming waste valuable time which could be better spent working on a plan. The carefree know this; but instead choose to wait. The Planner goes into work mode. And it doesn't matter which one of these three you are…. We all have one thing in common. Time! How you spend your time will determine your end!

Concerning Enemies

So, which one do you think is the most dangerous of all three types of people? The planner? The dreamer? Or carefree?

The planner can be extremely dangerous because he relies on facts and figures demonstrated traits and data. The planner doesn't have the ability to dream, so their attack is usually going to be straightforward in most cases.   They expect you to react in a designated manner according to outside stimuli, so they can begin the first phase of their plan: the beginning of your destruction. Planners can learn to be carefree within certain specified parameters. They usually lack the ingenuity of the dreamer; but being a planner is one step away from being a dreamer; in order to plan you must be able to visualize.   Once a planner has begun to let go of the reins, they begin to dream.
The dreamer is not usually threatening until they learn to plan. A hardworking planning dreamer is a triple threat! There isn't much they can't accomplish! You will usually get squashed if you go up against them.   You learn from the dreamer who works hard on his plans! Your worst nightmare is a dreamer who has become a visionary! Be very careful if you find yourself in a position to mock or step on another man's dreams! Generally, planners and dreamers won't attack anyone physically. Not true with carefree.
The carefree man doesn't care if he goes to jail for assaulting you! He doesn't care if he destroys your property! He won't give it a second thought when he decides to walk up to you and punch your lights out! He lives in the moment! And if by chance, you have just done something to get his dander up (put him in a rage) he will lash out physically without thought! Without remorse! Without the fear of repercussions. The carefree can be very care **less** but they are hardly ever care **full**.
When dealing with people you don't know always use discretion. Anyone can step into your life and in one moment destroy everything you have sacrificed to gain!

Discretion [dəˈskreSH(ə)n]
NOUN
 the ability to deal with situations in a way does not <u>offend</u>, <u>upset</u>, or <u>embarrass</u> people or tell any of their secrets.
"she knew she could rely on his discretion"

The Po Man's Guide to Breaking the Poverty Cycle

synonyms: circumspection · care · carefulness · caution · wariness · chariness
YOUR Health and YOUR Safety

I have learned we are supposed to spend our youth working hard and saving to ensure when you are older you will be well off financially. We are not, however, supposed to spend our youth damaging our bodies and ignoring our health and safety only to waste all of the money we saved to spend on medical bills when we are older. This is simply a warning, something for you to consider the next time you decide your job is worth getting hurt. You can get another job. You have one body, don't allow anyone to threaten you, bully you into doing anything you believe to be unsafe!

Diet
I won't begin by harping on the tenants of eating right, but I will harp on a diabetes free diet.

Diabetes
Diabetes type II is quickly taking over in America, not for all the hype reasons they will tell you but simply because of processed foods. The problem is most Americans can't afford to not eat processed foods! Do the math, eating healthy **requires more money.**

Here are 13 ways to avoid getting diabetes.
- **Minimize Your Intake of Processed Foods**
- Cut Sugar and Refined Carbs From Your Diet...
- Work Out Regularly...
- Drink Water as Your Primary Beverage...
- Lose Weight If You're Overweight or Obese...
- Quit Smoking...
- Follow a Very Low Carb Diet...
- Watch Portion Sizes...
- Avoid Sedentary Behaviors.
- Eat a High Fiber Diet
- Optimize Vitamin D Levels
- Drink Coffee or Tea

Consider taking these herbs:

Curcumin
Curcumin is a component of the bright gold spice turmeric, which is one of the main ingredients in curries.
Research has shown it can be very effective against arthritis and may help reduce inflammatory markers in people with prediabetes (66Trusted Source, 67Trusted Source). There's also impressive evidence that it may decrease insulin resistance and reduce the risk of diabetes progression (68Trusted Source, 69Trusted Source).

Berberine

The Po Man's Guide to Breaking the Poverty Cycle

Berberine is found in several herbs and has been used in traditional Chinese medicine for thousands of years.
Studies have shown that it fights inflammation and lowers cholesterol and other heart disease markers.
In addition, several studies in people with type 2 diabetes have found that berberine has strong blood sugar lowering properties.
In fact, a large analysis of 14 studies found that berberine is as effective at lowering blood sugar levels as metformin, one of the oldest and most widely used diabetes medications.
Because berberine works by increasing insulin sensitivity and reducing the release of sugar by the liver, it might theoretically help people with prediabetes avoid diabetes.

Exercise
Static stretching also appears to reduce strength and power (explosive strength). Warm-up (low intensity activity prior to work, **exercise** or sports) appears to reduce **injury** risk.... Studies in basic combat training show that both high and low BMI increases **injury** risk.
Dynamic stretching is a movement-based type of **stretching**. It uses the muscles themselves to bring about a **stretch**. It's different from traditional "static" **stretching** because the **stretch** position is not held.
7 best low impact exercises, suitable for all fitness levels.

1. Cycling. Hop on the bike for a low impact option that can get your heart racing and muscles well and truly switched on...
2. Rowing machine.
3. Elliptical machine.
4. Zumba class. **Zumba** is a fitness program that combines Latin and international music with dance moves. **Zumba** routines incorporate interval training alternating fast and slow rhythms to help improve cardiovascular fitness.
5. Bodyweight strength training.
6. Yoga.
7. **TRX** (a.k.a. "total resistance **exercise**")

Accidents
Most auto accidents are caused because people are not paying attention to either the road ahead or the other maniacs are on the road with them. Slow down, take a step back, never allow yourself to be in such a hurry, you forget your surroundings. Stay alert! Stay alive!
Most on the job accidents are caused by people ignoring the safety policies put in place at work. Don't take shortcuts, there is no reason to see your hopes and dreams destroyed; because, you didn't take things seriously once injured there is no going back!

On the Job Injuries
Maximum Medical Improvement (MMI) occurs when an injured employee reaches a state where his or her condition cannot be **improved** any further or when a treatment

The Po Man's Guide to Breaking the Poverty Cycle

plateau in a person's healing process is reached. You are as good as you are going to get. Getting an **MMI** Rating **after** a **Texas** Work Injury. **Texas** and Florida are the only states that have a **time limit** of 104 weeks to reach **MMI**.

What is an FCE medical test?
A functional capacity evaluation (**FCE**) is set of **tests**, practices and observations are combined to determine the ability of the evaluated person to function in a variety of circumstances, most often employment, in an objective manner. Physicians change diagnoses based on FCEs. Once the FCE medical test has been completed, the physician will give you an Impairment Rating. Some doctors have been known to look at guidelines for return to work and relied upon those when determining whether a Claimant has reached Maximum Medical Improvement. Another doctor examining the same Claimant may rely more on the fact little to no treatment has been done and with an injection and an interdisciplinary therapy program the Claimant should show improvement and argue; therefore, said Claimant is not a Maximum Medical Improvement.

Once you are given an Impairment Rating, your Temporary Income Benefits (TIBS) will stop and your Impairment Income Benefits (IIBs) will start. The maximum pay rate is less for IIBS than for TIBS and your benefits may be lower as a result. Or in most cases you will receive a lump sum payout. **Once this is done you are on your own.**

Don't delude yourself, I reached MMI and got an 11% Impairment Rating. I was given steroid shots for my back before I was given the FCE medical test. My back was OK for a year and then the problems returned. Everything is designed to push you through the system fast enough for the treatments to appear as though they are working. Once enough time has passed and those treatments wear off, it's too late. And if you had a lawyer, they will charge you out the butt during this whole process. They will charge you simply for updates on your records which simply means: because they can and they will.

But don't take my word for it, get hurt, you will find out the truth.

The Po Man's Guide to Breaking the Poverty Cycle

Which Type of Boss Do You Work For?

I've noticed from experience that there are six different sorts of people you will find in charge of you at work. I will name them and give you a few examples of "how" to deal with them. And don't share this with others people can be petty when angered or when they get fired, they will tell your supervisor everything you told them. Be smart.

First: We have the little Napoleon, they probably got bullied in school and now they want revenge on the larger guys so they talk down to everyone. Most of their answers will be tinged with sarcasm or some minor form of subtle ridicule designed to make you feel as small as they are inside.

How to deal with Napoleon

These guys are very insecure and are cowards at heart so you are going to have to give them a BIG nickname. BOSS should suffice. You will also need to give them positive reinforcement— a lot. Such as "Dang, boss you sure know your stuff" or "I'm glad we have you here I would have never figured that out on my own!" If you are building them up, they won't be so focused on tearing you down.

Second: We have the Super-Positive Liberal, he/she can't accept the fact: that things go wrong. They never want to hear anything that might be considered negative even if it is the truth. Liberals are ruled by their feelings and will exude a superior moral outlook that you hirelings simply wouldn't understand. They are at heart: women. So, they will tell you that they are male feminists and expect you to behave as they do and practice groupthink. The liberal doesn't care much for free thinkers or anyone who might dare to disagree with their outlook on life.

How to deal with the Super-Positive Liberal

Liberals can be tricky, they are always probing, trying to get you to reveal more about yourself so they can feel superior. Keep your answers short and to the point. They will be the first ones to attempt to get you to lie for them, regardless of what that lie might cost you. When in doubt, say nothing or tell them you have to think about it. If they don't approach you, leave them alone. When they ask you to do something outside of your scope let them know that you don't know: how or ask them to show you how it's done. But you must say it neutrally no emotions, no inflection. They never say no to their boss so you will have to shoulder a heavy work load.

Third: There is the Racist Tyrant, they always say, that they're not racist or whatever; but they will take every opportunity to impose their racial jokes upon you, make subtle inflective remarks meant to offend. Their goal is to get you to react so they can escalate the situation. Their main goal is to make you frustrated, flustered and or violent so you can be fired.

The Po Man's Guide to Breaking the Poverty Cycle

How to deal with the Racist Tyrant
You can usually win this type over by being professional and attentive. It won't be easy, but you are going to have to weather the storm.   Until they see that they can't rattle you. After the storm, they usually leave you alone. When in doubt treat them like Napoleon it's harder to mistreat someone who appears to look up to you. Feed his ego when it's true. Don't make up lies, he'll see through them and hate you more.

Fourth: The Workhorse Slave Driver. Now this guy will work you hard! He wants to get things done quickly. If it were up to him, he would do it all himself, but he needs help, that's why they hired you. I have had: black Workhorse Slave Drivers, I've had a white Workhorse Slave Drivers and I've had Hispanic Workhorse Slave Drivers and two Asian Workhorse Slave Drivers. Color seems to be irrelevant all these guys are the same! They want to get things done. They don't want to talk about it. They don't want to have meetings and take votes. They want to get it done and out of the way. Don't ever bring up race with this guy! They hate lazy people only.

How to deal with The Workhorse Slave Driver
As long as you show up on time and don't shirk your duties you will have no problem with this guy. But you will work hard. The only way to get ahead of this guy is to plan. As soon as you finish one task, ask for another. And you keep doing this until you die from exhaustion or they run out of things for you to do. Once you run out of things, he wants done take the opportunity to ask him to assign you to a project you want to complete.

Fifth: We have the Envious. Once they know: your skill set is better than theirs, you are in for one hell of a ride! They won't like you and they will be afraid that you're going to take their position. He/she will always make little sly remarks that are funny to them and others but not to you. These little sly jokes will be relentless and they will take every opportunity to put you down on the sly. Basically, these jokes are little warnings, designed to let you know who's the boss!

How to deal with the Envious
Never brag to them! Never even think of putting them down! You deal with the envious boss a little differently than the others. You want to let them know that you don't want their job at all. Be emphatic. You want their knowledge and it's going to take you a long time to learn what they know so they don't have anything to worry about. You just want to learn and be number two. Let them know: your job is to make them look good! The more they teach you the better they will look. You also want to present ideas to them in such a way that when the conversation is over, they think the idea was theirs. And when they steal your ideas, say nothing!

The Po Man's Guide to Breaking the Poverty Cycle

Sixth: The guy with the God complex is ALWAYS RIGHT! He is on top and you are a peon. They can dish it out but they can't take it! They take everything personally. They will belittle you in front of others. They will berate you in front of others. They never want to give you a raise. They will take credit for your work. They are erratic and can't seem to make up their minds. They thrive on creating fear, chaos and a high stress work environment.

How to deal with the guy with a God complex
In most cases with these guys all you have to do is feed their ego. Befriend them. Let them know often: they are one of the best you've ever seen. Tell them you want to be just like them and ask them to take you under their wing. You can argue with them a little, not much! Present your arguments as questions. Once they begin to shoot it down angrily, drop the subject. As long as they're not angry, you're good to go! Make them angry and you will have to deal with their wrath! These people are control freaks. In their mind, no one can get it done correctly except them, so they will micromanage the hell out of you! You're going to have to learn how they think, anticipate them and do what they would have done in your place. Once you get to the point where you always do what they would want, in any given situation they will trust you. They will give you latitude and most important praise you!

Seventh: Mr. Cool is in a class all his own. When it comes to joking around at work, they can dish it out and they can take it. Mr. Cool will never let it get personal or take you seriously when you get a burn in. They don't belittle. They don't berate. When they make a joke at your expense it's usually designed to motivate you and it usually works! Mr. Cool looks out for his people and will often cut you some slack. He likes his team and doesn't want anything to happen to one of its members. Mr. Cool will motivate you and push you to become better than you are at your job. Mr. Cool will not put up with Toro caca!

How to deal with Mr. Cool
Never take advantage of Mr. Cool. Betray his trust and you are in for a world of hurt! Get him in trouble and you have just signed your death warrant! Mr. Cool doesn't like repeating himself. Mr. Cool is a closet RAGE monster! Make him rage and you are toast! Stay on his good side and everything will be fine. Never cross Mr. Cool!

There is also the **Eighth** boss, this is the one which you will become. "How?" you ask. You take all of the attributes, the good ones from every boss you encounter and make them your own. Simply drop all of the things you hate. But here's a newsflash: If and when you become: the boss you're going to have to be able to play the a-hole card. It's not that you need to be an a-hole all the time but you're going to have to be one when the situation dictates. Trust me. There are times when your people will take away your ability to choose! I have tried being the good guy, the nice guy, the cool boss that everybody wants. At first, the people will love you, they will praise you to others; but eventually, they will become jealous and envious and attack you in any little way they

The Po Man's Guide to Breaking the Poverty Cycle

can; because they feel that they can never be anything like you. Just remember when you're the boss, you will be dealing with lots of different people that have not learned to break their circle, only they will be working for you.

Automation and LEAN

I feel the need to insert this small section which is a warning here. You should be aware of the impact automation and LEAN are having on the job market. No one wants to go through the hassle of finding a respectable job and find out in six months your new position will be phased out. This small section is here simply to inform you of the next coming phase here in America. It will also give you something to think about before you except that new job. After the LEAN detour we get back on track or you can skip this section and go to Dealing with Employment Agencies.

Now, I understand most millennials don't want to work with their hands, they want easy jobs where they can sit behind a desk and stare at a computer for eight hours. Easy-peasy job and life is fine. These guys are single and have no desire to get married or have a family. They just want to work at menial jobs such as working for McDonald's or retail stores or anything in the same venue so they can collect a check, go home and play video games. I have news for those guys, those jobs are going to be phased out! Automation is on the rise and it's here to stay!

In the future, these low skill jobs will be replaced by robotic automation. Look at Walmart, they already have self-service checkout stations everywhere and maybe only three cashiers actively working on the floor. The employees were not sufficiently warned and the shoppers quickly adapted to the new change! You came in the store one day and there they were self-service checkout stations, brand spanking new and ready to be used. Oh, shoppers may have noticed the change, figured out their favorite cashier was missing, may have complained, but gradually everyone got used to the idea. After a month or two no one said a word. The world moved on. They just brought their cart up, read the directions on the screen, learned to scan their items and paid like it was the most natural thing in the world. It was more convenient. How do thousands of cashiers lose their jobs? More than 10,000 people lost their jobs and that was only in 2013.

They say, in the next 10 to 20 years, more than 3 million people are going to lose their jobs due to automation and that's here in America! So, if you have one of those low skill jobs like customer service, phone center, stockers and so forth. Start building skills now. Oh, it gets better! They have self-driving cars and trucks, big ones! Your friend the truck driver is targeted and these tech giants are locked and loaded! Drivers of all sorts are on notice: you may wake up one day soon to find yourself replaced by an automated truck. Technology at its finest! The era of the low skilled worker is ending! It is closing in on you rapidly. **Now is the age of automation, skills and vocations and there is no getting around it.** For the would-be worker, there is no way out except vocational training or some savvy new idea. You could become a programmer or some sort of engineer, even then your job may become obsolete. So now, instead of worrying about the next guy being able to come in and take your job, you're going to have to worry about the next

The Po Man's Guide to Breaking the Poverty Cycle

machine they buy to speed up production or the next software upgrade. You are going to have to prepare yourself for the world that is coming. Skills are going to be needed! And let's not forget about LEAN manufacturing.

LEAN manufacturing was first implemented in the auto industry and introduced to American corporations as the next BIG THING! It was slow at first and now it's branched out everywhere! You can't escape Lean anymore. Now you have so many seconds to do a required task! You must be cross-trained so you can be moved anywhere to meet the needs of the company. Everything is broken down into standard work. And standard work is set up so you produce more, work harder, faster and get the boot if you make mistakes more than once. If you do not meet your numbers, you get the ax. LEAN has absolutely nothing to do with helping the worker. Lean is all about greater productivity, which means if they can put a robot in your place, you are history. Don't believe me, go to any manufacturing plant and get a job you will find out quickly. I like to say LEAN means lean on your people! Work quicklier faster!

The state of Japan because of LEAN
https://www.businessinsider.com/japanisfacingadeathbyoverworkproblem20183

This note is taken from an Asian boss on YouTube

For decades, Japanese working culture was notorious for the long hours put in by company employees. But in recent years, there have been efforts to combat this culture of overworking. In August 2019, Microsoft conducted an experiment in its Japanese offices where it gave every one of its 2,300 employees Friday off. And days ago, **they announced this caused worker productivity to increase by 40%.** Yet in a society where demanding work and devotion to one's company has long been the norm. So how exactly do normal Japanese people feel about this kind of work life balance? We hit the streets of Tokyo to find out.
I viewed video after video and discovered Japan is rapidly aging and there are not enough people taking care of the elderly and not enough young people having babies. They are not having babies because they are always at work. Now when women are always at work.
Well-rounded images and extended arms for as many options are available such as adjustable Masters front wheels 3 months ago
Well, if I was a 25yr Japanese woman from a family of an only child, just finished university and now have to find a job in a country where everyone is over qualified and there's not an abundance of good paying jobs because their all taken and I have to look after both my parents and my grandparents and might even have to worry about looking after my spouses' parents or grandparents, I wouldn't want to have a kid. That's 5 people I have to look after not including myself or if I plan to have more than 1 kid or accidentally have twins. Parents plus grandparents plus own kids plus I'm pregnant and can't go to work and have to look after my kids equal my spouse has to take care of 11 people with his job.

The Po Man's Guide to Breaking the Poverty Cycle

Other really good comments:

Jun Abejo3
It's a proven fact higher educational attainment among women will make them career oriented, marry later in life, or not at all. They will bear one, or two babies or none at all due to old age. Young girls coming from rural areas with lower educational attainment could be those willing to be a wife and mothers in the traditional Japanese way. Sad to say, many of these girls are scouted, duped, tricked and lured with big cash to work in adult video entertainment and other demeaning businesses jeopardizing their chance to lead normal married and family life. This further aggravates the low birth rate trend.
Now I know you're thinking I live in America, what does this have to do with me? Everything! Here in America, they are adopting Lean programs or Lean type programs every day. So little by little, we going to end up just like Japan, working ourselves to death. Lean is a vehicle they will use to usher in this new era in America where people begin dying from overwork.

Michal Turlik1

A GLOBAL society is based only on the workforce can only accelerate human annihilation. Now Japan is one of the first countries need to face the fast decrease in population growth. They are trying to fix the problem by adding women in all the work areas, but this will only increase the GDP in the short term. Then they should figure out how to let people make children. When you are forced to work hard, even 10, 12 hours per day, how much can you expect you will be able to find a good and attractive partner with whom to create a family and a common life together? Usually, people who live in Tokyo have only time to sleep and if you do not meet your soul mate during your school years you are almost screwed. We are going to not have any time free almost everywhere on planet Earth. Remember it is up to us to make the change and to reestablish a good balance between work and our personal life needs. In other times we could call the whole scenario one word only: slavery. The labor cost is constantly decreasing (not only in Japan) which automatically forces people to work more which still automatically means to have less time to live as human beings. All those financial indexes going up and down are only speculations and money is being added or subtracted by mere database/digital entries. I am almost sure the time has come to rethink the whole significance of the human presence on planet Earth.

Now, this guy gets it! If we keep following Japan and LEAN, we are next!
HYPERLINK "https://www.youtube.com/channel/UC3vcVLxgAOG457c2EwlZdCA"
Let's get back to the subject. When choosing your next job, keep automation and LEAN in mind. There will be no escaping them.

The Po Man's Guide to Breaking the Poverty Cycle

The Work from Home Craze

The work from home craze is here to stay because people don't hate working, they hate their work environments. No one wants to have to wake up early, drag themselves out of bed and force themselves to make that long drive to work all the while, hating their destination. Everyone has seen those ads, those scams, promising a better tomorrow. Live the dream! Sign up with us and work from home! Everything you have always wanted in a job and you get to do it from the comfort of your own home! Sometimes it's nothing more than being in the right place at the right time!

You have to understand that most people aren't seriously looking at the types of skills they are going to have to possess in order to perform these jobs. They are caught up in the dream. The dream sounds amazing. Who wouldn't want to get up in the morning, roll out of bed and immediately begin to go to work without ever having to get dressed? I say again, a great many of these people who get these jobs have **excellent skill sets** and probably got in at the beginning first-in-line so to speak. So, you, being a Johnny-come-lately, will have more of a problem when it comes to getting your foot in the door. I'm not saying it can't be done, I'm simply stating a fact most people will not make it. If you are still gung-ho about working from home, you will have to ask yourself some serious questions. Did you go to school for journalism? Have you been writing for years? How many years of data entry do you have? Have you worked in these environments before attempting to get the work at home position? Are these opportunities legitimate?

If you begin to look at today's manufacturing industry and even most other environments, most of these companies go to agencies. Do you have a listing of these agencies? Are you familiar with how they work? Do you know anyone on the inside? I'm not trying to pour salt on your dreams, I am stating simple facts. In my opinion, you have to know someone that has already done these things and is willing to assist you.

The simple truth is that a lot of these positions were filled early and now these companies are bursting at the seams with applicants, all more qualified than you. And most of them are already on the waiting list. They will get first call; you are not even on the radar.

So, let's discuss these websites that are popping up everywhere. Have you personally spoken to any of the people that actually found a way to become successful at this venture? You read the reviews but reviews can be faked. If I build a website, does it also stand to reason, that I might be able to write my own reviews?

Have you ever noticed that all these gurus on YouTube have no problem with giving you the addresses to these websites? Let's be logical about this when most people find a good thing, they don't tell anybody about it! And if they do tell anyone, it's usually their closest friends and no one else. They don't go outside and scream it from the rooftops. They maintain a low profile and no one is the wiser. How many times have you watched

The Po Man's Guide to Breaking the Poverty Cycle

infomercials and the founders of these great companies ask you to send in $29.99 and they will let you in on their little-known secret?
 The simple truth is, work from home jobs are like get rich quick schemes. Everybody wants in on the action and only 2% of the people that sign up will actually be able to make it work!

 Now that I have sufficiently rained on your parade, I can tell you that Flex Jobs is legit. Simply enter this address:
https://www.flexjobs.com/jobs?gclid=EAIaIQobChMIhcf54NKD5wIVQP7jBx0cCgyAEAAYASAAEgJd9fD_BwE

So, with a little bit of research, you can find work from home positions. But, as I said before, you will have to be highly skilled. And if you were thinking about writing, proofreading and the like, I hope you are prepared to present your work portfolio upon request.

Yes, there are Customer Service jobs out there.
Amazon https://www.amazon.jobs/en/locations/virtual-locations

If you can type really well, you could try **TranscribeMe,** you will have to pass several tests. All you need to do is enter this address and register, then they will give you the requirements. https://workhub.transcribeme.com/Account/LogOn?ReturnUrl=%2f

Check out this article: https://finance.yahoo.com/news/40-legit-companies-pay-home-090340602.html.

Did you get all fired up, before you realized the amount of experience and knowledge they will require? Temper your expectations and come back down to earth.   This is going to be a long ride! Freelancer, Clickworker and Upwork.   I tried them.   Nuff said!
 Mystery shopping is cool for a hobby, but you will never make enough money to support yourself.   It works, just not the way you think.   You get a shop, sometimes you have to spend your own money and after the shop is accepted, you get reimbursed.
 The work from home package handling/shipping scam don't fall for it! Not only is it illegal, you could be shipping stolen goods or any host of other things! You can even find yourself facing jail time! Tampering with the mail is a federal offense!
Let's be honest about this, there is no such thing as an easy work from home job that you get through an email or a classified ad! If you get an email from a company and if the email address has anything to do with Gmail, 90% of the time it's a scam!

The Po Man's Guide to Breaking the Poverty Cycle

Starting All Over Financially

What can I actually say about starting over financially? It's one of the hardest things that any man will ever have to do but easier than you think. I have lost everything 3 or 4 times before I turned 50. I'm actually starting to get good at it! It's like someone is taking a portion of your life (we'll call that your heart) and ripping it out without mercy. The first thing you will want to do is crawl up into a little ball and cry like a baby. Go for it—if it helps. After all no one can understand what it feels like to lose everything unless they have lost everything! All that struggling and all that work might seem to have been for nothing. So, I'd say, the healthiest thing to do is go ahead and play the blame game, rant and rail against the heavens if you must. Once your emotions have subsided, then it will be time for action!

The very first thing you need to do is make an assessment. What, if anything, do you have left? What are your options? Do you still have a job? Do you have any incoming resources? This is the initial planning stage of your big comeback! One thing I've learned about starting over financially, there really is no such thing. Let's call it a huge setback. Now you may think I'm crazy for saying this but in some ways, it is actually a good thing! This will be your opportunity to put everything into play that you have learned because now you are going to need everything that you know!

I started all over financially at least 6 times in my life and I can tell you from experience the first time always feels like it's the end of the world! The second time feels like you destroyed the country and the third and so forth, is more like: here we go again. The truth is, the first time is always the hardest! Picking yourself up after you have crashed and burned is not an easy thing to do! And by no means do I take it lightly. But there's only one thing you have to remember, nobody else is going to do it for you!

So, get up! Take up those reins and guide your life back to the point from which you fell! I watched many men start all over after divorces and major setbacks and I can honestly tell you that in most cases they usually end up better off than they were before! It goes back to the old adage give a man a fish you feed him for a day. Teach a man to fish and he will feed himself for life. Once you have endured, fought battles, scrimped and saved and clawed your way back to where you want to be, nobody can take that knowledge from you! Nobody can magically come in and wipe away all of that experience! You know what it takes to get there! You know what it takes to maintain what you have! You know what pitfalls avoid! And if, heaven forbids, you ever fall again, you know who you can trust and who you can't! All of these things will make coming back a heck of a lot easier, no matter how many times you fall!

I'm not saying you're not going to have anger or animosity! I'm saying, you will know how to get over it! Take this setback as an opportunity to show yourself and the world that no matter how many times you get knocked down, you will always get back up! Show them you will never stop! You will never cease to strive! Scream it to the world,

The Po Man's Guide to Breaking the Poverty Cycle

"You can slow me down: you can get in my way, set obstacles in my path; but you cannot stop me!

A man who can learn from his mistakes is dangerous in deed! You will be compelled to never make the same mistakes again! And every time you see anything that remotely looks like the things that brought you down the first time you will dismiss them or her with extreme prejudice! So, let's get into the meat. On the next page are 11 points to be considered and addressed:

The Starting All Over Checklist
1. Assess your situation. Do you have a place to stay? Do you have food to eat?
2. Assess your finances. How much money do you have to work? Will it be enough for your new start? How long until your money runs out? Budget your way back!
3. Do you still have transportation? What mode of transportation can you use until you can afford a ride?
4. Do you still have employment? If not, what steps are you going to take to find employment?
5. Are you free to travel anywhere?
6. Are you going to have any assistance? Is there anyone willing to help you or will you have to do this all alone?
7. How much time do you think it's going to take for you to get back to where you were? If all of your necessities are still in place you're only dealing with time. If all of your necessities are not in place how much time until you restore them?
8. What shortcuts can you take? Nobody can take away your knowledge! Nobody can take away your skills! Nobody can take away your earning potential! All of these things are going to lift you up faster!
9. What are your immediate goals? What are some of the smaller goals you can accomplish? What are your long-term goals? Your first an immediate goal is to make sure that all of your necessities are taking care of…meaning a place to live, food, transportation and a job, incoming funds. If you have a job and a place to stay, then you can make any plans you need to make, suffer through any hardships you need to suffer through with a roof over your head. Once you have a firm foundation, you can build any future you like.
10. Do you have a plan? Which of my short-term goals do I have the power to attack right now? Establish a budget which will bring you out of the hole you find yourself in.
11. Can I repair my credit in less than seven years? Or am I going to have to bite the bullet? Do I have collections? What's the smallest collection I can pay? Your collections are part of goalsetting. Collections should be addressed in order of smallest to greatest.

HEALTH

If you have your health then you still have the ability to tackle any obstacle that may come into your path. If you do not have your health, then your first order of business will be to find out how to receive any medical assistance you may need or believe you require. Even if it's just something you want to get checked out so that you can have

The Po Man's Guide to Breaking the Poverty Cycle

peace of mind. But if you're younger, it is more than likely you have your health, so you can skip over this section, if you do not, read on.

If you do not have your health, you don't have medical insurance or any means by which to acquire the medical aid that you need, there are options. Is there a free clinic? Are you a veteran? If you are a veteran, you need only report to your nearest VA and get a checkup. The VA will require that you register at a clinic near you so they can get you into the system. You are going to need your DD form 214, State ID and a place where your mail can be sent. The VA has lots of options if you are homeless or you lack certain essential items. Once you are registered, the VA will set up appointments for you so that you get the medical assistance you need. If you don't know where to start:

https://www.myhealth.va.gov/web/myhealthevet/home or type the address into your browser.

If you are not a veteran:

Programs for People who are Homeless or at Risk of Becoming Homeless
There is a state-by-state listing
http://www.homelessassistance.us
https://www.hhs.gov/programs/index.html

The Po Man's Guide to Breaking the Poverty Cycle

The Truth About Women and Your Money

Why are you looking for a woman? The answer to this question will tell you how and where your money will be spent. I will attempt to explain the types of women that you will encounter and how things usually end. Maybe, you will be no worse for the wear. Maybe, you will find yourself totally bankrupt and emotionally devastated.

Companionship/Friendship
If you're only looking for company and you just want to hang out with female friends, then chances are you will spend your money eating out, going to movies and shopping of some sort. Guys who are only looking for friendship from women are usually trying to satisfy a need. They don't want a girlfriend or wife but occasionally, they get lonely and want female companionship. They can live without the sex. Your money will usually only be spent on you. As a friend, you may find yourself having to pay her way when she is a little short on cash, the very same thing you'd do if she were a male friend! You bring yours; I'll bring mine and we will enjoy the little we have together.

Sex
If you're just looking for sex, chances are, you will spend most of your money drinking, paying to get into clubs, buying clothes so you look good in the clubs. Buying drinks for women and eating out. If you're trying to wine and dine many different women, it is going to cost you. I'm not trying to tell you how to live your sexual life but this book is going to be useless to you if your libido will not allow you to save or go without.

Girlfriend
A girlfriend is simply a pretend wife, without the bonds of matrimony. So, expect to spend all of your money in most of the same ways you would if it's something serious. Women like to be seen. Being seen is going to cost you. If it's not something serious then you will mainly spend your money as though you were looking for company and/or sex. If you're not living together, then you will occasionally have to pay some of her bills. Unlike a wife, your girlfriend is a never-ending expense and, in some cases, this is the same with the wife, but not often. So, you have to pay all of your bills and you will pay to entertain your girlfriend. This can get very expensive. Women like to be seen and they like to brag.

Wife
A wife usually comes with a family, if you have not planned out your moves before you make them, you can get in debt and in over your head very fast! There are no dowries, like there used to be back in the old days. And most American women are walking financial disasters. They believe that you should work hard. You should provide! And

The Po Man's Guide to Breaking the Poverty Cycle

at the same time keep her happy. This can be seriously expensive and exhausting if you don't marry a sensible woman.

In most cases you're going to be dealing with one of Four Different Types of Women:

The Destroyer or Feminist
The **Feminist** hates men deep-down inside and through no fault of her own, will do everything she can to destroy you mentally, financially and emotionally. To put this into context she wants your money and your seed as long as you're a good provider. She wants to run the relationship and tell you how to spend your money. Preferably on her. She is not going to stand by your side, nor does she believe she should. The relationship will usually be one-sided and if you don't like it, you can hit the road. In some rare cases, she has her own money and will want to turn you into her soy boy. But like most men, you will be expected to hand your money over every payday and she will give you your weekly allowance. If you want to spend money on something, you are going to have to go through her first. And if your reasoning isn't good enough then you are going to simply go without.

The Destroyer
The Destroyer also known as the Psycho Crazy B, will often start off innocent and sweet. You know someone you can take home to your mother. But little by little, as time passes by, little red flags will start popping up everywhere. She will learn everything there is to know about you not out of love or some sense of duty but she'll know how to destroy you later. The Psycho Crazy B will call your job to get you fired. She will damage your property. And these days, she will attack you physically and expect you to take it like a man! And if you refuse, she will do her best to have you thrown into jail and have your freedom taken away. She can't be reasoned with and she knows the best way to hurt you is through your wallet. Never give her access to your bank account! Never buy property with her! Never co-sign for her vehicle! She will pawn your things and rip up your clothes. She won't be satisfied until she has left you homeless and destitute. Once you break up with her, film every encounter, you will need the recordings to stay out of jail or to get a restraining order. So, when you meet a woman and she starts quoting anything that sounds remotely like psychology run the other way!

The Western Party Girl
The Western Party Girl is a unique creature, she hits the bars for one of three different reasons
1. She considers herself to be a playgirl which means she can do what a man does sleep around with as many men as she wants with no consequences.

2. She loves being the center of attention and hates sitting at home. She always has to be entertained and loves drama.

The Po Man's Guide to Breaking the Poverty Cycle

3. She wants to find a good-looking man who is also a provider. Someone who will take care of her and probably her children. Most of the guys that go to clubs aren't looking for a wife, but this one is on the hunt. She is more interested in your seed than you. When the time is right, she'll get pregnant, make you pay for everything and put you on child support.

The other Western Party Girl is usually on drugs or into drugs and is only looking for a good time. The moment you try to get serious and want her to clean up her act that is the end. Her idea of a good time is sex, drugs and insert music of choice. You're not going to pay for sex per se, you're going to pay for all the other little inconsequential needs that she has like food, shelter transportation and of course, more money for drugs. If you are dealing with a woman that's into drugs things can go wrong on so many different levels. If you continue to deal with her, you, my friend, will reap the whirlwind!

The Faithful

You must understand by faithful I'm strictly speaking in matters of sex her being with another man. I'm only speaking of that aspect so don't go reading more into the text than I have written! Although they are hard to find here in America they are out there. Don't get happy, they also expect you to be faithful and kind. Now the faithful woman can be an enigma she can be a club girl. She can be a feminist and or destroyer. She can also be a drug user, but those are rare. Just because a woman is faithful doesn't mean that she can't be all of the above. She won't mess with anyone other than you, which means her entire focus will be on you. Even if that focus is hell-bent on your destruction.

The Virtuous

I have promised that there will be no Bible thumping in this book. So, there will be none! But I can't properly explain the motives of this woman without bringing up her prayers her wishes and her desires. No matter which type of man she finds she's going to want him to make some changes. The virtuous woman has dedicated her life to God! She may accept a man that has not done the same in the beginning but she will allow no one to inhabit her space or give her body to that has not done the same! She understands people can change and she will demand it! She will stand by your side; she will obey you but only as you obey God! Deviate ever so slightly in such a way that she believes will reveal your true motives and she will drop you like a bad habit! She wants a man who is suitable to her calling. Someone that will help and not harm! Someone who will enhance and not decrease! She will go through anything there is with you hoping for that which is to come. Destroy her hope and she is gone! Destroy her dreams and she is gone! Fulfilled them all and she will never depart from your side! It won't matter if you fall into hard times! It won't matter if you are attacked! It won't matter if everybody else speaks ill of you! As long as she believes you are the man that God gave her only death will separate her from you.

The Po Man's Guide to Breaking the Poverty Cycle

I was going to give this big spiel but I don't think that's necessary. The truth of the matter is simple! As long as you live on this planet, having a woman, having a family, will cost you money! The idea is to make sure the juice is really worth the squeeze!

Furnishing a Home or Apartment

Rental Furniture
Never buy rental furniture! Buying rental furniture can be worse than getting a payday loan! If something goes wrong you can and will find yourself in a bind really quick. With business practices such as "rent-to-own," the contracts are categorized as leases, stores can avoid state usury laws and other regulations. You will find yourself in a position where you're paying 3 to 4 times more than what the furniture is actually worth. **You can easily find yourself saddled with super-high weekly payments even if you choose the monthly payment option.** Most renters will find themselves defaulting on almost 75% of their lease agreements. I know you won't like this but you're better off going without and putting your furniture into layaway. These rental stores won't tell you that you are signing a rental contract not a purchase contract! So even after you paid it off you will have to continue paying! **Always READ THE FINE PRINT!!** In some states if you try to opt out you could find yourself going to court to face the possibility of jail time. Rental companies have a "trump card" which they can use to "legally force you" to uphold the rental contract. And no. They won't tell you this upfront! In the state of Texas where I live, there is an obscure law that states the rental company can file a criminal offense report, they can actually have you arrested and jailed! And if you refuse to pay them, they can file felony theft charges against you if you don't continue to pay their extortion charges. In a lot of the court cases filed, most of the people had already paid thousands of dollars by the time they defaulted. But if they didn't pay the remaining balance, they could face theft of service charges even if they returned the goods. It's outright legal extortion. **Don't be a victim. I repeat! Stay away from rental furniture and appliances!!**

Alternatives to Renting Furniture
Being in a hurry is your greatest enemy! Never rush a purchase that's more than $100. Always do your due diligence look the items up, see if they will fit into your budget. Will you be able to pay the monthly payment twice? Your goal is to help yourself. Not put yourself in a financial bind! Stop and think! Don't dig a hole so deep it would take you years and bankruptcy to get out of it. The old adage is true, **take your time, do it right.** And don't try to look this stuff up on your phone! You need to be able to contrast different sites! You will need a PC or laptop so that you can look at the monitor!

Classifieds

The Po Man's Guide to Breaking the Poverty Cycle

The links below are only a few of the classifieds you can find online. You can also find your local green sheets or white sheets or whatever free classified publication offered in your area:
https://www.classifiedadslocal.com/free-classifieds/furniture-for-sale.html
https://forsale.oodle.com/furniture/
https://claz.org/furniture.html

Layaway--In Store Only
Before you go hopping into your Bentley and head for the nearest Furniture store do some online research. Try this link: https://firstquarterfinance.com/furniture-stores-with-layaway-plans-online-offline/. Check out the stores nearest you and familiarize yourself with their layaway options! The purpose is to give you a good idea of where you stand. So, you know what you can and cannot afford! And if something goes wrong, you will know if you can or can't get your money back!

Online Sales
Nowadays, there are many online furniture companies that also offer layaway plans. Check out the link below:
https://influencedigest.com/other/top-20-online-furniture-stores/

Yard Sales
Don't be too proud to ask friends and family if they know of any yard sales or the good places where you can get a deal. Check out the link below this article has lots of good tips and advice.
https://www.thespruce.com/shopping-for-furniture-at-garage-sales-1391350

RTA Furniture: Ready to Assemble Furniture
Before you go thumbing your nose at the idea, most of this furniture will cost you 20 to 30% less than furniture that's already assembled. You can find some really awesome online sales, deals and opportunities you may never have found in any other furniture field. I have purchased bedroom sets, bookshelves, tables, chairs and a host of other items which I assembled myself. If you choose to go this route, just remember to replace the cardboard backing with a piece of 1/8 inch to ¼ inch fiberboard or plywood this will give your new furniture the stability that you're looking for you'll thank me later. The object here is to furnish your place. Later when you have more money, time and the ability to shop around you can buy the items you want.

https://www.overstock.com/Home-Garden/Furniture/Assembly-Required,/assembly,/32/dept.html
https://www.cymax.com/RTA-Furniture--p1.htm
https://swiftbed.com/pages/ready-assemble-furniture

https://www.amazon.com/ready-assemble-furniture/s?k=ready+to+assemble+furniture

The Po Man's Guide to Breaking the Poverty Cycle

https://www.walmart.com/search/?cat_id=0&facet=category%3ABox+Springs&query=ready+to+assemble+furniture

Wholesale Furniture
I went looking for anything I could find that would help you, the reader.   I also added the links that I found, hoping to give you a general idea of what's out there hopefully I succeeded. This is my limited effort to get you to learn the power of research. No one is going to just hand you anything, you need to get in the habit of looking at things when there is a need! This must become something that you just do, something you can stop yourself from doing so that you learn to never go into anything without looking it up and doing your due diligence.   No one is going to just give you anything, especially information! **Your job is to find a way where there is no way.**   As I said before, no one can stop you, but you. You can be lazy and not check any of these links out but I advise you to look before you leap in all things! Some of these places have really awesome deals.   Some of those places are typical.   Keep looking until you find the best possible deal for you! **Expand your search parameters if you have to but under no circumstances should you ever be satisfied with someone else's research!**   At the end of the day, I could write 1200 books but if you never take the opportunity to seek what you're looking for on your own who will really be at fault?

Wholesale Furniture Brokers
https://www.gowfb.com/collections/sectional-sofas

Liquidation.com
https://www.liquidation.com/auction/search?query=TQ3xL222Tyj49f2ckN2pKN1aeNu2&flag=new&sort=close_time&ascending=1&_per_page=30&_page=2

All Modern
https://www.allmodern.com/gateway.php?&url=https://www.allmodern.com/&refid=MX79645962249795.Bohemian%20Dining%20Furniture~bb&pcrid=79645962249795&device=c&targetid=kwd-79646136302382:loc-190&channel=BingToF&msclkid=a3b3021f8f7110d12e985c0da560203a&utm_source=bing&utm_medium=cpc&utm_campaign=AM.S.US.Ms.Top.Core%20Style%3ABohemian.Match%3AB&utm_term=Bohemian%20Dining%20Furniture&utm_content=AM.S.US.MS.Top.Core%20Style%3ABohemian.Match%3AB.Room

Living Spaces.com
https://www.livingspaces.com/?msclkid=36e21cd28b3314e4a23442c0a1c7002c&utm_source=bing&utm_medium=cpc&utm_campaign=Beta%20-%20General%20-%20Same%20Day&utm_term=%2Bcheap%20%2Bfurniture%20%2Bstore&utm_content=(general)%20furniture%20-%20stores%20-%20cheap

Furniture Depot
http://www.furnituredepot.com/bedroom-furniture-dressers-c-29_13.html

Facebook Marketplace – they sell everything! Just make sure you don't get scammed.

Social Security Disability

Here are 10 of the most common conditions that are considered disabilities.

Arthritis and other Musculoskeletal Problems
We depend on our muscles and joints to help us move in both our everyday lives and at work. When arthritis and other musculoskeletal issues strike it can make it difficult or impossible to work.

Heart Disease
According to <u>WebMD</u>, heart disease is estimated to be responsible for a whopping 17% of all of the health costs in the U.S. today. As the condition worsens, it can become impossible to continue working.

Lung or Respiratory Problems
COPD and other lung ailments are a common reason to file for disability benefits. Lung conditions can affect people of all ages, making it difficult to breathe.

Mental illness, Including Depression
Mental health conditions, including depression, can be just as disabling as physical health conditions and are a common reason for filing for disability benefits.

Diabetes
Linked to other causes on this list, including obesity and heart disease, diabetes is another common cause of disability among people in the U.S.

Stroke
The effects of a stroke can range from very mild to life-altering. Depending on the severity, after a stroke, the victim may not be able to work again, at least in the short-term.

Cancer
The impact of cancer and of standard treatments for it can be disabling.

Nervous System Disorders

The Po Man's Guide to Breaking the Poverty Cycle

Multiple Sclerosis, Alzheimer's, Parkinson's, ALS, Epilepsy and other conditions that affect the brain and nerves are common and can affect both the young and young-at-heart alike.

Injuries Sustained in Accidents
Anyone of us could become injured at any time as the result of an accident at home, at work, or anywhere else. When those injuries impact your ability to do your job, you have a disability.

What to Expect
We're writing to let you know that we successfully submitted your application for disability benefits. We submitted your application through Social Security's online system because it's the fastest and most reliable way to ensure they start processing your claim as soon as possible.

In the next few weeks, Social Security will likely send you a medical release form and a summary of the application to review and sign. When you receive the summary, please look it over to ensure all the information is correct, then sign and return it to Social Security as soon as possible. Social Security needs your signed application summary and medical release form before they start processing your claim. If there is any incorrect information in the summary, please let the office know so they can correct it. Should read like this:

We're writing to let you know that we recently mailed you a secondary signature package with additional forms for signature. These documents allow us to request your medical records as well as provide us with additional copies of claim documents in the unlikely event SSA misplaces your originals. It is important that we receive them as soon as possible to continue working on your claim, so if you have any questions about them, please let us know as soon as possible.

The Work History Report - Will ask you to describe the work you did over the past 15 years. DDS uses this information to determine if you are still able to perform those jobs with your current conditions.

The Function Report - Adult questionnaire asks about your everyday life. DDS wants to know how your conditions affect your lifestyle and ability to do daily tasks.

When you receive the questionnaires, please complete them to the best of your ability, review the questionnaires to ensure that theirs is nothing in YOUR responses the DDS might misinterpret or use against your claim.

The Examination - You may be called in to submit to an examination by a disability specialist.

The Po Man's Guide to Breaking the Poverty Cycle

How To Shop Online for Clothing

Learning to shop for clothing online you have to be a little savvier than most people think. It seems as if all your problems can be solved by a simple click of your mouse. Not true. You have to know: your sizes, arm length, waist measurement and the length of your inseam. You are going to need to master your item descriptions as well, this will allow you to accurately find any item that you might be searching for. Seek and you will find. Shopping online isn't for everyone. You are going to have to be able to know "when" to type such things as single pleated, double pleated, cuffed and relaxed fit as your descriptors. You will definitely need to know: what type of fabrics you're seeking to buy as in the examples below:

Example #1: Men's "Olive Green" Pleated Cuffed Dress Pants (36/32) NEW NWT $125
Example #2: Bocci 100% Silk Shirt Size 2XL Olive Green Stripe MEN'S
Example #3: Paul Fredrick Black Wool Double Breasted Sport Coat with Metal buttons 44R
Example #4: Men's Genuine Lambskin Leather Trench Coat Jacket Full Length Over Coat MT03
Example #5: NEW Claiborne Men's Dress Pants Sz W 36 X 32 L Black Slacks Pleated Cuffed NWT
Example #6: NEW Levis Men's 550 Black Relaxed Straight Leg Jeans 36x32

One small descriptive "word" not included in your search parameters can mean the difference between an awesome buy or a nightmare return. You also have to take into account that the photos may not give an accurate representation of the item you're attempting to buy. NWT= New with tags. Now remember your mastery of product descriptions is all there is that stands between you and the greatest buys you'll ever make online. I can't stress it enough pay close attention to descriptions you'll thank me for this later.

Things you're going to have to know

I'm only adding this section into this book because I made some excellent purchases at the cheapest prices! And found good-quality items I could not have afforded otherwise. The objective is simple: to get what you need and/or want while saving as much money as possible! In most cases choosing normal sizes will work for you, in other cases the

The Po Man's Guide to Breaking the Poverty Cycle

description should display runs one size small or runs large only you know your body sometimes normal sizes will not work for you. In everything you do your objective is to save as much money as you can while still getting an excellent product! In order to do this successfully you are going to have to be willing to search until you find the correct items at the best prices.

 I wear a 44R Dress Coat or Jacket or a 2XL in normal running sizes. In Slim fit that would be a 3XL so you have to be very careful when you're reading product descriptions. Look for the words "true to size" or sometimes the items will run small and even run more than one size too large. It will take some effort on your part, but you are going to have to practice until you know what you are doing.

 Shoes are a little harder to master, sometimes it's a hit and miss but once you figure out which sizes to go with it will be a simple matter of picking out the shoes that you like. For example: in the Asian and EU sizes I wear a 43. The same size in the US I wear 9 ½ W. Most of the time I have to settle for a 9 ½ D. But now, that I've gotten older and I guess my feet fatter I've moved up to a size 10 D. I've had improvised when I bought shoes that were a little too small. They still fit barely, but the shoestrings were too short! So, I bought new strings. Problem solved. So, I you're going to buy something from Asia, I would suggest buying the cheapest you can find at first to make sure they fit.   Or you will discover after trying them on, you have to go up one size. Once you figure out what your size is you should always buy the same size unless the description specifically says it runs small or runs large. Don't get comfortable always check and double check when it comes to your shoes! It can be a real pain to return them.

 Chest measurement My chest size is 52 inches or 2XL. If you have been shopping long enough you will know what sizes you can and can't get away with.

Garment length Some guys are going to need the extra length. I usually buy the regulars but only you know your body. So, if you're taller always buy items a little longer.

My sleeve lengths usually run 34 to 35 inches or I can accommodate 36 to 37 inches. Neck Size My neck size is a whopping 18 ½ inches that's why have to go up in size from a XL to a 2XL. The closer your sizing is to the norm the more deals you can find. I have missed out on a lot of deals because of my thick and fat head. The larger the next size the more the shirt is going to cost you.

 Shopping for hip, stylish, but decently priced clothing for men is next to impossible! Women have it made! There is no reason we should have to pay nearly $80 for a pair of dress pants! Or $40 for a really nice dress shirt! I don't have time to shop in person or the stores near me just don't have the selection I'm looking for or they're ALWAYS out of stock, mainly the sizes I need and want.   I have searched high and low so that I could offer you a listing of online stores that offer wallet-friendly clothing, so you can make your own trends AND STAY on-budget.

1. **eBay:** I have found some of my greatest buys on eBay, everything from dress clothes to compression shorts. Back when I was younger, I was always on the lookout for what I called "club clothes"!

The Po Man's Guide to Breaking the Poverty Cycle

2. **Amazon:** These guys have almost anything you can think of and they will ship many of your favorite pieces to your door within two days with a Prime account.

3. **Walmart.com:** Don't laugh, you can find some really nice buys online, high quality athletic wear and more. I buy all my work pants online and save a lot of money because of their online specials!

4. **Target:** Yeah. Laugh it up. But you can also find some pretty nice shirts, slacks, vests and other things that guys like to wear. These days it's hard to get a nice pair of socks without emptying your bank account.

5. **TJ Maxx:** This classic discount store has been around for nearly 3 decades. You can find designer buys at a *fraction* of the price. I shouldn't really have to explain anything about the store to you because most people have heard of them.

6. **Old Navy:** Not much to say about Old Navy. Everybody knows about them because of the commercials. They have plenty of good clothing at good prices.

7. **JC Penny:** This chain has always been there; at least for as long as I can recall! They have always carried the latest trends, the newest fashions and fashionable items most people would love to get their hands on. Back when I was growing up, a hundred years ago, we would go downtown and walk through the JC Penny store wishing for the day that we could afford to buy some of the clothing we saw for sale.

8. **https://www.contemposuits.com**. This website has a lot of nice dress clothes, I won't say that they are cheap; but you will find a lot of nice items without ever leaving your house.

9. **https://tripleblessings.com**. Here you have a special type of suit jacket and blazers. Maybe this store is more my style but who knows: maybe we have some of the same tastes.

10. **Sears.com:** This classic store will offer many online only discounts that will keep you coming back for more! I've shopped at Sears a great many times and found lots of great buys! You have to do a little searching; but you will find them!

New and Used Items
11. **Swap.com:** This is one of the best new and second-hand online sites I've ever seen! And the 2nd best is right below. These guys carry items that are brand-new for rock-bottom prices! You just have to be willing to do some searching. Go figure.

12. **Poshmark.com:** An online store that carries many new and second-hand top label items. You will be amazed at some of the awesome buys you'll find on their site!

The Po Man's Guide to Breaking the Poverty Cycle

AND IF YOU CAN PULL OFF SLIM-FIT AND YOU ARE SMALL ENOUGH FOR ASIAN SIZES

13. (**#1**) **Theleesshop.com:** Where do I begin! Style and class! These guys have some awesome fashions snazzy jackets and coats that you haven't seen anyone else wearing your level you just need to make sure that you get the correct sizes.

14. **AliExpress.com:** retailers from all over Asia just be sure that you know your Asian sizes or your son will get everything you buy.

I've heard of some of these sites but I have never used them personally.   I have, however, checked out their websites just to be sure that they would fit my narrative.

1. **Nordstrom Rack:** the perfect compromise for anyone who loves Nordstrom, but isn't exactly made of money. They carry many of the same brands (including classic designer pieces), so you can get your favorite high-quality items.
2. **Boohoo:** a UK-based store that adds up to 100 new items every day. Sometimes you'll find deals, sometimes you won't. Sometimes the normal price will be the deal.
3. **Cotton On:** Australian retailer that specializes in unique basics you'll wear all the time.
4. Express.com: For way more than inexpensive trendy gear. Their prices are nice!
5. **6pm:** the Zappos outlet you didn't know you needed.   All your favorite brands, for less!
6. **American Eagle:** They have some cool stuff.
7. **H&M:** Which you probably already know about, for good reason. This Swedish store has basics, eco-friendly lines and does regular collars with top designers to bring you the latest fashions.
8. **Hollister:** High quality clothes that definitely aren't just for teens anymore.

Shopping online is king, whether you're looking for something in particular or just want to treat yourself!
There are thousands of stores coming online every day that we've never heard of! Some of them will be posted on eBay and other selling sites. Once you find these gems, share them with your friends or don't.
All you have to do is search for a little while and buy. Sometimes you may have to wait. But never forget, the object is to get good quality clothing and/or accessories at the best prices possible!
You can also build your dream wardrobe and drive all your friends crazy with the really cool stuff you find. If you don't need it, don't buy it. Don't get addicted to shopping!

The Po Man's Guide to Breaking the Poverty Cycle

Ramblings, Tips and Tidbits of Advice

Tenacity noun
the quality or fact of being able to grip something firmly, grip.
"The sheer tenacity of the limpet"

synonyms: persistence · pertinacity · determination · perseverance · doggedness · tenaciousness · singlemindedness · strength of will · firmness of purpose · strength of purpose · [more]the quality or fact of being very determined; determination.

"You have to admire the tenacity of these two guys"
the quality or fact of continuing to exist, persistence.
"The tenacity of certain myths within the historical record"

Tit for Tat battles of Wit
There is nothing wrong with the male bonding ritual of burn for burn, as the blacks used to say, ranking on each other. But don't do it at work unless you KNOW the person, you are engaging WILL NOT TAKE YOU SERIOUSLY! If you are at home and someone engages you and you know they can't take a joke, walk away and/or Cut Slings!

Mind Training Tip#5
I am not allowed to quit! You are going to need this little mantra a lot more than you think! There are going to be times when your tenacity must be the mental trait you have access to at the time. When you are frustrated and want to give up you must constantly tell yourself, "I am not allowed to quit! I can do this...!"

Life Tip#1
Never put yourself in a position where the outcome will cost you your future!

Life Tip#2
If you have an angry friend that's always causing or getting you into trouble Cut Slings!

Life Tip#3
Whenever you start a new job, establish your boundaries right away! Don't hope they will get the hint. Later it will move from annoyance to frustration next thing you know you are going to get physical before you can stop yourself. If you don't like being

The Po Man's Guide to Breaking the Poverty Cycle

touched, make it known the first time someone touches you. You don't need to be rude, just make it plain make item know you are not joking.

Life Tip#4

If you have a friend who does drugs, never let them ride with you in your vehicle or enter your house! If you are the one does drugs, then you have just wasted your money, this book will not help you.

EMERGENCY CASH!

Take $200, fold it up and put it in that hidden pocket of your wallet. Leave it there and forget about it! I can't tell you how many times this has saved me!

Ramblings

Changing the way, you think

Your mind does what you tell it to do, so you have to learn how to command your brain and have it execute without you even being aware. When you desire a change, you must mentally project what you desire and what you would have your brain accomplish and reinforce that change by speaking out loud and professing the change you desire. The desire is to make your brain get the message. Being smart is a choice, but if you want to knock down that wall fast, read, read, read.

Take every opportunity to increase your memory recall. Bind certain keys were going for you so you execute functions in your subconscious. You should always engage in memory building exercises.

I cannot express to you how vitally important it is for you to have a computer, a working computer you can use. I have learned one thing talking to people who come from bad backgrounds and poverty none of them have a computer at home so their outside influences are limited by garbage. Seek out friendships with people but don't ask him for money and don't ask him for help asked for advice or guidance. They will gladly give advice or guidance. Make friends with people who know more than you. Ask him to teach you. He will love the fact you want to learn. Build friendships with people are striving. Your friend failed and they can tell you shortfalls without you ever making mistakes or going at it alone.

As long as you expect a TAX REFUND you are still Po! Rich people want to limit how much taxes they pay, they will look for deductions, contribute or whatever all in a calculated way to ensure that they owe NOTHING at TAX time! If you are looking forward to TAX time, you haven't MADE IT yet!

Alphabetical Index

Advance Fee Loans.......Pg.87-88
Alison Courses...............Pg.68-69
Associates.....................Pg.130
Auto Parts.....................Pg.176
Automation and LEAN....................Pg 203-205
Avoid Grouping! !!.....................Pg.135
Bad Company Corrupts Good Character............Pg.124
Big Money Sunny Syndrome.......Pg.11
Birth Certificate Corrections...................Pg.191-192
Bi-Weekly Budget..............Pg.22
Buying Good Cheap Tools...........Pg.-186-190
Car Title Loans.................Pg.91-95
Carlton Sheets........................Pg.13-15
Child Support...................Pg.179-180
Codecademy...............................Pg.70
Cooking like Mom or Better.................Pg.184-185
Cosigning a Loan....................Pg.99-100
Credit Scores.....................Pg.71-74
Cut Slings........................Pg.127
Dealing with Employment Agencies...............Pg.139
Disputing Errors on Credit Reports...............Pg.75-80
Do I know Where My Money Is Going?......Pg.7
Don Lapre........................ Pg.16
Don't Fall for Get Rich Quick Schemes!......13
Dry Cleaning.........Pg.30
Fixing Your Credit...........Pg.81-86
Fixing Up Your Ride..........Pg.12
Flexible Spending Accounts................Pg.177-178
Forgiveness: The Key Unlocks the Doors to Progress.......Pg.125-126
Four Different Types of Women......... Pg.211-212
Furnishing a Home or Apartment....................Pg.214-216
Getting and Giving Good Advice at Work.................Pg.165

The Po Man's Guide to Breaking the Poverty Cycle

Giving Money……………….Pg.32-34
Grocery List………Pg.29
Groupthink…………………….Pg.128
How to answer the TELL ME ABOUT YOURSELF interview question………Pg.162
How to Answer BEHAVIORAL INTERVIEW QUESTIONS Using the STAR Method…Pg.163
How to Shop Online for Clothing………Pg.219-222
Initiative……………….Pg.133-134
Kevin Trudeau……………………..Pg.15-16
Khan Academy Courses……………Pg.66-67
Knowledge, Wisdom and Experience are 3 different things.Pg.48-49
Know Your STUFF!............Pg.40
Learn to Take a Joke…………….Pg.124
Life Choice Examples………Pgs.24-28
Mantra How to ALWAYS WIN………………………….Pg.174
Matthew Lesko……………………………………..Pg.16-18
Mental Laziness You Hate To READ!!....................Pg.134
Monthly Budget……………..Pg.22
Moving Money Around…………………Pg.31
Obtaining Computer Skills, YOU NEED and Lack…………Pg.50-51
Overtime……………Pg.9
Payday Loans……………………………..Pg.89-90
Placeholders……………….Pg.31
Prepping For Hard Times………………Pg.-181-183
Research! When You Don't Know!!…….Pg.43
Resume Samples…………..Pg.140-160
ROBERT KIYOSAKI)………..Pg.18-20
Russ Dalbey……………………………….Pg.15
Sacrificing For a Better Life…………………………..Pg.193-196
Social Research - ALWAYS BE AWARE……………………Pg.164
Specialty Merchandise Corporation (SMC)………..Pg.18
Start small and learn to Dream Bigger……………Pg.175
The Character Hack for Physical Laziness…………Pg.132-133
The Copycat Wins in the End……….Pg.39
The Elephant in the Room………………………Pg.5
The Enemies of GOOD Planning and Sound Decision Making…………Pg.172-174
The NEVERS at work………………..Pg.126-127
The "Real Deal" About Your Credit………………Pg.101-105
The Rock, the Sponge and the Diamond in the Rough…….Pg.42
The Rules for Clubbing…………….Pg.12
The Seven Problem-Solving Steps……………………Pg.169-171
The Truth About Women and Your Money……….211-213
Too Much Information TMI……..Pg.130-131
Toxic Friends……………………Pg.127
Udemy Courses…………..Pg.52-65

The Po Man's Guide to Breaking the Poverty Cycle

Using a Credit Card………………………Pg.96-98
Using Credit Cards - How to Build Your Credit……………Pg.106
Using Credit Cards: How to RAISE Your Score…..Pg.107-109
Using your 401(k) as an Emergency Savings Account……………..Pg.34-35
You Spend All of Your Money at the Club …………Pg.11
Your Next Raise……………..Pg.10
What to Look for in a New Job………..Pg.161
Weekly Budget…………………….Pg.21
Which Type of Boss Do You Work For?………………….Pg.200-202
Whip Up A Quick Budget……….Pg.23
 YOUR Health and YOUR Safety…………….Pg197-199
Starting All Over Financially………..Pg.208-210
Social Security Disability……….Pg.217-218

If you have any questions, I can be reached at askfdspaarkman@aol.com
I also have a new website : https://fdsparkmanbooks.com/

I'm also going to start posting on YouTube Budgeting tips and stuff. I could use some ideas.

If you like the book please leave a good review. I know I got scatterbrained sometimes, but I was trying to load this book with useful info!

The End